THE TRUE GLORY

The Royal Navy: 1914–1939

THE TRUE GLORY

The Royal Navy: 1914–1939

Max Arthur

'There must be a beginning
of any great matter, but the
continuing unto the end until
it be thoroughly finished
yields the true glory.'
Sir Francis Drake, 1587

Hodder & Stoughton

British Library Cataloguing in Publication Data

Arthur, Max, 1939–
The true glory: the Royal Navy, 1914–39
1. Great Britain. Royal Navy – History – 20th century
2. Navies – Great Britain – History – 20th century
3. Great Britain – History, Naval – 20th century
I. Title II. Phillips. Roland
359′.00941

ISBN 0 340 62301 2

Typeset by Hewer Text Composition Services, Edinburgh
Printed and bound in Great Britain by
Butler & Tanner Ltd., Frome and London

Hodder and Stoughton
A division of Hodder Headline PLC
338 Euston Road
London NW1 3BH

Contents

List of Illustrations

The blockships, *Intrepid*, *Iphigenia* and *Thetis* sunk at Zeebrugge. (*Imperial War Museum*)

Seaman on board HMS *Barham*. (*Imperial War Museum*)

HMS *Queen Elizabeth* triumphantly flying the flag of Sir David Beatty and preceding HMS *King George V, Ajax, Centurion* and *Erin*. (*Imperial War Museum*)

Royal Marines and sailors of HMS *Southampton* at Murmansk 1919. (*Royal Marines Museum*)

Royal Marines alongside their six-inch gun in Siberia. (*Royal Marines Museum*)

HMS *Renown* manoeuvring at speed. (*With kind permission of Captain Harry Hodgson*)

Duke and Duchess of York aboard HMS *Renown* in 1926. (*With kind permission of Captain Harry Hodgson*)

Royal Marines embarking for China in 1927. (*Royal Marines Museum*)

HMS *Bee* on the Yangtsze River in 1927. (*With kind permission of Captain Shannan Stevenson*)

Fairy Flycatchers on the deck of HMS *Eagle* in 1931. (*Imperial War Museum*)

Men of HMS *Exeter* on the return to Devonport in December 1939. (*Illustrated London News Library*)

Families scanning the list of survivors of the HMS *Royal Oak*. (*Illustrated London News Library*)

Foreword

by Admiral Sir Jock Slater GCB LVO ADC, First Sea Lord

Max Arthur has created a successful format for the memories of the men and women who served in the Royal Navy during the First World War and the inter-war years. He has done this by giving the survivors of the period, many of whom are over ninety-five, the opportunity to tell their story in their own words. Leading Stoker Jack Cotterell brings the effort of shovelling coal to life, especially when the *Gloucester* cracks on steam to have a go at the *Goeben* in 1914. The Battle of Jutland in 1916 is vividly recalled by former Midshipman Brian de Courcy-Ireland in his account of the sinking of *Invincible*. The inter-war period contains accounts of action against the Bolsheviks in Russia and incidents in China, and on the lighter side, Lieutenant Commander Harry Hodgson telling of being taught the Charleston on board *Renown* by the Duchess of York (now the Queen Mother) in 1927. At the other end of the scale Surgeon Lieutenant Roger Lancashire gives the most graphic account of the carnage in *Exeter* during the Battle of the River Plate in December 1939 and his valiant effort to save life and limbs.

These are the personal recollections of some of the men and women who *were* the Royal Navy between 1914 and 1939. Together they reflect both the tedium and the highlights of life ashore and at sea during a fascinating period in our naval history.

Author's Preface

What I have sought to do with *The True Glory* is to capture something of the spirit of the men and women who served in the Royal Navy between 1914 and 1939 and learn of their daily life in peace, war and civil unrest: it is not intended as a formal history of the Royal Navy for that period. The book is based on taped interviews with the contributors. In some cases, however, where I have been unable to find a survivor of a particular period or incident, a written account has been included.

The rank given at the start of each contributor's account is the highest held during the period to which the account refers.

Each account is a chapter in itself, a chapter in the life of the person who related it. Apart from the opening three accounts, I have, whenever possible, arranged them in chronological order. Because these are personal accounts, not cold histories, the order in which I have placed them will sometimes seem imperfect. The opening three accounts belong to the oldest known survivors. The oldest living naval officer, Commander Harry Hodgson, is followed by the oldest living Royal Marine NCO, Sergeant-Major George Finch and then by the oldest living Royal Naval rating, Able Seaman Jack Gearing. All are aged over 102. However, the oldest living Royal Marine officer, Brigadier Roy Smith-Hill, is included in the period concerning Russia in 1919.

The lengths of these accounts vary, some are many pages long as in the case of Captain Thomas Jameson, RMLI, whereas others select the most affecting moments. In some cases, the same contributor appears three or four times to tell of different events at separate periods. To give the accounts an historical context I have included a short history of the Royal Navy from 1914 to 1919 at the start of the book and prior to the accounts of the inter-war years, have included a second short history to cover this period to the beginning of the Second World War.

While the manuscript was in the press the local Exeter paper, the *Express and Echo*, telephoned me to say that they had found a survivor of Jutland. Knowing there are less than ten alive, I was delighted. I was able to talk to Bert Pester who had recently celebrated his 102nd birthday. In a firm, west country voice, he told me of his early years delivering bread on a horse prior to joining the Royal Navy at the outbreak of war. At the battle of Jutland he and his friend had carried shells in a canvas bag to the gunners on HMS *Centurion*. He still felt strongly about the dead of that battle, eighty years ago. A few days after our conversation he slipped quietly away in his sleep. Bert Pester, like the contributors to this book, had faced the rigours of training, understood the discipline, had enjoyed the camaraderie and in the face of adversity, had shown courage, compassion and the humour that this country has come to expect of its senior service. That tradition still continues.

A further volume of personal accounts from the outbreak of the Second World War to the present day is in preparation.

Throughout the writing of this book, it has been my privilege to meet many fine men and women. These are their words – I have been but a catalyst.

Max Arthur
Hampstead, London
July 1996

Author's Acknowledgements

I would like to thank all members of the Royal Navy who told me of their personal experiences and who, throughout the writing of this book, gave me their support and co-operation. Sadly, a place could not be found for everyone's story, but all deserved one. I would also like to thank the wives and families whom I met or spoke to, whose stories also deserve to be told.

Throughout the writing of this book I have had co-operation and help from many sources and I would like to thank them all: Commander Graeme Moodie and Commander Ducan Ferguson of the Department of Public Relations (RN); Captain Bob McQueen and Hugh Mair of The Royal Naval Association; Lieutenant-Commander Mike Coombes of the Association of Royal Naval Officers; Lieutenant-Commander Mike Lawrence of the Fleet Air Arm Officers Association; Commander Jeff Tall, Director of Royal Navy Submarine Museum, Gosport; Graham Smith, Naval Secretary (OMobS); Jim Allway and Anton Hanney and the staff of the *Navy News*; Captain Tony Newing, RM, Editor of *The Globe and Laurel*; Captain Derek Oakley, RM, of the Royal Marines Historical Society for the use of extracts from Special Publication number 10 and 12 which deal with the accounts of Captain Thomas Jameson and Sergeant Harry Wright; Major Mark Bentinck, RM, Corps Historical Records Officer for assistance on 6th Battalion RMLI; Matthew Little, Archivist, Royal Marines Museum; Peter Kemp, Peter Hart and Brad King of Imperial War Museum; David Saunders and colleagues of the Gallipoli Association; Norman Gilham, RFC/RNAS Veterans Association; Captain Roger Hill for his interview with Captain W. R. Fell; Kyle Tallet for background details of RMLI; Len Fogwill, Secretary of River Plate Veterans Association; all the nursing and residential homes such as Pembroke House, Gillingham, The Royal Alfred Home in Eastbourne, and The Star and Garter in Richmond, all of whom gave me kind assistance and who provide such excellent facilities for retired gentlemen of the Royal Navy; George Cheesman and fellow members of Royal Marines Association, Victoria, Australia; Albert Gearing for kindly supplying the picture of his father for the back cover of the jacket; Mrs S. Smith for supplying tape recordings of her late husband, Stan; to Colin Peacock for additional material on his late father, Eric.

I am most grateful to John Winton, naval historian, who kindly read through the manuscript and made valuable suggestions, and Ian Drury, military historian, who has written the historical notes. On the publishing front, Richard Cohen commissioned the book; Roland Philipps, Publishing Director of Hodder and Stoughton, waited patiently and was totally supportive throughout; as was Angela Herlihy who dealt diligently particularly with the amendments. My editor, John Bright-Holmes, offered constructive advice and encouragement and I am much in his debt. Ellen Kinsella was most helpful in my early research, Sarah Mnatzaganian and Sacha Baker both transcribed extremely complex tapes and organised the material very skilfully; Carolyn Mallam transcribed the remainder of the tapes as she has done for all my books and I thank her. Vice-Admiral Sir John Roxburgh and Rear-Admiral David Kirk offered sound advice throughout this book and I am most grateful to them. I should also acknowledge my indebtedness to *The Royal Navy Day by Day*, by A. D. Sainsbury (published by Ian Allen in association with the National Maritime Museum), an invaluable reference which I have consulted to provide my chronology of naval events from 1914 to 1939. Finally I would like to thank Cecil and Fanny Lewis, and Don and Liz McClen, who have been a constant support. To the many others too numerous to name, who have given me information and co-operation, please accept my thanks.

PART ONE

The Royal Navy, 1914–1919

HISTORICAL NOTE

At 11.00pm on 4 August 1914 the Royal Navy was ordered to commence hostilities with Imperial Germany. Its most modern battleships were already assembling at the desolate Orkney anchorage of Scapa Flow that was to be their base for the duration of the war. The fleet had been fully mobilised for the summer exercises and the First Sea Lord, Prince Louis of Battenberg, had kept it together as the political crisis in Europe worsened. Five battle squadrons were concentrated at Scapa Flow: twenty dreadnoughts, five battle-cruisers and eight older capital ships; the English Channel was guarded by no less than 27 old battleships and 21 cruisers.

For the previous thirty years, the numbers and capabilities of the world's battleships had been an index of strategic power, studied in the same way that nuclear weapons have been since World War II. Imperial Germany had sought to challenge Britain's long cherished status as the world's premier maritime power. And it had lost. The declaration of war found the brash new German fleet still significantly outnumbered. Having read so many novels in which foreign navies attempted to land an invasion force in Britain, the British public expected an early trial of strength – a twentieth-century Trafalgar. But the German fleet stayed in port, its commanders and its Emperor acutely conscious of the odds.

The Royal Navy's responsibilities extended far beyond its primary role of countering the German fleet in the North Sea. There were three battle-cruisers and over thirty other warships in the Mediterranean. Cruisers were on station in the Atlantic, the Caribbean, the Pacific, the Indian Ocean, off West Africa, South Africa, and China. Its global reach was soon demonstrated as German commerce was swept from the seas, and a blockade imposed on Germany that would slowly but surely strangle its economy. Expectations of a headlong confrontation between the rival battlefleets were soon dashed. Admiral Jellicoe, commander of the British Grand Fleet, as the main force at Scapa Flow was soon christened, refused to risk his heavy units off the mine infested German coast. The close blockade of Napoleonic times was an anachronism. Germany's 'High Seas Fleet' (Hochseeflotte) refused even to venture far into the North Sea. The first major clash took place on 28 August 1914 when British light forces raided the Heligoland Bight. After a running fight in poor visibility, three German cruisers were sunk, but only after the characteristically bold intervention of Vice-Admiral Sir David Beatty's battle-cruisers. As the two British squadrons were ignorant of each other's presence, and British submarines lying there in wait had no idea British capital ships were taking part, it was fortunate that a 'friendly fire' incident did not mar the operation.

Germany achieved its revenge a month later, when three British cruisers patrolling off the Dutch coast were attacked by a single submarine, U-9. Several officers had expressed anxiety about this 'live bait' squadron and its vulnerability, but all published memoranda seem to fear a surface action with an overwhelming force of German cruisers, not an attack from beneath the waves. How the underwater threat could be so little appreciated remains a mystery, especially since Captain Johnson of the *Cressy* had spent three years commanding a flotilla of Royal Navy submarines, but on 22 September, *Aboukir, Hogue* and *Cressy* were sunk in succession. *Aboukir* went first and her consorts stopped to pick up survivors. Over 1500 sailors drowned.

In its quest for a 'place in the sun', Germany had lavished vast sums of money on a naval base at Tsingtao, China. In 1914 the cruiser squadron based there vanished into the Pacific before the port was invested by the Japanese. On 1 November the Germans were intercepted off the coast of Chile by a smaller British squadron which brought them to action despite what proved to be hopeless odds. The elderly cruisers *Good Hope* and *Monmouth* were sunk with all hands, including their courageous commander Rear-Admiral Sir Christopher Craddock. Galvanised by a defeat that was reported around the world, the Admiralty despatched two battle-cruisers to the South Atlantic. That very week, German battle-cruisers carried out the first of a series of bombardments of British towns on the east coast, killing civilians in an attempt to lure an isolated British squadron to its destruction. 'Where was the Navy?' the Scarborough coroner would ask after another attack in December.

With two battle-cruisers detached to avenge Craddock, *Princess Royal* covering the Canadian troop convoy, and the dreadnought *Audacious* lost to a mine, the Royal Navy's numerical advantage had been dangerously eroded. On 16 December the Germans came within an ace of success as Admiral Warrender's second battle squadron nearly clashed with the entire High Seas Fleet. Luck, typical North Sea weather and the timidity of the German Admiral combined to save the day. Meanwhile, the German Pacific squadron had the ill fortune to raid the Falkland islands just as the British reinforcements were coaling there. Against the 12-inch guns of the battle-cruisers *Inflexible* and *Invincible*, the armoured cruisers *Scharnhorst* and *Gneisenau* could only hope to win time for their lighter consorts to escape. Only one, *Dresden*, escaped annihilation, and she only survived to skulk off the Chilean coast until sunk in March 1915.

In January 1915 the Royal Navy began to reap the benefit of an intelligence windfall: the capture by the Russians of an intact German naval code book. A sortie by the German battle-cruisers was discovered in time for Beatty's battle-cruiser squadrons to intercept them at Dogger Bank. Although the Germans promptly turned for home, the inclusion of the armoured cruiser *Blücher* in their raiding force slowed them down. German gunnery proved incredibly accurate, Beatty's flagship HMS *Lion* suffering grievously, but the odds promised a major British victory. Unfortunately, periscopes were sighted and the British turned away. A catalogue of signal errors then led the battle-cruisers to concentrate against the already crippled *Blücher*, while the remainder of the enemy squadron made good their escape.

A month after the first major clash in the North Sea, an Anglo-French squadron bombarded Turkish coastal defences at the Dardanelles. In a daring – some said foolhardy – plan, six old battleships shelled the outlying Turkish forts into submission. A further bombardment on 25 February encouraged a larger force to penetrate the straits and break through to Constantinople. With their capital at the mercy of the fleet's guns, it was hoped the Turks would sue for peace. Unfortunately, the attempt to force the Dardanelles failed on 18 March when the pre-dreadnoughts *Irresistible*, *Ocean* and the French *Bouvet* were sunk by mines. On 25 April, British and Imperial troops were landed at Gallipoli, taken ashore by small boats, often commanded by teenage midshipmen whose steadiness under fire attracted comment from many army units. The Australian/New Zealand (ANZAC) Corps would win undying fame during the Gallipoli campaign, but the Turks could not be dislodged. Perversely, the evacuation eight months later was a model of success. During the stormy night of 9 January 1916 the entire force of 16,000 men was withdrawn from under the noses of a vigilant and resourceful enemy, without a single life lost.

If Dogger Bank was frustrating for the Royal Navy, it exerted a paralysing influence on the German high command. For the rest of 1915 the dreadnoughts of the High Seas Fleet skulked in port as the Grand Fleet continued its regular patrols off Scotland. In May 1916, again reacting to timely signals intelligence, the Grand Fleet put to sea for 'another bloody sweep' as one officer described it in his diary. But on this occasion the elusive enemy was brought to action.

Both fleets were preceded by their battle-cruiser squadrons, the British battle-cruisers being supported by the four 'Queen Elizabeth' class 15-inch gun fast battleships. As at Dogger Bank, the German battle-cruisers were outnumbered, but their gunnery was deadly accurate. HMS *Indefatigable* exploded and sank in the first ten minutes. HMS *Queen Mary* blew up too, prompting Beatty's oft quoted remark that 'there seems to be something wrong with our bloody ships today'. Pursuing the Germans until he ran into the main body of the High Seas Fleet, Beatty reversed course. He drew the Germans north, transmitting tantalisingly vague reports to Admiral Jellicoe aboard the fleet flagship, *Iron Duke*. Winston Churchill famously observed that Jellicoe was the only man on either side who could have lost the war in an afternoon. Acutely aware of his enormous responsibility, Jellicoe nevertheless manoeuvred the Grand Fleet with a sure and confident touch. Deploying into line of battle at just the right moment, he placed 24 dreadnoughts squarely in the path of the oncoming Germans, crossing their 'T' as if on one of the peacetime exercises in which he had excelled before the war. First the battle-cruisers, then the enemy main body came under a devastating fire. But by evening, and in executing a simultaneous sixteen-point turn, the German fleet had sped back into the mist.

Jellicoe had placed his fleet across the Germans' line of escape. Desperate to regain port, the German admiral reversed course too early and ran into the British battle line again. Only by ordering his battle-cruisers to attempt a potentially suicidal run at the British van did Admiral Scheer manage to break contact. The German battleships vanished into the gloom. They were not to be seen again until their surrender over two years later.

Scheer broke through the British light forces following Jellicoe's battleships, and despite a succession of close-quarter battles throughout the night, no British ship managed to signal *Iron Duke* with the news. The old German battleship *Pommern* blew up when torpedoed by a British destroyer; the crippled flagship of the German battle-cruiser squadron, *Lützow*, was scuttled, but the rest of Scheer's capital ships reached port safely – some so badly damaged they would be in dockyard hands for many months. Unrealistic public expectations, combined with clumsy public relations by the Admiralty fuelled the idea that Jutland had been a British defeat. The British had suffered more casualties and lost more ships. Yet it was the British Grand Fleet which was at sea the following day, ready to renew the fight. The German navy had no intention or capability to match them.

The German war effort was increasingly frustrated by shortages of strategic materials. Despite some ingenious improvisations, German industry was permanently handicapped and the nation unable to feed itself. Although the British public was to be bitterly disappointed by the battle of Jutland, the German civilian population would remember the end of 1916 as the 'turnip winter'. While the German battlefleet failed to break the Royal Navy's stranglehold, its submarine force began to exert a similar pressure on the United Kingdom. Even while fettered by international law, and compelled to conduct a 'restricted' campaign against British merchant ships, the German submarines inflicted appalling losses on trans-Atlantic trade. Once Jutland confirmed the inferiority of the German surface fleet, the U-boats were unleashed. Free to attack without warning, they came perilously close to victory in 1917. Merchant ships were being sunk faster than replacements could be built; Britain's umbilical cord across the Atlantic was about to be severed. Anti-submarine weapons were developed, but locating a submerged U-boat proved extremely difficult. A heavily-patrolled mine barrier helped defend the English Channel while mine-laying in German waters accounted for several enemy submarines. Merchant ships with concealed guns, 'Q-ships', achieved a few spectacular successes but the ruse was persisted with long after enemy captains were wise to it. Promoted to First Sea Lord, Admiral Jellicoe was eventually prevailed upon to revive the eighteenth-century tradition of convoying merchant ships. Early Admiralty objections were proved to be mistaken as the introduction of convoys drastically reduced sinkings. The German assault on neutral shipping finally persuaded America to declare war. The USA's giant economy sustained only a tiny peacetime army, and it would take over a year before America could deploy significant land forces in France. Germany made a desperate attempt to win the war on the Western Front in the spring of 1918, but it ended in failure. Imperial Germany and its allies were finished.

The Royal Navy played a key role in the defeat of Imperial Germany. It transported the Army to France and guarded the Channel for the next four years. The British army expanded from 250,000 in 1914 to 5.7 million in 1918, the vast majority deployed and maintained overseas by the Royal Navy. At the outbreak of hostilities enemy seaborne trade ceased, German colonies were overrun and their ocean raiders intercepted and sunk. The blockade of Germany severely handicapped enemy industry and eroded civilian support for the war. The Grand Fleet was denied a glorious victory in battle, but its achievement was in no doubt as its squadrons assembled in 1918 to receive the enemy surrender. The once proud warships of the High Seas Fleet steamed into captivity at Scapa Flow, controlled by committees of mutinous sailors.

Lieutenant Harry Hodgson

Up to 1903 all young men going into the Royal Navy as officers joined *Britannia*. When the Admiralty decided that we should build up a big fleet for the war which was bound to come with Germany, the officer intake was doubled. Instead of sending more cadets to Dartmouth, however, they decided to use the outbuildings and stables of Queen Victoria's old home at Osborne on the Isle of Wight. The first lot of cadets went to Osborne in 1903, and I joined at the age of thirteen in the spring of 1906.

In my group were ninety cadets who had come from various preparatory schools and were all about the same age. I was one of nine boys from Stubbington House School, Fareham, which had for years trained boys for the Navy. Each group formed a term, each term being named after a famous admiral. We were the Blake term, ahead of us was Drake and ahead of them was Rodney. The main teaching concerned the technical requirements of a naval officer, as well as ordinary schooling. I spent two years very happily there. The only unfortunate moment was when the whole College went down with mumps. There were not enough beds for everyone so I was moved to Haslar, near Gosport, and a pretty grim place it was in those days.

Blake term left in the spring of 1908 and went on to Dartmouth. The College had been built on the west bank of the River Dart close to the old *Britannia*. There we were following six other terms. We increased the technical part of our education and for each term we were given a project. Ours was to construct a steam launch. We started at the drawing board and at the end of the year we had a two-cylinder steam-driven boat which we took up the Dart. We made every part of it. For recreation we did plenty of rowing in cutters, whalers, gigs and lifeboats. We learnt to do all we would be expected to do when we got to sea. We also played rugger and hockey and hunted with a pack of beagles. With my Welsh background I was selected for the choir and we performed a skit on *The Pirates of Penzance*. It had all been rehearsed when the voice of the cadet who was playing leading lady broke! I was asked to take his place and in three weeks I had learnt the part. The captain's wife fitted me out with a dress and corsets and a dark wig and I played 'Belinda'. My solo was encored and it all went down very well.

I passed out of Dartmouth in the spring of 1910 and we all went to the *Cumberland*, a training cruiser. We cruised around the British Isles and the Mediterranean. For a certain period as cadets we actually ran the ship while the officers looked on. After six months we returned to Portsmouth. We were then promoted to Midshipman. I was appointed to the *Temeraire* which was part of the Fourth Battle Squadron of the Home Fleet. I was very unlucky because we had a real bully for a Sub-Lieutenant of our gunroom. Something had gone amiss in his upbringing and he was determined to take it out on all his junior officers. He told one of the officers that he was going to beat every midshipman in the first six months. And he succeeded. I did three years in the *Temeraire*. Our captain was the brother of General Allenby and a charming man. During this period I spent three months on a destroyer for additional training. It was a hard time because I was expected to do the work of a lieutenant and my life was made uncomfortable by a martinet of a captain. I came back to the *Temeraire* and for the final year was a senior midshipman.

In the spring of 1913 I did my exam for First Lieutenant. We were examined in seamanship and navigation. The Chairman of my Board was W. W. Fisher who gave me a real roasting. Anyway we all passed and two months later we went on to Portsmouth for the rest of our examinations in navigation, in what is now the Naval Headquarters. Having passed we were made Sub-Lieutenant.

In 1913 I was appointed to the cruiser *Cochrane* and made Assistant Torpedo Officer to 'Freddy' Walker whose son, Johnny, went on to win the DSO and three bars and who was probably the most outstanding anti-submarine officer of the Second World War. With the tension building up on 29 July 1914 it was decided to send the whole Fleet to Scapa Flow. We all sailed made ready for war, darkened ship at night and guns manned night and day. When we got to the Orkneys the *Cochrane* and three other cruisers were sent to the Shetlands because the Admiralty feared the Germans might occupy the islands and make them a base from which to launch raids. We found no Germans and on our return to Scapa we saw a huge fleet of merchant ships. We were told which one belonged to our squadron. Myself and another officer went on board and found the ship was like a giant storehouse with every conceivable spare that we could possibly want. This was two days before the war broke out, and we were supposed to be a country unprepared for war!

Our first alert was when we were informed that Scapa Flow was to be attacked by submarines. Four of our cruisers were sent to intercept them. Can you imagine the foolishness of such a move? None of us had any anti-submarine gear or training, yet there we were outside the German (Heligoland) Bight spread out at five miles apart waiting for the submarines! On the second day out we all smelt petrol smoke. The Admiral ordered full speed towards the smoke and the Flagship *Shannon* rammed and sank the leading U-boat.

We then spent several weeks patrolling the Atlantic, checking all merchant ships and then, for several months, we patrolled the North Sea right up to Heligoland Bight. In April 1915 I was made Lieutenant and so had to leave the *Cochrane*. I was then appointed Second Lieutenant to the light cruiser *Forward* where I was made Gunnery Officer. Our task was to attack Zeppelins. We would get a signal, dash off to Heligoland Bight and try and shoot them down as they came home! But our guns were totally ineffective. Our 4-inch guns had a range of 10,000 yards and a 20-degree elevation. After out commander complained, the squadron was sent *without* anti-submarine equipment to the Mediterranean for anti-submarine patrols. After we had been at sea a while we were directed to the isle of Mudros at the mouth of the Dardanelles. The Gallipoli campaign had begun earlier that spring and, although we were not involved, we all marvelled at the evacuation from the peninsula.

We then sailed to Salonika to accompany troopships in the Aegean for fresh attacks on the Turks. We imposed a tight blockade on Greece, a neutral country, in case they decided to throw their hand in with the Germans. It was a most pleasant summer. However one morning the Chief Yeoman of signals came down to the wardroom with the message that the German cruisers *Goeben* and *Breslau* had broken out from Constantinople. We were the only ship between them and the Mediterranean so we immediately moved to intercept them, at full speed. The captain read the Service for going into action and told us that the two ships would be fought until they sank. Half an hour afterwards we got a signal to say: '*Breslau* sunk by mines, *Goeben* sinking' – so we missed that bit of action. The *Goeben* however managed to get back to port.

The *Forward* continued in the area, until the summer of 1918. During that period we landed a very accurate attack on the Turks, and the Greeks were induced into the war on our side. However it seemed more like playing politics than being at war. We then docked at Taranto in order to change crews.

We travelled up by train for seven days to Cherbourg. On board we were joined by a number of soldiers who had been through the thick of the fighting on the Western Front. We'd been rather isolated from such a scene. My mother had always told me to rope my carriage door but alas I did not heed her warning. On the last night we woke to find all our possessions had disappeared, including my boots, my precious camera, my binoculars. All had been stolen.

After leave in August I was appointed to the *Indomitable* and patrolled the North Sea in her until November when I was sent on a torpedo course on the *Vernon*. I was dined out on 10 November. The captain said in his farewell speech 'You will do six months on the *Vernon* and then return for the final victory at sea'. The war was over a month later! That is how little we knew. I had spent all my adolescence training for war, and all my adult life at war. But there was more to come.

Born in 1893, on 17 July in Queenstown, County Cork, Captain Hodgson is the oldest surviving Royal Navy officer.

Sergeant-Major George Finch,

Royal Marine Light Infantry

My mother died in 1907 when I was fourteen. I was the eldest of seven children so I had to leave school and get a job, which I did as an errand boy at Simpson's boot shop in Devonport. I got four shillings a week. One afternoon when I was out delivering I saw a fellow coming down the road in uniform: it was Tom Carey who was the errand boy in the chemist shop. I said to him, 'Hello Tom, what's all this?' 'I've joined the drums,' he said. I said, 'How much a week do you get?' He said, 'Seven shillings and three half pence, and I get the weekends off'. I said, 'I'm having some of that'.

I went home and told my father that I was going to join the Royal Marines Light Infantry. He was an ex-Marine himself and told me to think about it. I told him I didn't want to think about it, I wanted my birth certificate so that I could join up. Eventually he gave it to me and I put it into my pocket. I went to the barracks the next day and told them I wanted to join the drums. They gave me a medical and then a major asked me for my birth certificate. When I felt in my pocket, it wasn't there. He'd taken it, my father had taken it. The major was very good, he just said, 'That's all right, son. Sign here, and bring it in tomorrow'.

I went home and said to my father, 'I've joined up and I want my certificate you took out of my pocket'. He gave it to me and said, 'As you make your bed, so you lie on it'.

I joined up on 23 September 1908. I found out what my father meant on my first day at Stonehouse Barracks. We were given a mattress cover which we had to fill with straw, sew up the end and plump it down. So we made our bed and we laid on it! We also had one brown blanket and a sheet. My service number was Plymouth 14220.

Our day started at 7.00. We would exercise on the parade ground, then at eight o'clock we'd have breakfast. After that we'd go down to the cliffs to a place called the Drummer's Pit where we'd exercise on the bugle, fife and drum. I was lucky because I had learnt how to play the bugle with the Church Lads Brigade. We wore the pill-box hats. I also used to practise at home sitting in the lavatory. It used to wake everyone up! In the afternoon we had drum practice.

I loved the bugle. You see, I'm an isolationist, happy alone. I learnt all the different bugle calls, like Sunset, First Post and Last Post. They didn't want us to wear out the drums, so we used to cover a stool with a blanket and beat out the rhythm on that. We'd march up and down at sunset but when I was playing the fife I used to feel I was just making up the numbers. I couldn't get on with it. The bugle was my first love.

One day I was in the Drummer's Pit and the drum sergeant said, 'You're going to be the bugler of the guard when the Lord Lieutenant of Caernarvon presents HMS *Caernarvon* with a silk ensign'. That was a great honour.

Early in 1910 I joined HMS *Argyll*. We were in the Atlantic Fleet on our way to celebrate the Argentine centenary when we received news of the death of King Edward VII so we diverted, coaled ship at Bahia (now Salvador) and came home. The Atlantic was a sheet of glass all the way back. Hailey's comet was out for days and I'd never seen so many dolphins accompanying the ship. It was as if nature was paying its respects.

From Devonport, we were called up to London for the Coronation of George V. I was on duty as a bugler right in front of the Royal Box. I could see King George and the rest of the royal family all sitting there, the carriages going by, all the guards on horses. It was a glorious sight.

The next job for the *Argyll* was to accompany the King and Queen to India for the Delhi Durbar. I think we got that because we were one of the first ships to have wireless. It was my first trip to India. All us boys slept on the upper deck in hammocks. While I was in India I became eighteen and was rated a man: my pay went up to eleven shillings a week. We didn't do much when we got there. We lined up in a field, presented arms, then got back on the *Argyll*. It was a big occasion for the people of Delhi. We had come to show the flag and let the people see the new King and Queen.

I returned to Deal for training and then back to Plymouth with a Very Good Rating (VGR). I wanted further promotion. While I was there I paid sixpence to a drill instructor every Friday evening to help me become more efficient at drill.

My next job was as a corporal on HMS *Theseus* in Queenstown in southern Ireland, which was the base of the Fourth Cruiser Squadron. We were on a summer cruise when war broke out in August 1914. I was paid off from her and joined HMS *Oropesa*, a converted merchant ship. She was an 8,000-tonner, had one funnel, and she ran 14 knots to speed. We used to patrol from Scapa Flow up to Greenland, three weeks out and six days in. On one patrol my gun crew was on watch when the lookout shouted 'Corporal, what do you think that is?' I saw it – it was a periscope. I reported to the bridge 'Submarine off the port bow, sir!' The captain turned, then called 'Gun's crews close up, prepare to fire.' I had a loud voice and everyone moved quickly. My gun jammed and didn't fire, but the other two 6-inch guns at the stern opened up and hit the U-boat. Oil and bits and pieces came to the surface, but there were no survivors. If I hadn't recognised it and shouted, we'd have had it.

A few weeks later when we got back I was due to have some leave in Plymouth. We were all lined up ready to go: I was at the back. One of the chaps said, 'George, they're calling out for you'. I went to see the First Lieutenant who said 'Corporal Finch, you have been awarded the DSM'. I felt very proud.

Less than two years later the *Oropesa* was sunk off County Down by a U-boat 96, but by then I was on the *Drake*. We were involved in convoy duties between Scapa Flow and Halifax, Nova Scotia. We were on it for months. Of course we never heard anything about the Western Front; our world was just what we were doing.

I had my most frightening moment of the war on the *Drake*. Once, when we were carrying bullion we went through a gale. It was as dark as dark and the waves were miles high. I don't know how we kept going. We nearly capsized three or four times.

On 2 October 1917 we were carrying explosive and were torpedoed on the starboard side by a U-boat in the North Channel off Rathlin Island, about four miles north of the Northern Irish coast. Being a coal burner there was plenty of space where the coal had been used up, so the water just came in. I slid over the side and after a while was picked up by a motor boat and taken to Belfast.

I then went to the *Cordelia* as a Lance Sergeant. From there I became an instructor at Deal. Being trained in signals, I hoisted the flags to show the end of the war. But I stayed on in the Navy till 1932; that made twenty-four years service as a Marine. When I became a sergeant-major, I went to my father and said, 'I made my bed and I laid on it'. I think he was proud of me.

In 1996 Sergeant-Major George Finch was 102 and the oldest known surviving Royal Marine.

Able Seaman Jack Gearing,

I was born in Greenwich in 1894 when Gladstone was Prime Minister and Queen Victoria was on the throne. In 1907 I became an apprentice waterman and lighterman to my father who, like his father and his father before him, had worked on the Thames. I had to sign the same indentures as my grandfather had – they stated that an apprentice had to 'faithfully his master serve, his secrets keep, not waste his goods, nor commit fornication, contract matrimony, not play at cards, dice, tables, nor haunt taverns or playhouses or absent himself from his Master's service day or night'!

It was a hard life, but we respected each other, and we knew the ways of the tug captains, the pilots. We used to sail up from Faversham to London in our barge *Mayflower* with such things as hay, bricks and building material. On the return journey we carried home manure from the streets and stables of London for the farmers to spread on their fields. In 1912 I went up to the Watermans' Hall to get a licence. This entitled me to take a fifty-ton barge on the Thames single-handed.

In 1913 I could see how the world was going. So when war broke out I went to the RNVR recruiting office in Blackfriars and joined up. I became a naval man. I went then to Crystal Palace for square-bashing, including marching to Epsom Downs. I was in Benbow battalion, each battalion being named after an admiral. While I was there they created a balloon section, which I joined. We would go up in a basket beneath the balloon and would get up to about 500 feet. We were there to listen for Zeppelins. If we heard one we would call down. If the rope broke we had a grappling hook which you lowered down until it snagged on something!

I was next posted to Scotland, then Chatham, and on to Devonport where, in 1915, I joined the *Theseus*. I hadn't been on her long before we were told we were to sail to Gallipoli. A number of ships had attacked the Turkish fortifications, such as the *Queen Elizabeth* in February 1915. They did all right on the first lot of forts, but after that, all they hit was dirt. The Turks laid mines in the right places and did for the French battleship *Bouvet* and also put *Inflexible* and *Irresistible* out of action. The Navy on its own had failed and had to withdraw back to Mudros. It was decided that the Army would have to land and take on the Turks.

We were told we were going to Gallipoli by the captain, and that we were to tow the *Robert E. Lee*. We arrived at Mudros and took on board a battalion of the East Yorks to fight what was to be one of the hardest battles ever fought out. In France, you attacked over open fields with plenty of places to land, but here you had nowhere to land. It felt as if we were going straight to a mountain that could see everything.

As we got near Suvla Bay a two-seater British aircraft flew over us. I think he was seeking the protection of our gunfire, but he had been hit and came down near our ship. We put boats out, reached her before she sank and kept her up, but when we got the pilot and observer out, they were both dead. That upset us. They had been too long in the water.

We knew that the four hundred men of the East Yorks were mostly fresh from training and few had seen action, so every sailor was given two soldiers to look after. We gave them our hammocks, made sure they ate well and gave them our rum. You see, we knew that where they were going would be like Hell on earth, so we gave them all the love we could, because they were going to need it. There was all those feelings, all that silence. That's why I admire the British, they take it and they're quiet.

As we approached Suvla Bay on the night of 6–7 August, it was the darkness before the dawn. I stood on the gangway which had been fitted over the stern to allow the troops to walk down into the motor lighters. As the soldiers followed each other down with their rifles one got hit by a sniper and screamed out. I told him to shut up and put up with the pain or he would frighten the rest – that was my first scream of war. I was frightened myself. I took him down to sick bay. I was then put on a raft with a 5-inch gun and towed by pinnace into shore to land with the troops. I stayed with them for a day and then a picket boat came and took me back on board. Throughout the time we were there we bombarded positions with our five guns amidships, one for'ard and one aft. They were all 6-inch. I had never had any training in how to fire a gun but was made no. 2, the breech loader, on one of the 6-inch guns. Although I was frightened, I kept quiet because that was how everyone behaved. We were well protected against torpedoes by a 'blister', a steel casing which was about six or seven feet out from the ship and went all round. We were fired at, but the torpedo hit the 'blister' and did only a little harm to the ship. We had to retire for the day, but we were back the next day, all repaired.

On one occasion the anchor failed. It meant the ship was in trouble. I had to help the diver with his equipment while someone screwed his helmet on. As he worked down below he talked to me on the rope. The Turks must have spotted what we were doing, so all the time he was down there they were shooting at me. But I had to stay by the rope and work out what the diver wanted. When he finished his work he tugged away and I got him up. And still they were firing at us!

Each day when there was a lull we'd go in and collect the wounded. Some of them were terribly badly wounded, and all so young. Suvla Bay was reasonably flat and the soldiers had made homes for themselves or taken over where other battalions had been before they moved forward. I did my best to cheer them up and encourage them. But most of the time, I was quiet because there wasn't much you could say in the face of all that horror. It was important that they had their own thoughts, they had to come to terms with it in their own way.

Every Sunday we used to try and have a service on board and we sang hymns which were heard by the soldiers on shore. They told us how much it meant to them, so whenever we scrubbed the decks we sang out as loud as we could all the old hymns to inspire them: 'Onward, Christian Soldiers', 'Fight the Good Fight', anything that was rousing. It cheered us up too.

I saw quite a lot of the Turkish prisoners on shore. They were badly dressed and always wanted our boots, they were so poor; but they were wonderful fighting men. They didn't give way. We could see them fighting from the ship; they were good. We didn't feel any anger towards them, we had a respect for them!

We did get black towards the end. We weren't succeeding at all, all we were doing was losing a lot of men and ships. Every day we were bringing in different men, different faces, all tired, all beaten. And it was so hot that summer, so hot. Then, as autumn came on, we knew things were getting worse on land, even with the reinforcements. We were watching a picture of failure fought out by brave men. But that's what the British are like, they keep going right till the end.

When we withdrew on 20 December it was dark. The soldiers were all packed so tight and quiet in the barges making their way to the big ships. We never lost a man, which was remarkable. As we were steaming quietly away I thought of what 'Pincher' Martin, who had done twenty years in the Navy, had said to me a few days after we'd arrived at Suvla Bay: 'We're not going to be flying the Union Jack here'. He was right. We were never going to make it ours.

We spent a lot of time at Mudros and patrolled from there. After we left Mudros we sailed to Crete in early 1917 and we anchored at Suda Bay. While we were there we took over a mental hospital and our two ship's doctors, in their red aprons, were in charge. A number of ships were torpedoed in the area and we'd go out in our pinnaces to pick up survivors. The first lot I picked up on 8 March was from the SS Georgian, a troopship. The wheelwrights had made the handles and the sailmasters had sewn the canvas to make up about ten stretchers. We raced out as fast as we could and picked up all those survivors. I towed them in and had to make sure I didn't bump the wharf. We got them on the stretchers and I piggy-backed one of the chaps, a cockney, who had his leg hanging off. About half way to the hospital he stood on his one leg and said, 'Give us a fag, Jack' so I rolled him a fag and we both had a smoke, and then I got him to hospital. When

I went to see him the next morning he was dead – he had lost too much blood.

A few days later another troopship packed with men was hit in the stern. The U–boat fired another torpedo and a Japanese destroyer (they were on our side in that war) accompanying the troopship deliberately turned itself into the path of the torpedo and was badly damaged, but made it back to harbour. We helped them ashore with their dead and wounded. The Japanese then cremated their dead. Our shipwright made lots of wooden boxes so that the Japs could carry home the remains of their dead. That was a very brave thing the captain of that Japanese ship did – very brave indeed.

In January 1918 we had to deal with about 150 survivors from *HMS Louvain* which had been torpedoed. They had been carried to us by the *Colne*. They were all decent chaps, just out from England to join the *Europa* at Mudros. Sad scenes. We buried some of them with full honours ashore. Everyone was downhearted about the losses. We spent the rest of the war in that area.

One day in 1912 I was walking across Blackheath, and I saw a lovely girl whose parasol had blown away. I retrieved and mended it for her. We began courting. Then the war came along and I didn't want to leave her a widow so I couldn't marry her. While I was in Malta I bought some wonderful silk and lace. On leave in 1917, I got a dressmaker to turn the silk up into a wedding dress and we had a wonderful day. We were married for seventy-six years.

Born in 1894, Jack Gearing is, in 1996, the oldest known rating in the Royal Navy.

Leading Stoker Mechanic Jack Cotterell

I can remember, being about five at the time, the Boer War, and one particular song called 'The Boers have got my Soldier Da'. My mother, though, didn't take to the song at all!

At twelve I left school and went down the mines. About three years later I was made redundant. I went to the Poor Law who would give you a ticket for what you needed. No money, just a ticket for food or clothes or coal. After a few months I found a job in a steel works, firing the coal boilers. I had to walk an hour before I started work at 6am and an hour walk back. It was a very hard life, but the only one we knew; and we had fun swimming in the canal and doing things that boys do.

Georgie Day lived in Pontypool, and he was in the Navy. I used to like his uniform and of course he had tales to tell us boys of foreign places. So in 1912 I thought, that's it, I've had enough of coal, I'm off to join the Navy. I went to Bristol to sign on for seven years with the option of another five years. And what job did they give me? Stoker!

I went to Devonport for training and then was picked for the steam trial of HMS *Centurion*. The weather was awful rough off Portland Bill and we collided with a Swedish trawler. She went straight down. All we knew of it below in the boiler room was the bang. We must have hit her hard because her masthead lamp was flung on to our deck; there were no survivors. We had a lot of dockyard workers on board and they must have thought their end was near. Because we were damaged we had to return to Devonport.

In 1913 I transferred to the light cruiser *Gloucester* which burnt oil and coal. She had 6-inch guns, a pair for'ard and another pair aft, with batteries of 4-inch guns to port and starboard. She also had torpedoes. You could look down on to the lower deck and see them all lined up. She was very modern and very fast, about 26 knots. You had to really shovel to keep her going! When we were coaling I'd be on the winch. We always coaled at sea.

We left Devonport for Malta as part of a peace-keeping force holding the Greeks and the Montenegrans from each other's throats. When the war broke out on 4 August 1914 we were in Alexandria. We got news that the battle-cruiser *Goeben* with 11-inch guns and the cruiser *Breslau* were in the Mediterranean and we were to search for them. We found them coaling off Messina in Sicily. The order received was to 'shadow, not attack them', which seemed sensible because with our 6-inch guns you would not willingly take on the 11-inch guns of a battle-cruiser. We patrolled outside Messina for two nights. Then they both came out. Well, we stokers went mad, we made that much steam Captain Kelly had to phone down to tell us to slow down. That brought a smile to our faces! We chased them for two days. When we weren't stoking away, we'd go up on deck, where we could see the smoke of the German ships.

We thought *Goeben* might make a break north-east for the Atlantic but as she passed Cape Matapan we were told she was heading for Constantinople. At one point we steered straight at the *Goeben* in order to get between her and the Italian shore and to keep her in sight in the failing light.

The *Breslau* was obviously worried about our torpedoes and she made threatening passes. Of course, she could have blown us out of the water. All through the night, though, we pursued them. We were really working our hearts out down below while Captain Kelly kept them in sight, reporting their position all that night. The next morning *Breslau* had had enough. She dropped astern of the *Goeben* and crossed our course as if dropping mines. The captain saw through this and we opened fire at about 11,500 yards with our 6-inch guns. The *Breslau* returned fire and a shell went straight through one of our lifeboats hanging on its davits, which was a shock because I was sitting in the 'heads' at the time. I've never moved so fast in my life.

We got the call from Captain Kelly to increase speed. He turned the *Gloucester* and closed the range so that he could employ his full broadside. The *Goeben* didn't like this. She turned and opened fire again, but missed. We continued to shadow the enemy but from a greater distance. We were still working full out, but by mid-afternoon were running low on coal. At 4pm we heard that we were heading North 55° West at 15 knots, to coal. Our chase was over. We had been the first British ship to open fire in anger in the First World War and the first one to be hit. In the Admiralty report later we got this glowing account of the *Gloucester*'s action. It said the *Goeben* could have sunk us whenever she wanted, but that she'd been put off by our boldness, which gave the impression we had close support nearby. Then it said, 'the combination of audacity with restraint, unswerving attention to the principal military object constitutes a naval episode which may jointly be regarded as a model'. You couldn't ask for greater praise than that. Unfortunately both *Goeben* and *Breslau* escaped our cruisers ahead and made their way to Turkey. But we'd done our job. The *Goeben* and *Breslau* didn't come out again for a long time and, when they did, they ran into our minefields.

We returned to Malta and were there until October when we sailed to the Pacific to search for the German raider, the light cruiser *Emden*. In three months since the outbreak of war she had sunk seventeen merchantmen mostly going to and from Australia and New Zealand. We had been steaming for several days when we heard that, on 9 November, the Australian cruiser *Sydney* had battered *Emden* with shell fire until she was a virtual wreck and sank after running on to a reef.

We put into Bombay for what proved the hottest coaling of my life. Thank God I was on the winch again. But that heat, over 100°F and the humidity of 90%, was almost unbearable. As soon as we had coaled and cleaned up we were back shovelling coal into the flaming maws of those boilers. You had to do it carefully. It's a skilled job needing the firebed spread evenly and all the hollow spots filled and flaming to white heat. We wore blue tinted glasses to save our eyes from the white glare while we were looking where to spread the coal. The *Gloucester* had oil jets just below the grid of the fire.

Our next task was to pursue the *Kronprinz Wilhelm* which had sunk fourteen merchant ships in the South Atlantic. We arrived in the area on 28 March 1915 where we spotted a steamship. As soon as it recognised us it turned and sped off, but we soon caught up with it and Captain Kelly hoisted, 'Stop immediately. What ship?' They replied that they were the Dutch ship *Hendrick*. But our boarding party discovered she was the collier *Macedonia*. She had been ordered to wait in the vicinity to coal and resupply a raider. We took the crew, who were a pretty rough lot, off the ship, and put them down below. We put our prize crew aboard *Macedonia* and sailed her back to Gibraltar. On the way we got a message from the *Macedonia* that the captain (who was still on board) had given orders to the cook to poison our crew. But the cook refused and told one of our officers. We took the captain off and locked him up. He was tried and later shot in Gibraltar.

The *Kronprinz Wilhelm*, having realised she would not be able to coal, put into Newport, Virginia, and the crew were interned. The *Macedonia* was turned over to the authorities at Gibraltar. Her cargo of coal, ammunition and supplies was worth a fortune so we all shared in the prize money.

We then sailed for Scapa Flow from where we did mostly night patrols. After the Pacific and Southern Atlantic it was a cheerless place and the seas were very rough. After a while we moved down to Rosyth, which was much nicer, to join Beatty's Third Battle Cruiser Squadron.

Midshipman Henry St John Fancourt

I was born in 1900 and went to Osborne in January 1913. Our group of seventy joined initially at Osborne and stayed together throughout Dartmouth in the Grenville term. We later went on to do our Sub-Lieutenants' course together.

At the outbreak of war in August 1914 the senior term at Osborne was Blake. Instead of being sent on to Dartmouth they were sent to sea. Some of these young lads joined the Reserve Fleet which was being brought up to full commission in time for the big fleet manoeuvres which were taking place in July 1914. Three of the ships they joined were *Aboukir, Hogue* and *Cressy*, all rather ancient cruisers.

About a month after the war started the three ships were cruising at around 8 knots just off Sheerness and the Hook, supposedly protecting the Expeditionary Force. Then, up popped a U-boat with a young commander who couldn't believe his eyes. He put a torpedo into the *Aboukir* and, in good old naval tradition, the *Hogue* came alongside and lowered its boats to pick up survivors. The U-boat simply fired two torpedoes at the *Hogue* which went down pretty quickly. The *Cressy*, instead of learning a lesson from the *Hogue* and speeding off, went to the aid of the other two cruisers and was promptly hit by a disbelieving U-boat commander.

Fourteen hundred men lost their lives, including ten from Blake who were about fifteen years old. I really don't think the Navy knew what it was doing at this stage: it hadn't been at war for years.

Midshipman Frank Layard

I went to Osborne House at the age of twelve and then on to Dartmouth. But at the beginning of the war in 1914 all cadets were turned out of Dartmouth to join various ships. Some of the boys who were only a couple of months older than me were killed at the battle off Coronel and on the *Aboukir*, *Cressy*, and *Hogue*, sunk by U-boat in September 1914.

I, and five others of my term, joined our first ship, HMS *Indomitable*, at Rosyth in the Firth of Forth in September 1915. This is the moment at the beginning of every naval officer's career which he remembers most vividly. For me, at the age of fifteen, it was like going straight from school into an unknown adult world which I knew would be pretty tough, and I felt very apprehensive as I stepped out of the night train at Inverkeithing station. I had received my appointment while I was on leave at the end of two months' practical training at Keyham, where we had been sent after only two-and-a-half terms at Dartmouth. For some reason our sea chests, instead of being sent straight from the college to our ships, had been sent home and there was consternation among porters and cab drivers in London when asked to handle this huge and heavy article. It would not fit into a taxi and eventually it had to be hoisted on to the roof of a horse-drawn 'growler' which was the only way of getting it from Charing Cross to King's Cross.

We must have been a very comic looking lot as we came on board, with our youthful faces and squeaky voices. The ship had just finished coaling when we reported to the awe-inspiring figure of our commander, James Moreton, a very big man, covered from head to foot in coal dust. He christened us, 'the war babies' and immediately ordered an intensive course of capstan drill, which meant jumping down from the capstan with stiff legs to land heavily on our heels. This spine jolting performance was said to be a sure way to make our voices break. It had no effect whatever. We just had to wait for nature to take its course.

Our life as junior midshipmen in the *Indomitable* was hard but by no means as tough as in some other gunrooms at the time. It was traditional that the 'Young Gentlemen' must be taught that forgetfulness, carelessness and slackness could not be tolerated and that they must develop a proper sense of duty, responsibility and respect for their seniors. Much of this education was done with the aid of the stick, or the threat of the stick, and very effective it proved. Do this or forget to do that and the penalty was a dozen or half a dozen over the backside. Fair enough. But, when, as sometimes happened, the Sub-Lieutenant would say, 'All the young gentlemen are getting slack, half a dozen all round', you didn't know exactly what you were being beaten for, and it seemed unfair. Especially when, at one point, the Sub we had was six-foot-five with a strong right arm and an unerring aim!

A gunroom punishment book was kept and during our twelve months as junior midshipmen the records of beatings varied between the six of us. We took it in our stride, even the young officer who received half a dozen strokes on twelve occasions. But the lot of the junior midshipman was probably harder in the war because, owing to restricted leave and general boredom when in harbour, the senior gunroom officers found their amusement in bullyragging the young gentlemen. The Sub of the mess had great power which he could easily abuse and not that many captains, commanders or senior wardroom officers worried much about what methods were used so long as the behaviour and general discipline of the gunroom was good. One or two extreme cases of bullying came to light, leading to official enquiries and disciplinary action, and as a result the harshness of gunroom life was gradually eased. But it was traditional that continual chasing and much chastisement was an essential part of a young officer's upbringing. It never did anyone much harm unless carried to extremes and it certainly kept us up to the mark. There was here a danger, however, that these methods instilled into officers at a very early age too high a regard for, and obedience to, authority: a too strongly developed sense of the importance of rank and seniority resulting in the reluctance of junior officers to express their own opinions, and a too ready and unquestioning acceptance of those of their seniors. I think it tended to stifle initiative and fresh ideas and to create a tradition of rigid conformity. Yet this same system produced admirals and senior officers of the Second World War, many of whom proved to be brilliant and inspiring leaders.

Our gunroom contained three commissioned officers: the senior Sub-Lieutenant who was mess President; another Sub; and a one-stripe Assistant Paymaster. There were, as well, nine Senior Midshipmen and an Assistant Clerk who ranked as Junior Midshipman. The senior snotties, as midshipmen were called, who had only come to sea a few months before us, were all Public School entry and some three years older. We thought that the much longer training, which we had done, more than made up for the gap in our ages and we always regarded ourselves as their equals.

We took it in turns to be duty 'wonk' (junior midshipmen were known as 'wonks' and sometimes as 'warts') and this was a day when you had to be particularly alert to avoid trouble. The duties included calling the Sub, turning on his bath and seeing that he got up, being available at all times in the mess to run messages; dashing up on deck if the stove smoked to 'trim the Charley Noble', or in other words to turn the cowl on the stove pipe into the wind to prevent a down draught; being ready to jump up and light the Sub's cigarette, never forgetting to carry a box of matches and, in fact, acting as general dogsbody. You might be sitting on the settee in the dog watches reading or writing up some lecture notes (the junior midshipmen were never allowed to sit in the armchairs) when someone would shout, 'Duty Wonk, T. on the P.' (meaning tune on the phone). Up you would jump, wind up the gramophone, put in a new needle – choose a record and start it up. Before you could sit down again there would be a roar, 'Not that damned tune, you bloody wonk, put on . . . so and so'. The seniors all had their particular musical likes and we soon learnt what they were.

When asked a question you were never allowed to say 'I don't know' unless you quickly added, 'But I'll find out'. Then off you would dash to find the answer or hope that if you stayed away long enough the matter would be forgotten. If asked 'Why did you do this?' or 'Why didn't you do that?' you couldn't start your explanation with 'I thought' because you would then immediately be asked 'What happened to the man who thought?' Whereupon you had to go down on your knees and recite the sad story of the man who 'thought' and the three misfortunes which befell him in consequence. It went something like 'He thought he'd got his trousers down and he hadn't. He thought the French letter was all right and it wasn't. Then there was something about a baby!'

While still very new a junior midshipman might be told to go and get the key of the starboard watch from the quartermaster. Up he would go on deck and the quartermaster, knowing the joke, would refer him perhaps to the bosun who, in turn, would send him to the captain of the forecastle, or to the chief stoker, or the bandmaster, or the captain of the heads and so on endlessly until at last the unfortunate lad realised that the whole thing was a leg haul.

Certain silly bits of backchat were invented by our seniors for their amusement and we always had to be ready with the appropriate response. One which sticks in my memory is this:

'Utting,' someone would shout (why Utting and not Hutton I do not know).

'Sir,' Hutton would answer springing to his feet.

'What's the use of you?'

'None, bugger all, sweet F.A., sir,' he would reply.

He would then resume his seat amid howls of laughter. This little pantomime would be repeated day in, day out. We were easily amused in those days.

If at any time the Sub said 'Breadcrumbs' the junior midshipmen had to stuff their fingers in their ears and shut their eyes. Something was going to be said that was not considered fit for the ears of the young gentlemen. If on hearing the shout 'Negative Breadcrumbs', you looked up. This revealed that you had not stopped your ears properly. You were then banged on the head.

Shortly after our arrival in *Indomitable* we were 'christened'. This ceremony took place after dinner on a guest night. One by one we had to kneel in front of the Sub with a ship's biscuit balanced on our head and sing the christening hymn, 'Lord of power and Lord of might at this festival tonight'. When we reached the line 'Till the hand of grace comes down' the Sub brought his fist down with a tremendous bang, breaking the biscuit and nearly knocking you out in the process. The last lines then had to be sung fortissimo, 'Alleluia let us sing, hail to this our christening'.

However it was not always hard work and hard knocks on guest nights. Often they were good fun with the band playing in the flat i.e. cabin outside, a glass or two of sherry beforehand, wine bill permitting, a glass of port with 'The King' and permission to smoke afterwards. The evening generally ended up with a sing-song round the piano, or races over or round the chairs, or competitive games like pushing a penny as far as possible with the end of your fingertips and both feet behind a line and only one hand on the deck. We were taught all the bawdy gunroom songs and jokes and we learned to drink, sometimes to excess, and to smoke. All this before we were quite sixteen. Regrettable as this may seem, I do not think it did any of us very much harm, and we kept ourselves reasonably fit with games and the daily dozen at early morning PT on the forecastle.

Apart from these activities our everyday life on board gave us plenty of exercise. If sent on a message you could stand still just long enough to say, 'Ay, Ay, sir', and then you had to *fly*, and never should you be caught walking up or down a ladder; it must always be taken at the run.

We were lucky in having an exceptionally nice lot of wardroom officers who would frequently ask us in for a drink or a meal. We really enjoyed Sunday supper in the wardroom with a cinema show or a game of bridge to follow. A guest-night dinner was even better. There might be dancing in the wardroom flat, or our snotties' nurse, who was a great comedian, would amuse everyone by conducting the band or giving us one of his brilliant imitations of the comedian, Harry Tate.

In marked contrast was the seeming indifference shown by our captains. (There were three during my time in the ship.) We were never asked into the cuddy for a meal and in fact he seldom spoke to us except to give us an order or send us on a message. Captains and admirals in those days were remote and mysterious people who did not consider it necessary to establish a personal contact with those under their command and who, in consequence, were seldom seen. There was no attempt to keep ship's companies informed of what was going on and there was never an occasion, that I can recall, when the captain fell the men in to give them a pep talk. During my two years only once did the admiral of our squadron come on board and not once did we see Admiral Beatty; not even after Jutland. How different it is today.

Because, as midshipmen, we were still under training, our parents, even in wartime, had to pay the Admiralty £50 a year to supplement our meagre 1s.9d. a day pay. This extraordinary arrangement was brought to an end through a question in Parliament. A parent, whose young son had been killed at the battle of Jutland, received shortly afterwards a reminder from the Admiralty that the £50 payment was overdue. Nevertheless, after paying our mess bill, we were able to afford quite frequent trips to Edinburgh and the local golf course with occasional visits to cinemas and theatres which shows how far a few pounds went in those days.

Being under eighteen we were not allowed to smoke or drink spirits, but we were allowed a ten shilling monthly wine bill, which went quite a long way with port and sherry at 2d. a glass, and a gin at a penny. Gin was always Plymouth Gin. A tin of fifty Gold Flake cigarettes only cost 1s.3d. and on guest nights the junior midshipmen were allowed to smoke after 'The King'. I bought my first pipe in Edinburgh and lit it up at the next guest night. Long before it was finished I had to retire to the heads to be very sick indeed.

When in harbour we had instruction in seamanship, navigation, signals, torpedo, gunnery and engineering. Not only did our snotties' nurse amuse us socially but in his lectures he was full of little epithets. 'Seamanship,' he would say, 'is the application of common sense to the everyday happenings of maritime existence.' And he could really mix metaphors. If you were trying to think of the answer to some question he would remark, 'Silence is golden, but it cuts no ice'.

At sea we were in three watches acting as lookouts in the foretop by day and as assistant 4-inch gun and searchlight control officers by night. We also did bridge duties and, at least twice a night, we had to get cocoa for the officers on watch and at the end of the watch it was our job to go below and call the reliefs. It was really frightening climbing up the outside ladder to the foretop in bad weather, clinging on for dear life as the ship rolled about and the full force of the wind caught you. With a stern wind the climb was sheer agony. You tried to hold your breath as clouds of hot smoke from the funnel swirled around you. At some point you had to open your mouth to take a breath and then you would have a lung full of the filthy stuff that left you coughing and gasping. On finally reaching the top you pushed open the small trap hatch and struggled through; no easy task when wearing an oilskin over an overcoat over countless sweaters. I lost cap after cap overboard as I climbed up and down that mast.

Less dangerous were trips to the galley at night for cocoa. But even then you were dodging under the swaying hammocks, trying to keep your feet and balance the jug of cocoa as the ship rolled, and the smell, the heat and the steam in the galley was enough to turn your stomach. Calling reliefs required much perseverance and a special technique. No relief could be late, but also God help you if you broke the calling rules. Never, never could you shake or even touch an officer or shout at him. You had to switch on the light, call him by name, and tell him the time and report the weather, and repeat this until he was awake, then return over and over again until you saw him get out of his bunk.

Occasionally we would go into Edinburgh to have tea or play golf or go to the cinema. There would also be the occasional afternoon dance for junior officers at the Kintore Rooms arranged by the Edinburgh ladies. If there weren't enough volunteers for these events some of us were detailed off to attend and did so very reluctantly, at least I did, because at that age I was shy, I was very uncertain of my dancing and I was terrified of strange girls. I once appeared on the stage of the King's Theatre. Lady Beatty had arranged a charity matinee and the *Indomitable* was asked to provide a turn. We danced the hornpipe which seemed to go down rather well.

Running a picket boat was a wonderful experience, and a duty which every midshipman enjoyed. No modern motor-boat will ever match the beauty, elegance and dignity of the old steam picket boat with its sparkling bright work, scrubbed wooden decks and spotless paintwork. It was capable of 15 knots. Every midshipman took a proper pride in his boat's appearance and each week he would be expected to give the coxswain an extra tin or two of Bluebell polish. The crew consisted of a Petty Officer coxswain, two bowmen, a stern sheetman, a fender man, a stoker in the boiler room, and a stoker Petty Officer in the engine room. When a midshipman was in the boat he always took the wheel himself and worked the engine-room gong while the coxswain stood alongside keeping a watchful eye. The young inexperienced officer was in charge, but the older and greatly experienced Petty Officer was there at his side to help and give advice if required, and this relationship was accepted gratefully on the one side and without any resentment on the other.

On days when leave was granted all the picket boats of the Fleet would be waiting at Hawes pier, one alongside the other, having come in stern first in order to make a quick getaway. Each had an illuminated sign displayed on the top of the cabin. As the buses arrived down from Edinburgh the officers would stream on board their boats. With the engine opened right out, the whole boat throbbing and vibrating, the boiler-room fan roaring and sparks flying out of the funnels, a dozen or more boats, starting with the outside one, would go dashing off towards the ships lying a mile or two out. We looked on this return trip as a race and tried desperately to catch or out-distance the rest. In the excitement of the race, the midshipman could become very unpopular with his messmates, sitting huddled up on the top of the cabin, if he failed to ease down when the spray started to come over or if a sudden alteration of course brought water slopping in over the officers in the stern sheets.

There was a great temptation to try and show what a brilliant and dashing boat handler you were. To make a good alongside at high speed, judging the tide to a nicety and pulling up with a smother of foam under your counter as you rang down full astern, was a way of demonstrating your skill, but it did not always come off. A small error of judgement could result in a crash which could easily damage your boat, or if a strong tide was running, getting your bows either swept in and firmly wedged under the ladder or carried out while the bowmen desperately struggled to hold on to the boat rope. This created a very undignified and unseamanlike situation, which you could have avoided with a little more care and attention and if you had not been so anxious to show off.

Two incidents come vividly to mind when I recall my gunroom days. The first was the unforgettable sight of the Grand Fleet at sea. As you looked there would be just columns of smoke on the horizon. Then the cruisers spread ahead on the AK line would come into sight and then, at last, this huge armada of anything up to thirty battleships advancing in five or more columns surrounded by a close screen of destroyers. That was a spectacle the like of which will never be seen again.

Again I well remember a combined wardroom and gunroom picnic at Scapa Flow with a tremendous meal of bangers and bacon fried up on a large fire and much singing and vast consumption of sloe gin in the launch on the return journey. Little did we think at that time that within forty-eight hours we would be in the thick of battle. (See below, page 71.)

Naval Cadet Charles Drake

It was May 1913 and a very cold day. Exmouth term, which was just about to join Osborne, was lined up in two lines opposite each other on the South Railway Jetty at Portsmouth Dockyard. We were to be inspected by the First Sea Lord, Prince Louis of Battenberg, and the First Lord of the Admiralty, Winston Churchill. Prince Louis's son, later to be Lord Mountbatten, was a naval cadet in my house.

We were a diverse bunch. Among our entry we had C. B. Fry's son and W. G. Grace's grandson. Many of us were fairly impecunious and without private means. I remember the first time I put on my uniform my mother started singing from Gilbert and Sullivan. 'When I first put this uniform on, I thought as I looked in the glass, 'Tis one in a million, if any civilian, my figure and form can surpass'. She was terribly proud that her son was joining the Royal Navy.

Prince Louis of Battenberg had what I would call an imperial beard and Winston Churchill had a reefer suit and a yachting cap. Well, I was very young and didn't know who they were: I thought Battenberg was King George. You see I had never seen a good photograph in the paper of George V, I only knew he had a beard.

As they came down the line, Winston chatted away every now and again to one or other of the cadets who were all shuddering. When he was nearby, he suddenly turned round at right angles and pointed at me and said, 'What have you got at the end of that lanyard, boy?' I didn't like being called 'boy', but I was very frightened and pretty small, too. I said, 'A key, sir.' 'A key, have you?' said Winston. Then he said, 'Have you got anything else?' I said, very quietly, 'Yes, sir, a knife.' 'A knife, have you? Could you show it to me?' I pulled the end of the lanyard out and held it out to him. He said, 'Would you open it, please.' It was very stiff but I pulled very hard and out came the biggest blade. 'You've got that blade on that knife!' 'Yes, I have sir.' Winston held the knife in his hand and turned to the others and said, 'Now, my boys' – I think he called us 'boys' – 'when you get to the enemy, you must cut him down, cut him to bits!' Well, this was a rather horrifying remark to hear from the First Lord of the Admiralty. However, we all mumbled 'Yes, sir'.

My dear mother and another lady behind us heard this and were shuddering with fright. My mother was probably thinking, 'What have I put my boy into, cutting Germans to bits?' I thought Mountbatten's father looked a bit shocked too. But Winston moved off, laughing away. We were marched down in single file on to the tug to the Isle of Wight. We were then allowed a little bit of stand-easy time and we waved to our parents on the jetty as off we went to Osborne.

Boy First-Class Stan Smith

I was born on 23 March 1899 but from the age of two months I was brought up by my grandparents in Great Yarmouth, about twelve miles away, to give my parents a chance to build up their home. I was made a great fuss of and was absolutely spoiled. My nanny, Jenny Minns, used to take me out and about around town. As I grew older, I began to explore Yarmouth for myself. In those days all the streets were cobbled and filled with horse-drawn carriages and carts, and there were horse trams running from the south end of the town right through the centre and along the promenade.

My grandparents were very religious and we went to church three times every Sunday. I went to the Priory School which was run by the town's main parish church of Saint Nicholas. We wore caps bearing three yellow rings and the Yarmouth coat of arms. The uniform was velvet knee breeches, shoes with large silver buckles, a white lace shirt and collar and a small cut Eton jacket. I recall with some embarrassment that my hair, which was in curls, flowed down to my waist after the fashion of the day.

I was one of the first pupils at Yarmouth Grammar School which had just been completed. We had a lot of homework in those days, and I had five maiden aunts who would never help me whatsoever with my studies, but I couldn't complain, since they were all school teachers.

After I left school they bought me an apprenticeship as an electrical engineer. Electricity had only just arrived in Great Yarmouth; the trams were all being converted from horse power and ours was one of the first houses to have 'the electric'. When World War I was declared the whole population of Yarmouth seemed to be caught up in war fever and all the young men were rushing to join up for the forces. Everybody said it would only last about six months, so it seemed a good idea to be part of it. My old mate, Charlie White, and I did everything we could to assist the war effort even though we were only fifteen. However, we got the distinct impression that they weren't that hard up for recruits.

One evening, just as it was getting dark, a Zeppelin appeared over Yarmouth and bombed the town, damaging the fish market and surrounding buildings. This made us more determined than ever to join up and do our bit. We fished around for information and found out that we could join the Royal Navy at fifteen years and three months. We weren't going to let three months put us off, so we went to war by tram, to the nearest recruiting office at the coastguard station in Gorleston. Faced by our irresistible enthusiasm, the recruiting officer hadn't a chance. He agreed that we could join, provided that we passed the necessary examinations and got our papers filled in and signed by our parents.

We had to do a small educational test and pass a medical, which we both did successfully. The hardest part was getting the papers signed. Charlie's parents were highly unlikely to sign his, while I, with a doting grandmother and five maiden aunts to contend with, hadn't the ghost of a chance. Rising to the occasion with the best intentions, we signed each other's papers. They were unwittingly accepted as proof of parental approval and we were told to report the following day with nothing more than the clothes we stood up in.

The next morning I left a note for my grandmother on the mantelpiece in my bedroom and slipped out to meet Charlie. At Gorleston we were given railway warrants and a meal voucher. Then we were taken to Yarmouth station, put on a train and told to get off at Manningtree in Essex. From then on we were in the charge of a petty officer who took us by train to Harwich where we boarded a steam pinnace for the journey across to the Royal Navy training establishment at Shotley. Thus, for better or worse, at the age of fifteen we were in the Navy.

The most pressing matter at this point was the need to eat. We were given two boiled eggs and two thick slices of bread and butter; not the sort of meal I'd been used to. Still, it went down well on an empty belly. We were shown the dining-hall and the dormitory and allotted two beds before being allowed to wander around the barracks to get acquainted with the different classrooms and other buildings.

The following morning we were called at 6.00 am, given a basin of cocoa and two biscuits, and told that we had fifteen minutes to wash, dress and fall in on the football ground for PT. We had to run around the pitch for half an hour before going in for breakfast. After that we had to pass the doctor, the dentist and the barber who soon put paid to my curly locks. So ended our first day.

The following day the real business of training to be a sailor began when we were formed into classes and introduced to Petty Officer Slyfield. There were twelve in my class and it didn't take any of us very long to realise that he was a real old sailor, a tough salt who believed that sailors were born of vigorous discipline. He used to walk around brandishing a six-inch vent bit – a thin steel rod about six feet long – which he would use enthusiastically with the least provocation. Once we were at drill he exhibited a command of language which was in itself an intrinsic part of my naval education, displaying an intimate acquaintance not only with ourselves, but also with our mothers and fathers. He was even inclined to doubt whether we had any parents at all.

His job was to make sailors of us, and quickly, for there was a war on. For our part, we got on with the job and began to tolerate the insults. We learned gunnery, signalling, wireless and all the other mysteries of life at sea. Using a mock loader in the 6-inch gun battery, we had to heave projectiles weighing 100lb on to the loading tray; a feat of strength which taxed our young muscles to the utmost. We managed it, after a fashion, and eventually passed all our subjects. I was made a second-class boy and allowed to exercise my new-found authority by marching the class from one classroom to another.

However, any delusions of grandeur were quickly quashed by a visit to Shotley swimming pool. We had to strip naked at one end of the baths and, seated on stools, learn how to kick our arms and legs. Thus fortified with such basic theory, we had to parade up to the six-foot end and jump in one at a time. Survival was the only incentive to learn. All the instructor had to help you was a long pole and if you grabbed this you were pushed under again. You just had to grin and bear it, kicking and struggling to make it to the shallow end. It was at this point that I first began to understand the fear of the deep and appreciate the rigorous training. When a ship goes down and you've got to swim for it, there's no time for the niceties of a more leisurely instruction. We had to pass a swimming test in a canvas suit which stiffened up tremendously in the water. Our arms and legs were so stiff and sore as we kicked our laborious way for two lengths of the baths. I managed it, but afterwards I was more drowned than alive.

We were then transferred to HMS *Ganges*, an old sailing warship moored in the centre of the river, to learn seamanship. We were taught how to control and use oars in the various boats, including gigs, skiffs, whalers and cutters. We no longer had to endure PT in the morning. Instead they sent us over the masthead, which was a jolly sight worse. The ratlins were made of half-inch thick tarred rope which used to cut our bare feet to pieces. We were glad to come down the other side on our knees.

We also had to go out on the rigging which ran out from the shrouds to the edge of the crow's nest at an angle of forty-five degrees, so if you had shoes on, you'd lose your grip and be left hanging in mid-air. There was an escape route through lubber's hole near the mast, but neither the discipline nor the fear of failure allowed us to use this. I became quite expert at climbing the rigging. With one or two others I used to climb the mast in my spare time, to get into the crow's nest for a smoke. This was one of my first experiences in bending the Royal Navy rules and getting away with it, because we weren't allowed to smoke until we were eighteen. The extra-curricular practice stood me in good stead. When we had ceremonial occasions I was chosen as button boy, which meant I had to climb the mast and stand on the cap at the very top which was about one and a half foot square. The people down below looked very small indeed.

We were each issued with two hammocks, a set of clews and a lashing. Then we learnt how to put an eye in the lashing and how to sling the hammocks using a simple half-hitch which tightened up with the increasing weight put on it. There was a good deal of fun when we got into our hammocks for the first time. Some went straight over the top while others were swallowed up like Egyptian mummies. We eventually got the hang of it. A bed, two covers and two blankets made up the sleeping arrangements. Hammocks, though very nice to sleep in, posed a special problem in the mornings. Called at 6.00 am, we had to jump out smartly and lash our hammocks with seven complete half-hitches, all exactly the right distance apart, before stowing them away. Only then could we get away for our basins of cocoa and a couple of biscuits, get washed and be ready, twenty minutes later, for what the day might bring. When the petty officer came round in the morning with his 'Wakey, wakey' call, it was a scramble which had to be seen to be believed.

We gradually began to feel and perhaps even to look more like sailors, as we were kitted out for sea. They gave us four of everything – underclothing, white suits, navy suits, collars and everything a sailor needs, including a 'housewife', which was a rolled-up pad containing a sewing kit for patching up our clothes. Everything had to be identifiable so I spent some time attaching a piece of wood with my name carved into it to my gear. Navy coloured items had to be marked with white paint, white things with black paint and our boots and shoes acquired metal identification discs. We were then shown how to lay all these out for kit inspection, Royal Navy style.

Basic instruction on how to wash our clothes and keep ourselves fit and clean was not forgotten. We were put into messes where we had to make our own tea and peel our own spuds, exactly as we would have to do on board our first ship.

Back in Great Yarmouth, my battalion of aunts had never really got over the shock of my sudden departure, and thinking I would leap at the chance to return to my former cosy existence, they came down to Shotley to buy me out. I was sent for by the commanding officer, but maybe my training had been too good, stiffening my resolve to the point where nobody was ever going to call me a quitter. I looked at my aunts and I looked at the Navy, and although I was disillusioned, I stayed put.

Boy First-Class Charles Morris

I joined the training ship *Arethusa* in 1913. It was an old wooden ship, based at Greenhithe, which belonged to the Shaftesbury Homes. Although I wasn't an orphan myself there were plenty on board, it was like an orphanage on water. We got up about seven, scrubbed the decks, then after breakfast we were taught all forms of seamanship, rigging, diving and there was lots of swimming: it gave me a really good start for life. I was on board about twelve months before going to HMS *Ganges* at Shotley.

As a Boy First Class at sixteen I was taught mathematics, navigation and how to use a sextant. Good schooling. We learnt how to track the passage of a ship from one point to the next taking advantage of the tides, the winds and, because there were few giros in those days, we learnt how to understand the variations of the compass. We also had to climb the mast and dress the sails.

In April 1915 I joined the *Marlborough* at Scapa Flow. She was part of the First Battle Squadron, an 'Iron Duke' class ship completed in 1914, and led the squadron which contained the *Revenge*, *Hercules* and *Agincourt*. What a sight that was, all those squadrons of dreadnoughts. In the forbidding gloom, they were dark and massive.

On my way to join *Marlborough* I was stung in the eye by a wasp. My eye really swelled up so I went to the sick bay where they lanced it. I was in there four days. When I went back down below, I'd got something of a reputation. Everyone thought I was a fighter.

The *Marlborough* used to go out to sea for two or three days at a time. Of course, she was a coal-burning ship and used to take on about 3,000 tons of coal at a time which could take up to twenty hours. Everyone on board took part. It was hard, but it brought officers and men together; we had to work as one. All the hands were piped 'clean into coaling rig!' This meant we could wear almost anything to cover ourselves, some really fancy head gear was used which helped brighten the task. As the collier came alongside we'd scramble on to the holds and hold the bags while others filled them. There was dust everywhere. There would be four big Able Seamen filling my bag and they didn't care if they caught your knuckles. It was done as fast as possible because there was competition between ships to see who could coal fastest. The bags were hoisted on to the decks of the *Marlborough* by derricks. Then it was transferred to barrows and wheeled to the chutes. We'd only have about half an hour for meals, usually two large slabs of bread with bacon or cheese washed down with a big bowl of tea. Then back to work.

After we'd loaded it all on, we then had to hose down the ship before we could go below to wash ourselves. There weren't any showers so four of us had to wash in one bucket of cold water. Coaling was tough, very tough.

We got sixpence a day, but beer was a penny ha'penny a pint and porter (ale) was a penny. We'd enough to pay for extra eggs and bread. The only drink on the ship was rum and we weren't allowed that until we were twenty-one and we couldn't smoke until we were eighteen. If we were caught smoking it was cells for two or three days on 'low diet' – in other words, bread and water.

We used to get the news of the war relayed by wireless from a station in Cornwall. It would be typed up and put on the noticeboard. We were learning about the Western Front and the terrible things that were happening. But for us it was another world away.

Signalman Eric Peacock

I became interested in the Navy when a friend told me of his experiences in the Mediterranean. But I was under age and undersize at the time, so I had to wait until I was fifteen and three months in May 1913 before I could join as a 'Boy'.

I did my seamanship training at Devonport on *Powerful* and then on the *Ganges* at Shotley. After qualifying at the Signal School in Portsmouth I was allocated to HMS *Irresistible*, which was part of the Fifth Battle Squadron based at Portland Harbour. There was great excitement on board when war was declared on 4 August. Within a few days the squadron under the Flagship *Prince of Wales* sailed from Portland for channel patrol, accompanied by much cheering from the other ships and the Army manning the guns on the breakwaters.

We moved at economical speed between Start Point and Dover in single line for roughly six weeks. During this time I got to know about coaling. We would drop into the Isle of Wight and as much as 1,400 tons would be hoisted aboard in bags by derricks from the collier. Apart from those on duty, the whole ship's company took part with us boys usually in the dumping stations, throwing the empty bags to the collier. We got blacker and blacker as the day went on. A week later we would be back doing the same.

Three cruisers patrolled east of Dover northwards. We often sighted them and signalled greetings. They were the *Aboukir*, *Cressy* and *Hogue* and we were very saddened when we heard how they were all sunk by one submarine.

On 26 November we were at Sheerness. That day, as all days at 8 am, we were indicating by flags the state of coal, provisions and water. It so happened that *Bulwark*'s hoist was a bit adrift and so we were watching her. As her flag reached the top, there was a terrific explosion and then the startling realisation that the *Bulwark* was no longer there, just an open space between adjacent ships, calm water and bits and pieces floating. It was devastating.

Early in January 1915 we sailed from Chatham to a secret destination, in the company of the battleship *Majestic*. Our chief yeoman, a wily man, had spotted some details on the captain's chart, and said quietly to us, 'I hope you all have your whites and cap covers'. This meant warmer climes. We arrived via Malta at Tenedos, an island near the entrance to the Dardanelles. We were told we were going to bombard the area and then force a passage through and shorten the war! Throughout late February and the first two weeks of March we were kept busy bombarding short gun positions and the village of Krithia. We also landed demolition parties to blow up any enemy guns still standing after our bombardment.

On one occasion I went ashore. Landing in whalers at Kum Kale on the Asiatic Coast there was no trouble until we neared the gun positions, which consisted of big mounds of earth with the gun on rails in between, easy for running into firing and returning. Fire opened up from various points and one or two of the party were wounded, but the Royal Marines went into action and the demolition party got on with the job of putting the guns out of action. The firing ceased, and it was decided to proceed further inland. Until then I had done nothing but remain near the CO and keep all my equipment intact – a tidy load – for, besides my side arms, service revolver, ammunition, cutlass and necessary trappings, I also carried two semaphore flags, white and blue Morse flags, boat-flashing lamp and candles. I moved around with my pistol cocked for instant action and ready to frighten any Turk that appeared! We came to a big wall, apparently one end of a rectangular burial ground, and, as the firing appeared to come from the further end, it was decided to split the party, move up each side and charge round the end and annihilate the enemy. This we did but only to make a lot of cheering noise and meet each other! The sniping continued while we made our way to the whalers, one marine dragging a wounded comrade on a spade. I broke my pistol and littered the flag deck with six empty cartridges. I don't know who I fired at, but I must have had a good time!

The day of 18 March remains clear in my mind, as it was our biggest attack on the Turkish gun positions. Many battleships and destroyers (British and French) moved into position from west of the entrance into the Dardanelles towards Chanak. My action station was with the Fire Control Officer, in the foretop, high on the foremast, manning the voice pipe to the captain. Action continued throughout the afternoon with relays of up to four battleships stationed abeam moving forward as the leading ships got far enough and turned about to make way for the next line. The bombardment was severe and ships were hit. Apart from my excitement in passing and receiving messages, the Gunnery Officer had also climbed into the foretop and we had a direct line to the fire-control room. So I knew what was going on, and also had a magnificent view of the whole area. The first real shock was hearing a heavy explosion and seeing the French battleship *Bouvet* listing and gradually disappearing, all in seconds.

The action continued; other ships were hit by gunfire and there were big splashes in the sea around us from near misses. I was completely occupied with control work when, suddenly, there was an awful crunch, the ship shuddered and began to list to starboard. It seemed quite a bit to those of us in the foretop! There was a complete silence for a few seconds and then the Gunnery Officer ordered 'Everyone out of the Top'. One by one the crew went down the ladder, leaving myself and the two officers to follow, when the GO said, 'Off you go, lad', and down the ladder I went. Then just before I reached the lower top, a shell hit the foremost funnel and I let go the rungs on the mast and fell on to a number of gym mats which had been stored there. When I reached the upper deck I was yellow from the fumes. The Turks now decided we were a sitting target and guns from each side of the Channel concentrated their fire and made several hits. I remember looking towards the bridge and seeing the captain leaning against the rails at the same time as I heard the order, 'Abandon Ship'. As I slipped into the water I was worried about a new pair of boots obtained on repayment from the Slop Room only the previous day, which were slung round my neck, but I never saw them again. I was soon picked up and taken to *Queen Elizabeth*.

After the *Irresistible*, the QE was a wonderful ship, with spacious mess deck and plenty of room to sling a hammock. I transferred to the cruiser *Phaeton* and travelled to Mudros during a violent spell of weather, when I experienced the worst bout of sea sickness I ever had: the ship was pitching and wallowing, hitting 'milestones' every few seconds. I turned myself almost inside out, not an ounce of bile left inside me and, as we entered harbour, I was hanging over the rail like a wet towel.

At Mudros I was chosen as part of a landing party led by the chief yeoman of the *Irresistible* to land at 'W' beach, Cape Helles. We spent a lot of time preparing. The only spare uniforms were khaki, but to maintain our pride we stencilled 'RN' on to our cap ribbons.

We disembarked from the *Euryalus* with the Lancashire Fusiliers. As we moved towards the shore, tows were returning with the dead and wounded. The invasion force had been seen when Very lights were fired by the Turks, so rifle fire came from every point along the cliff top. There was also barbed wire in shallow water and on the shore. Somehow we got in bows-on, between bodies and wire. As I jumped out of the boat I had to try and keep hold of my signalling equipment, because that was vital – I wasn't any good without it, for, as soon as we hit the shore, and despite enemy fire, we had to keep up our signals to our ships covering the troops landing. The Turks made several determined attempts to drive us into the sea. I found myself creeping forward, like an infantryman, and banging away with my .303 rifle. But really it was the Lancashire Fusiliers who held the day. They were marvellous.

The first forty-eight hours were the most hectic as far as our unit was concerned. The Lancashire Fusiliers, with support from those who had landed on 'X' and 'V' beaches, gradually pressed back the Turks who had prepared trenches almost up to the water's edge, but at tremendous cost of life. On one occasion I was standing alongside an officer from Army Signals while he was reading out the words being transmitted. All of a sudden he was hit and badly wounded. Everyone back on the ship thought I was dead because I rolled away out of trouble when he went down. It wasn't just rifle fire that was so hard to endure but the heavy Turkish artillery from Kum Kale. That was constant – there was no peace. All the time we were kept busy: it was semaphore or morse flag by day, box lamp in the dry batteries, or boats flashing lamp at night. Later, when we got more established, we used a heliograph for hourly communications with Tenedos, which was about twelve miles away.

We slept where we could, when we could, pulling a waterproof over us when it rained, and could it rain! The enemy aircraft used to drop a load of darts which dropped in showers which was pretty miserable. As the weather improved we could grab a swim, but corned beef and biscuits was still our daily diet.

During my time there I got dysentery really badly. I managed to get hold of some flour and drink a basin full of flour water. I didn't go near a bog for three weeks! Living in dugouts, and lying on sandy soil, meant that everyone became infected with lice. Even if you got rid of your old clothes and put on new ones they still came back. They would recommence attack as soon as you were dressed. Neither flame nor water could kill them! The heat, the unburied dead carcasses, and the rubbish brought in a plague of flies. Mealtimes were a nightmare because everything was black with flies. One particular lunchtime, eight Royal Engineers rigged up a table close by us and sat down to eat their bully beef. A shell burst and killed them all. We only found pieces when we went to help them.

As the months went on we saw Turkish prisoners. We all admired them as fighters, but they were mostly filthy with torn and tattered uniforms. They'd had no pay for months and very little to eat. Yet still they shelled and shot at us. I even got reprimanded for not taking adequate precautions during shelling!

Our wireless transmission station was visited by quite a few senior officers including Sir Ian Hamilton and Lord Kitchener. We also saw a lot of Commander Samson of the RNAS. Every aircraft that flew over to us was Samson. He really was a hero, he seemed free to fly where he wanted.

Rumours of a possible evacuation came through to us before anyone else. Units began to disappear. We then heard that Suvla and Anzac beaches had been successfully evacuated with no casualties. By now, December, the weather was raw cold. Yet we couldn't believe that the Turks would let us simply slip away. But they did, and on 8 January 1916 we left from the pierhead. Of that 20-man naval party I was one of the first on to the beach on 25 April 1915 and one of the last to leave. I was ten days off my eighteenth birthday.

Ordinary Seaman Tom Spurgeon

I was brought up in the East End of London and was just sixteen when war broke out and I joined the Navy. I went to Chatham for a few months of general seaman's training and then, at Christmas, was sent up to join the *Ark Royal* at Blyth in Northumberland where she was being converted into a seaplane carrier. Originally she had been laid down as a collier and, as the only carrier designed to carry sail, she had a mizzen to keep her head into the wind.

Every day it was snowing and absolutely freezing. We were told we'd have to scrub the decks with this brick type thing, a holystone, so-called because we had to get down on our hands and knees to use it. You know, bare feet, rolled-up trousers; well, we didn't fancy that in the freezing weather so one of my chums threw the bricks overboard! The captain fell us all in and said, 'If someone will come forward and tell us why they did that, everything will be forgotten'. Nobody did.

We were all put on 10A punishment which meant, instead of falling in at 6 am, we fell in at 4 am. And four o'clock on the Northumberland coast in winter is very cold. I thought to myself, if this is the Royal Navy I wish I'd never joined. But slowly we were getting the ship into shape, polishing brass, scrubbing the decks, making everything spotlessly clean. The 'Jaunty' (the Master-at-Arms) used to follow the captain around with his notebook and pencil and woe betide you if he found anything not perfect. That jaunty always seemed delighted if he could jot something down. Any boy caught smoking meant that the jaunty could give him 'six of the best'. It hurt even watching it.

On 1 February 1915 we sailed to the Dardanelles. I think we had been sent after the *Goeben* and *Breslau* but nothing came of it. Aircraft were still in their infancy then but we had on board six seaplanes with folded wings and four land planes which could take off from the deck but had to land on an airfield. All were held below in a big hold. On each side of the ship was a crane which would lift them up on to the deck. We would open out the aircraft wings, then check them. Once everything was all right the pilot would get in. The cranes would then swing the seaplane over the side and lower it down into the sea. Sometimes a motor-boat would tow it away for a suitable place to take off and away it would go. The only weapon on board, apart from two 112lb handbombs, was the pilot's revolver.

The aircraft were kept very busy spotting for the ground forces and also guiding submarines. The planes would go out early morning and then report back. We lost one of the pilots, Viscount Torrington, and his observer. They were forced down by the enemy. We lost other aircraft shot down.

One of the top pilots of the Royal Naval Air Service (RNAS) was Wing Commander Samson. He was everywhere, a real daredevil who could use some choice language when he wanted. He was a grand character whom we all admired. He sent a note to our pilots: 'Observers always carry rifle, proper charts, binoculars; life-saving device or petrol can; watch if not connected to aeroplane. Pilot carrying out observations: nail pad to instrument panel!!'

Through binoculars we could see some of the fighting on land as sometimes we were only five hundred yards from the shore. We saw the Australians arrive. I was particularly impressed with their tents which had a metal structure inside and were easy to erect. But everyone seemed to have arrived too late because the Turks were well dug in and prepared. When soldiers came down to the beach with the wounded we'd send a party out to take them back to various ships. There was a French hospital ship nearby, the *Duguay-Trouin*, and in April they took on board the poet Rupert Brooke who was very ill. He'd been bitten on the lip by a mosquito and it had become poisoned. Unfortunately he died. He had insisted he didn't want to be buried at sea, so they decided to buy him on the island of Skyros. They chose a place in an olive grove. There wasn't time to put a name on his coffin so one of his friends, Arthur Asquith, the son of the Prime Minister, used a cauterising iron and burnt his name into the coffin. His grave was lined with sprigs of olive and flowering sage. At the foot of the grave the men from his platoon of the Hood Battalion planted a white cross. There was a great feeling of sadness everywhere. It had been so sudden. Only a year before he'd written his poem called 'The Soldier'.

The *Ark Royal* stayed throughout the action at Gallipoli. Our food was mostly corn beef and hard-tack biscuits. We were bombed from the land as well as by German aircraft. We only had 6-inch guns so there wasn't much we could do in reply. We used to pull into Mudros for a rest, but we were bombed even there. The Zeppelins were a real danger to us, because you couldn't hear them coming. The searchlight used to catch them, though.

When we finally left Gallipoli I was a bit sad because it hadn't been a success and there had been a lot of death. As a young man I couldn't understand what it was really all about.

Private Joe Clements

Royal Marine Light Infantry

I was born in Caterham in 1898 and at thirteen went to work as an errand boy for a local grocer. We worked six days a week and sometimes on a Saturday till 9 pm. I used to pull a two-wheeled cart for miles in all weathers for 2s.6d. a week. Sometimes on a Wednesday half-day the boss gave me half an apple.

I tried to join the Navy at thirteen and was bitterly disappointed to be turned down. On the 18 August 1914 I left home and walked the seven miles into Croydon and tried again to join the Navy. I was told the Navy was full up but I could join the Royal Marine Light Infantry, so I signed on for twelve years. My age was sixteen and five months so the recruiting officer advised me to go outside and have another birthday. That same evening we were put on a train to Deal and didn't get to bed till midnight, but of course we were up the next morning at 5.30. We were taught how to drill, how to shoot and how to swim in a canvas duck suit. In November I joined the brigade of the Royal Naval Division which had returned from Antwerp and three weeks later was posted to the machine-gun section. On 1 January 1915 we left Deal for a three-day march, but I suppose, looking back, we had in truth left to go to war. We marched 18 miles one day, 25 miles the next, and 25 the last day, all in full kit. Then they put us on a train to Blandford where we were billeted in a village school. The King and Winston Churchill inspected us so we knew we were going to the Front. It is funny how people don't tell you, yet you know. The 1st and 2nd RMLI were to be part of 3rd Machine Brigade, 63 Royal Naval Division, alongside the two Anson battalions.

On 26 February we embarked on the *Franconia* and, after a week, arrived at Port Said and stayed there two weeks training in the desert. Then we boarded the *Alnwick Castle* and stopped off on the rocky island of Lemnos which was very bleak and the right place for manoeuvres. So we were well prepared for anything though we didn't at this point know where we were going. On 24 April we were told we were to make a dummy landing at the Gulf of Saros at the top of the Gallipoli peninsula. We did this to distract the Turks while the main force of troops landed at Cape Helles. We came ashore in six small boats pulled by a steam pinnace controlled by a young midshipman. We were told to make a lot of noise in the hope that the Turks would pull their army away from the south. Well, we made a hell of a lot of noise, but there was no one there, so we got back on the boat and sailed down to Gaba Tepe and landed on the night of 29 April, the day after the Australians.

It was a bit chaotic as the Australians seemed to have discarded all their equipment on the narrow beach and climbed up the side of the cliff with just their rifles and ten rounds. The impetus of the push had carried them over three ridges, but of course the Turks were well dug in and counter-attacked. The Australians couldn't hold them and eventually ran out of ammunition and made their way back to the first ridge where we took over. As quiet as we could we went up the gully in the dark each following in the footsteps of the chap in front. Eventually we made the rocky ground of the first ridge. I fixed up my Maxim machine-gun behind sandbags at the end of a gully, then sat and waited. It was still dark when we heard trumpets blowing as the Turks came at us in droves from the other end of the gully from where we were positioned. I didn't have to take aim, I just fired and mowed them down. You couldn't miss, there were so many of them. It was like firing into a mass of bodies gelled together.

Eventually they withdrew. But they came again seven times that night and each time we drove them back. Come the dawn, they had gone, only the bodies were left. A young lieutenant came across later that morning to tell us that we were moving on. I was about to dismantle my machine-gun when he noticed that I only had a few rounds left in one of the bands. He told me that he had never fired a machine-gun and asked if I'd show him how to do it, which I did. He sat down behind the steel guard and sandbag and fired away and then suddenly slumped back, a bullet through his head. A Turkish sniper had managed to hit him through a very small slit in the steel guard. A young man killed by an unlucky chance.

From there we were moved by lighter to Cape Helles. After looking around at the forts and the effect of the first naval bombardment, we sorted out the beach, then made our way up the slippery communication trench to our new position. On the way up there was an arm sticking out so we all shook its hand saying, 'Hello, Johnny.' We took over from one of the Anson battalions. The trenches were about six foot deep and on top we piled sandbags about three feet high, front and back, and on top of that was concertina wire. You certainly didn't put your head over the top because you were only about 150 to 200 yards from the Turks. I fixed my machine-gun between the sandbags with a firing step below. The Indian Army brought us up food on mules, but it was bully beef and biscuit for the first three months. Then one day we were issued a loaf of bread to share between seven men – it was such a change! Occasionally we'd exchange some bully for curry and mix that with the beef.

We needed to get water but the Turks used to mark the point of the stream we were using and put snipers in. Because I was still a boy I didn't ever get my rum ration but my mother sent me packets of Navy Cut cigarettes. We soon discarded our sun helmets and used a forage cap or balaclava because there were no steel helmets then. Forever in our clothes were lice. You could never destroy them and of course there were the flies, flies on everything, your food, your skin, your face and of course on the dead bodies out in no-man's- land. About 20 yards in front of me was a dead Turk. Everyday he became more bloated until eventually he burst. The smell was dreadful, but we seemed to take death in our stride.

Our daily 'stand to' was at dawn and from then on it was two hours on, one hour off. We'd usually get fired on either by snipers or from the heavy artillery which sometimes used shrapnel shells – they were really nasty things. On one occasion I ducked down with the rest of the trench and felt something hit my back. It had hit the webbing and hadn't pierced me. I was very lucky. A great drain on our nerves was 'Asiatic Annie' – a big, heavy gun – which was fired from some distance. You could count in seconds how long it would be before the shell landed.

I had my machine-gun trained on Krithia which was probably just over a thousand yards away where there was a road used by mule trains. We would fire and make the mules jump about a bit. At night we were sometimes told not to fire in certain directions because we had patrols out. One night the Gurkhas were out there, so we were keeping a close watch. Out of the dark came this voice to warn us not to shoot, 'All right, Tommy, all right'. Then I saw this smiling face coming in and it wasn't till he'd got in the trench that I realised he was carrying the head of a Turk! He had used his kukri.

As the summer went on water points were organised and we used to take it in turn to fetch it back in a bucket. One day while I was out, the Turks opened up on the reserve trench, then mid-way, and finally dropped a shell on my machine-gun post, and killed my no. 2, Jock Twycross, and wounded four or five nearby. That could easily have been me. I was sorry to lose him because we had shared a lot together. But then that is war.

On 4 June we didn't see the attack by the Collingwood battalion but we did see the repercussions. The Collingwoods were brand new, had never seen action, and were ordered to attack, 800-strong, in glaring sunlight shortly after noon. Many did not get further than the parapet before being mown down. By the next day they had lost 25 officers and around 600 other ranks. The remnants, as they passed by us, were in a bad way.

Come November 1915 it got very cold. There was continuous rain which filled up the trenches, so we had to sleep on the parapets. The Turks did the same, I suppose. We had an unspoken truce and didn't shoot at sleeping men. But it was so cold and we were always wet. On Christmas Day we were in the firing line and were served one slice of pudding and seven dates. Two days later we went down into our dug-out to change our clothes only to find our packs with our clean washing under three feet of water. We managed eventually to dry them out. Then, for another treat, they put us into the firing line for New Year's Day.

The first we knew of the evacuation was when the French moved out on 1 January. We spread out into their trenches to extend the line. We didn't know that Anzac and Suvla beaches had already been evacuated. On 8 January we began to destroy food and rifles that were not needed. We then tied empty sandbags around our feet, secured our water bottles so that they wouldn't clank around, and at midnight we moved off. I carried my machine-gun for over five miles in the dark until we reached the beach. As we were walking 'Asiatic Annie' fired several shells. We had come to hate her throughout our time at Gallipoli. The Turks didn't know we were going. Firing from the Asiatic side, Annie had always been a law unto herself.

We clambered on to a lighter and were carried out to the *Prince George*. The crew looked after us and gave us a meal of bully. As soon as I'd eaten it I fell fast asleep on the deck down below and the next morning we arrived in Mudros where we'd left from in April the previous year.

In those nine months the Royal Naval Division suffered terrible casualties. We had lost 1,653 killed, another 600 had died of their wounds. A further 238 had died of illness, and over 5,000 had been wounded.

Private Hubert Trotman

Royal Marine Light Infantry

I was born in Abingdon in 1897, the year of Queen Victoria's Diamond Jubilee. When I was eleven I won a scholarship and went to Abingdon Grammar School. I left school when I was fourteen because I was wanted in the family bakery business. I had always worked in the bakery after school and at weekends; it was expected of me and I wanted to do it. But it was a job that never finished: it was all hours. As you finished one day you seemed to start the next.

We were one person my father and me. He was my world: I had worked with him from the time I could walk. He was so proud of me when, at thirteen, I won first prize at the Agricultural Hall in London for my loaf. I got first prize again later, out of 3,000, for my Hovis ginger fruit cake. So he wasn't very happy with me joining up, so I waited until Christmas was over and joined on 30 December 1916. All my pals had joined up so I wanted to be with them. We had all been through OTC at school. Most of them are lying out in France now and their names are on the War Memorial.

I joined the Royal Marines and took a train to Deal to start my training. The month's training was tough. I can tell you that that was a training. Fifty men to a squad and each squad had a sergeant instructor. By God they were tough on you. You couldn't even move an eyelid unless the sergeant told you to. They were tin gods, those sergeants, but they turned out some real fighting men. From there I went to Blandford for my small arms training. It was there that I heard of General Trotman of the Royal Marines. I didn't know it at the time, but he was my father's cousin and there was a strong physical resemblance. He wanted me to take a commission but I told him I wanted to be one of the boys; they were a great bunch of lads, my squad.

Towards the end of the training came the hard bit – a test of skills with an officer observing. The officer followed each man separately on his horse. He carried a clipboard and took notes. We were told we were on active service. You would be walking along with fixed bayonet, looking for the enemy, when all of a sudden he would blow his whistle and a wooden head would pop up, and I would have to shoot at it. With different blasts of the whistles something else would happen and it went on like that throughout the course. Another thing we had to do was run a mile in full marching order in a certain time.

We were fit when we went from Blandford to the Somme in early April 1917 with the 2nd Royal Marine Battalion. We took over the trenches the Germans had vacated. They were full of mud. I saw a lot of men invalided out with trenchfoot but it didn't happen to me because I never took my boots off. The whole of the time I was on the Somme all I had to eat was bully beef, tinned beans and hard dog biscuits. Occasionally we would get a loaf of bread between six of us. It used to come up in a sandbag. If it was raining it would be wet. If the bloke carrying it slipped over, it would be muddy. I always remember the water was the colour of lime. From the fighting around Gavrelle there were many dead, some had been there for ages. We could only work at night and it took a long time to clear them. We couldn't bring them back to our lines, it was a case of pitching them into an old trench or shovelling in what was left of them. Then we used to fill the trench in. There were hundreds of bodies: it seemed endless. They had advanced on the German trenches and had simply been wiped out.

We then went up to Vimy and the brickfields of Lens and

I got attached to the Canadians for a while just after they had taken Vimy Ridge. I was with a Canadian sergeant in the line one night. He said he'd stand watch while I got some sleep. As dawn broke he woke me. I looked ahead and could see masses of Germans about to counter-attack. You could see their helmets bobbing along above the mist. The sergeant said, 'Keep your head down a minute while I think what we do about this'. I said 'I know what I'm going to do, I'm running for it'. I ran and didn't stop until I reached Bully Grenay where I knew there were some Marines.

I was there for a few weeks. I remember one time we were in a ditch and I was asleep standing on my feet. In a dream I heard my Dad calling me to get up. I woke to find I was up to my waist in water. I was so tired I think I would have drowned. Many did.

Then it was time for leave. We travelled in a box car to Calais. We were as lousy as cuckoos. When we got to Calais we had to head for the fumigator. But there we saw a queue a mile long. We were told the boat sailed in half an hour and if we didn't make it, we would lose a day of our leave. So those of us at the tail end of the queue broke off, went down to the docks, and damn me, we just walked on to the boat. We hid down below until it had sailed. So we disembarked unfumigated. That night I got as far as Paddington and the next day I caught the first train to Didcot. When I got home, just to take it in and breathe the familiar smell of the bakery again, I stood outside the shop for a while. Then I opened the door and shouted, 'Mother I'm outside. I'm home'. 'Come in,' she said, 'come in'. What a sight I must have been. I hadn't changed my clothes for months. I had a beard and I was in a hell of a state. She took one look at me and tears rolled down her face. She said, 'I'll clean you up'. 'No', I said, 'you can't do that yet.' I put my hand in my armpit and took out a handful of lice. 'Look,' I said. 'Lice, hoards of them, I can't come in like this.' I put them back where they came from and went up to the hospital to see the matron. She knew me well, because I had visited her on my rounds when delivering bread to the hospital. She said, 'Hubert, we will soon fix you up'. She put a large sheet on the ground outside. 'You stand on that. Empty your pockets and then take all your clothes off'. Then she put me in a big bath. When I got out I asked about my clothes. She told me she had put them in the copper, lice and all. I had to spend my leave in civvies. When I got back to Deal I was still in civvies, and so was called up on the carpet. I explained to the officer and everything was all right.

When I got back to France I was burying the dead again. We also used to go out on raids to catch prisoners for interrogation. The Germans were tough buggers and we lost a lot of men doing it. We were also engaged on working parties.

In May, one chap had a large flat, heavy parcel arrive for him from home. When he opened it, it was a steel breast plate and back plate with a strap over the shoulders. Off went the working party, leaving the man with the armour behind with one other chap. When we got back we couldn't find them. We dug around and around. All the while there was a great deal of shelling going on. Then we found them, both dead. One was called John Bull and the other was Eric Coates. We took them back and buried them beside the road. No one would touch that breast plate, it was just left there, no one wanted it.

'Woodbine Willie', the vicar, used to come around to give Bible readings. We didn't go there for the Bible reading, we went there for the fag you got afterwards. Mind you, if he'd given us a fag before he started, he would have had an empty house. On 6th July we were with Woodbine Willie when a sergeant came along and shouted, 'Come on you buggers, out you come'. He didn't use ecclesiastical language. He told us that the watch had seen Jerry out in front and that he was up to something. Seven of us went out that night into no-man's-land to sort them out. All at once I don't know whether it was artillery, mortars or what, all hell went up and so did I. Down I came with a bump. I laid there in the mud until I got my breath back. My left leg was numb. Two men had wounds and the other four were killed.

I crawled back towards our lines and managed to get under the wire. I was carried to the doctor's dugout in the side of the trench and from there down to the first field dressing station. Then I was put into an ambulance with a lot of others and driven over rough roads to a hospital. There were dozens of orderlies standing there and dozens of stretchers as well. They kept coming and taking men away and then they got to me. I was picked up, then put on a sort of spiral shoot and when it stopped I was taken off the stretcher and put on a conveyor belt. When that stopped, I was taken off and stripped, then x-rayed. The nurse painted rings and arrows on my leg, there were so many. When I looked, my ankle to the knee was a mass of wounds, it looked as if I had been riddled with a shotgun. Later I was taken to a little bay full of people in white coats, all lined up. I was asked to count to ten. The doctor stuck a gauze over my face, I got to four and the next thing I remember was coming to in a hut full of stretchers. The next morning I was put on to a light railway which had four stretchers to a truck and a little engine at the front. We steamed off and I think we went everywhere it was possible to go and ended up at Etaples where I was put in a hut with only one bed. I felt very low. Later the matron came in, looked at my leg and then picked me up in her arms as if she was cradling a baby and took me to a hut where there were other wounded men. She was either very strong or knew how to lift, but she also understood what my mind wanted. I was then sent to Boulogne by train to be sent home on the hospital ship, *Princess Elizabeth*. I remember looking out of the porthole and seeing the white cliffs and thought that I was passing from hell into heaven. I was taken to a military hospital in Endell Street in London. When I was getting about on crutches I was bumped up on to one of the lions in Trafalgar Square and saw the Americans arrive in London. They were quite a sight, fresh-faced and eager. They could have had no idea what they were going to as they came under the arch into Whitehall and down the Mall towards Buckingham Palace. My wound kept me out of action for more than nine months. Just as I was nearing recovery at Chatham they were asking for volunteers for the Zeebrugge raid. The General called a parade and said to the men, 'I am asking for volunteers for a very hazardous operation. Those not wanting to take part take one step backward'. Nobody moved. This became 'A' Company of the 4th RMLI Battalion which raided Zeebrugge.

At the end of August 1918 I was sent back to France to join the Hood Battalion, part of the 63rd Royal Naval Division, in time to face the tailend of the great German onslaught. As we got nearer the front, heavy shells started falling near the train, so we got out and took cover in some shrubbery near a wood. We could hear a tremendous fight going on ahead and saw the wounded walking past – drained. After an hour we were ordered forward and we went down into a valley. The Germans kept coming on wave after wave, but we stood our ground. At one point I was standing alone in the shrubbery with dead men all around me. I thought, 'I'm a fool standing here waiting for a sniper to pick me off'. So

I dropped down amongst the dead. When the next wave of our men advanced I got up and joined them. We were fighting for a couple of days but the Germans were resisting all the way.

We then rested and our numbers were made up. When we began to move forward again the roads were full of wagons, guns and transport, everything was moving forward. We marched for a couple of days, not on the road, but on either side.

One night we came across a row of guns that stretched for half a mile along each side of the road. They were wheel to wheel, so close together, that we had to squeeze between them in single file. We rested up on the side of a hill. Then just before dawn the battery to the right opened fire, then the one to the left. Flares started to go up, then a mass of shells, and the flames from the guns all lit up the sky, just like daylight. It was such an amazing contrast to the quiet we'd had while resting.

As soon as the barrage ceased we moved forward. This was the battle for the Hindenburg Line which the Germans were going to defend stoutly. Six tanks were with us and we smashed through on a wide front. We then got to the second line and the tanks broke off, three turned left and three turned right and we were left out in the open. We were faced by the German 3rd Marine Division. We let them have it, and they let us have it, bullet, bayonet, butt and hand to hand. It was the hardest fighting of my war. After ten hours fighting only ten of us came out. We were then relieved by the Highland Light Infantry and we dropped into a dugout at the side of the road to rest. A Highland officer found us asleep and called us all of the names under the sun. He thought we had been hiding. After being in that fight we were very angry. I told him that, if he swore at us again, he would have ten bullets and ten bayonets stuck into his fat belly. That put paid to him, he about-turned and legged it. We heard machine-guns start so we got out of the dugout and made our way to the rear. As we were walking back we found one of our galleys beside the road and they asked us where the Hood Battalion was and we replied that as far as knew we were it. We had some tea and fell asleep at the side of the road, they covered us up with blankets. When we woke we found that more men of the Hood had come back. That raised our spirits.

We had a week out of line and in October the battalion moved forward to attack Niergnies. We didn't meet a lot of resistance.

From then on we seemed to be moving forward, village to village, field to field. I remember going to a place where the foliage and the shrub had been cut down to about four feet high and barbed wire had been interwoven in the shrub, we lost a lot of lads there. One night seven of us under a lieutenant got into a ditch. I fell asleep, but not for long, because I was awoken by a terrific storm. I was soaking wet and the ditch was running with water well above my knees. I could see the Germans moving towards us. The lieutenant opened up with the Lewis gun and it jammed. I cleared it for him and we drove them off. We knew they would return in the morning. The lieutenant told me to find the captain and explain our position. I said, 'Where is he, sir?' He said, 'On our right somewhere, see if you can find him. You had better take Tully.'

As we were creeping across to a copse we came to a canal with a tree lying across it to block any barges. Tully decided that he was going to straddle this tree like a horse and ease himself across. He was doing very well but when he got to the middle there was a crack and Tully fell off into the water and didn't come up again. A sniper had got him. I had to get across, so I got down into the water, turned on my back, holding my rifle above me and pushed with my legs until I got to the other side. I was soaking, but squeezed myself out and made my way from cover to cover with a few shots at me until I got to the copse. There were bodies about, both ours and Germans', but nothing living until I got well into the little wood where I saw a fellow sitting with his back up against a tree. I said, 'Hello, chum, what's happened to you?' He pulled back a waterproof cape that was covering his legs and there was two raw stumps with jagged bones and blood pouring from them. He pointed and said, 'My legs are over there'. And there were two legs laying there, a couple of yards away. I got my first aid kit out and did all I could. I lit a fag for him and told him I would get help for him as soon as I could. Well, it was a long time before I got to the other wood, but when I got there I found the captain and a few more of our boys. I gave the captain my message and told him about the wounded man. I then went back with the stretcher bearers to get him. When I got there he was dead with the Woodbine still between his lips. He was put on the stretcher. As they were about to pick him up, the other said, 'Hold on, we got them left to right, he'd hate to go back lop sided!'

Not long after that incident, I was out with an officer looking for our Lewis gun crew. We never found them. They had simply disappeared. Later the Germans shelled the wood with gas. I put my mask on, but my eyes were stinging and everything was strange, but I was OK. That night a line of white tape was put out. At dawn we came under shellfire, so we had to move to high ground where of course the Germans had machine-gunners on the hill. We fought our way to the top. When we got there, I saw a sight that I will never ever forget. I can still see it today. Looking down, I could see, left to right, two lines of khaki troops moving forward with the sun shining on their bayonets. They were flashing red and yellow up and down the line. We settled down to watch their advance but the Germans opened up on us from the woods down below. We then had a tremendous fight with them down below before making it to another piece of high ground. This time it was like being on the edge of a cliff looking out to sea, but we were looking out on green countryside and there, down in the bottom, was a whole squadron of German Uhlans. They were dismounted and lounging around. We opened up on them and the place was one mass of loose horses. I only saw one man, riding low on his horse, get out of the valley.

In the first week in November we were still advancing, still fighting hard and losing men. We knew nothing of the proposed Armistice, we didn't know until a quarter to ten on that day. As we advanced on the village of Guiry a runner came up and told us that the Armistice would be signed at eleven o'clock that day, 11 November. That was the first we knew of it.

We were lined up on a railway bank nearby, the same railway bank that the Manchesters had lined up on in 1914 (the 2nd Battalion of the Manchester Regt defended this area on 23 and 24 August 1914 during the Battle of Mons). Some of us went down to a wood in a little valley and there found the skeletons of some of the Manchesters still lying there. Lying there with their boots on, very still, no helmets, no rusty rifles or equipment, just their boots.

My recollections of Armistice Day was that the guns just stopped, we pelted each other up to eleven o'clock, then stopped.

The Royal Marine band came up with a general at its head who said, 'You men stand firm'. I asked him if the war was really over, he said it was. Some lout behind me shouted, 'I thought it was, sir'. The general asked why and the lout replied, 'Because we can see a general in the front line'.

After he had gone I went to sleep on the railway bank. When I woke up there was a big pile of equipment on the ground and no men. So I climbed on to the top of the bank and saw them in the nearby village. When I got there they were all in the brewery, sticking their heads in the vats and having a big suck and coming out shouting like dogs coming out of water!

On 23 April 1919 I was demobbed. In the RND's short life we'd had over 7,500 killed and 3,000 had died of their wounds or in other ways. That evening I got as far as Didcot but there were no more trains, so I had to walk the seven miles home and got there at midnight. My sister was there to meet me and my mother. We kissed and jabbered away. Then my mother went to fetch my dear father. She came rushing out of the bedroom. 'Hubert, your dad has gone to pieces, he's just laying there like a log, he just passed out.' He had heard my voice and was totally overcome. With all the Royal Naval Division's casualties I don't think he ever expected me to return. He must have felt he'd heard my ghost. We did what we could for him. I went to bed at two and started work in the bakery again at five.

Midshipman Brian de Courcy-Ireland

In 1907, when I was seven, I met a sailor who was on leave and he shot me a line about how wonderful the Navy was. I decided there and then that I would join. Neither my father, who was a country parson, nor my mother, tried to dissuade me. I had two brothers who later served on the Western Front and both of whom survived. Fairly unusual for three sons to survive the Great War.

I was brought up in a village about six miles outside Bideford in Devon and, apart from an odd trip to paddle in the sea at Paignton, I never really left the village. In September 1912 my father accompanied me to London for my interview for the Navy.

It was my first time in a big city. I was one of 360 who wanted to become a Naval cadet at Osborne; they took eighty. At the interview one member of the board asked me (I'm sure, looking back, in a most friendly way) how many arches Bideford bridge had? I replied that I was astonished none of them knew! I was a bit surprised I got in, especially after they asked me to look at the clock and tell them the time in French. I simply told them the clock had stopped!

I enjoyed Osborne although it was pretty strong on discipline. Alongside our ordinary education we were taught Naval skills such as navigation, but the education was certainly biased towards the Navy. My term was Grenville and I remained in that when I went on to Dartmouth. In my last term at Osborne, in the summer of 1914, I was appointed to the *Centurion* for the Royal Review of the Grand Fleet at Spithead. To see all those ships together, fully rigged, was a tremendous sight. The high spot for me was being allowed to man one of the six-pounder guns for firing the Royal Salute. It really was the last great moment of the British Navy. Sheer power and might. We will never see its like again.

I joined Dartmouth in January 1915 and left in December of the same year. The term before us, the ones who'd been there at the outbreak of war, were sent to sea, and a number of them were lost on the *Hogue, Cressy* and *Aboukir*. That was sad news to receive but we knew our turn was coming and were looking forward to it. It was an unsentimental world really; the war was on, get on with it.

I travelled up from London on the Naval train which ran almost daily to Thurso in Caithness, whence we crossed over by steamer to Scapa Flow. There were stops on the way up at Inverness and Invergordon. I remember well the break at the latter. Outside the station a large funeral procession was passing; there seemed endless coffins. No one would talk, but we learnt afterwards that it was the dead from the *Natal*. As a result of an internal explosion, she had blown up in harbour on New Year's Eve while there was a children's party on board.

My first appointment, on 2 January 1916, was to HMS *Bellerophon*, a dreadnought of the Fourth Battle Squadron based at Scapa Flow. She was armed with ten 12-inch guns, one twin turret forward, one on each beam amidships and two in the centre line aft. I was a junior midshipman or, more commonly called in our gunroom, a 'wart'. I was fifteen and a half. To remind us that we were, in the eyes of our seniors, just warts, we were all given a good sound dozen lashes by the Sub (Sub-Lieutenant). So from day one we knew our place and what would happen if we stepped out of it.

Of course there were the more standard traditional initiation rites and evolutions. One of these, 'providing bumph', involved running to the officers' heads (lavatories) to collect a clean brown sheet of bumph paper (lavatory paper) and return it to the gunroom. The first wart back got a glass of port and the last a dozen on the backside. I got a dozen because I failed to notice there was an officer sitting on the toilet when I took the paper and left him nothing at all! The worst punishment was mast-heading, where you were sent to the crow's-nest. That was dreadful because of the roll of the ship and the cold. But the hardest task was for the duty midshipman who had to climb up to the top to give the chap his meal. Meanwhile, down below in the gunroom, if a Sub stuck his fork into one of the overhead beams all the junior midshipmen had to leave because officers were going to talk about ladies. In our first year we were looked after by a Snotty's Nurse. He'd make sure you behaved and did some work. We were traditionally called 'snotties' because in the old days of the Navy midshipmen could not afford a handkerchief and so would blow their nose on their sleeve. The Admiralty brought this practice to an end by having three buttons sewn on the cuff.

In the early part of 1916 we were doing sweeps of the North Sea. The *Bellerophon* was accompanied by the other dreadnoughts of the Fourth Battle Squadron, *Benbow, Temeraire* and *Vanguard*, but we were not involved in any incident. I recall how cold it was and how unpleasant a place Scapa was. We were a coal-burning ship and had to take on 3,000 tons every few months. In fact I spent my first Christmas Day in the Navy coaling ship, starting at 5.30 am and finishing at 6.00 pm. Anyone who was not on duty, and it didn't matter if you were a schooly (schoolmaster) or the padre, you had to take part. As a midshipman you spent an hour holding the bags for sailors to fill and then an hour working the winches to the derricks. You'd alternate throughout the day.

We usually got a corn beef sandwich at midday and when it was all over you had to scrub the ships clean. When we'd finished we'd have to get the bath ready for the senior midshipmen. When it was finally our turn the twenty-four of us junior midshipmen would have to share two-thirds of a bath of water spread between four tray baths each of which held about four inches of water. Again the senior midshipmen had use of them first. By the time we came to use them it had the consistency of pea soup and was very black. After a day like that we were flagged out, but it was part of a pattern of life.

On 31 May 1916 we guessed that something was up. We knew nothing, we just had a feeling. I was positioned in one of the 12-inch turrets working the dumaresq course and distance calculator. You had to put your course and speed on it and then what you thought was the course and speed of the enemy. Then you would work out the deflection to which you had to turn your guns aiming ahead of your target, read the range and pass this down by voice pipe.

We went into action some time after five o'clock. In the afternoon we were kept busy in the turret and I reckon *Bellerophon* fired about a hundred rounds of 12-inch. At one point we were rung up to be told we had sunk a German destroyer. During a lull we came out of the turret to get some fresh air and there, floating around us, was a whole mass of bodies and debris – some of our sailors were cheering because they thought they were Germans, but unfortunately they were from the *Invincible*. It was a terrible sight and my first experience of death.

Then it was back to the turret. The shells were loaded up from three decks below; all this involved about a hundred men to each turret. It was a precise drill and that drill occupied your mind during the battle as did my own work on the dumaresq. I must say the guns made quite a noise when they fired, though we did have things stuck in our ears. Then of course there was the reverberation of the ships as the guns went off, but you steadied yourself for this. You could see the enemy's flashes from their guns, but we were never hit.

For the night action I was on the bridge which, looking back, was exciting for a young midshipman. Captain Bruen was in command. The sailors called him 'Tiny' because that's what he was. He was completely unemotional. We continued firing into the early hours, then disengaged. We didn't really know what had happened until we got back and I felt a bit depressed because the press reports of the Jutland battle were rather bad. I also read of the casualties and found I had lost thirteen of my term of eighty, with whom I was quite friendly: one was Anthony Eden's youngest brother and the other was Admiral Sir Percy Scott's son. So the ship went into a bit of a depression for a few days, but we all suffered it together because we got no leave. We simply went back into routine.

A short while after Jutland I was taught an example of how to conduct yourself under stress. I was Midshipman of the Watch on the bridge at the time. We were waiting to weigh anchor when a commander came up to Captain Bruen, I could see he was rattled. The captain was watching the Flagship through his glasses, waiting for the signal to come down. The commander said, 'Captain, I beg your pardon, sir, I'm sorry to report that the Captain of Marines has just shot himself', and then he said, 'No, he's not shot himself, sir, he's cut his throat'. Captain Bruen just lowered his glasses, slowly looked at the commander and said, 'Oh, cut his throat has he, cut it badly?' The commander said, 'I'm sorry, sir, I'm afraid he's dead'. 'Oh, he's dead is he? Well, see to it, Commander, will you.' And then he returned his gaze to the Flagship and in the same voice said, 'Signal, weigh anchor'. That was quite a lesson.

Ordinary Seaman Fred Pedelty

I was born in Bladon near Newcastle in 1896 and worked as a miner before I joined the Royal Navy Reserve in 1913. At the outbreak of war I joined up. In early October I went with the Drake Battalion of the Royal Naval Division to Belgium, where we were to try and defend Antwerp against the advancing Germans. All we did was join the retreating Allied forces who couldn't hold the enemy. We simply got orders to join an organised retreat. The casualties were low, but we did have a brigade interned by the Dutch.

We came back and were given a hero's welcome by the local people before we were sent on two weeks leave. My officer, Lieutenant Wells, told me that I would be better off on a ship, so I was posted to Chatham. After a few weeks there we had to volunteer for either gunnery or torpedo. I had six months training at Sheerness on torpedoes and searchlights.

My first posting was to *Engadine*, a seaplane-carrier based at Liverpool. She was no more than a floating hangar which had been a cross-Channel ferry before she had been converted. She had three Short folder seaplanes stowed on the after deck. By the time I had joined her she'd seen quite a bit of action. On Christmas Day 1914 she was involved in the first ever naval air attack. Along with two other requisitioned ferries, the *Empress* and *Riviera*, she made a raid on Cuxhaven. Only two of the nine planes found Cuxhaven and four were lost. When she took on the *Emden* and *Nordeich* in January 1915 three of her aircraft sank before they could take off.

I had been sent to the *Engadine* because the aircraft carried small torpedoes. We operated on patrols in the North Sea from Harwich. We used to be accompanied by destroyers and cruisers because we were very vulnerable to attack. We did launch some of our aircraft on reconnaissance, but on the whole we weren't a success, so we were moved up to Rosyth.

We patrolled out with the battle-cruiser squadron, but we were seldom called on to use our aircraft. On one occasion we were in harbour in Hull and I was in the cinema with my girlfriend. All of a sudden a notice went up recalling all servicemen to their stations. I dashed back to the *Engadine* to be told to operate the searchlight. I was having a job getting it going, but eventually got the beam working and caught this Zeppelin in the spotlight. This had been a great menace to the east coast. The ships opened fire but he diverted to Grimsby and attacked there. While we were on patrol on 31 May we began to pick up little snippets from the signalmen that something was afoot. There was a lot of speculation, and excitement.

At about 2.45 in the afternoon of 31 May we were not far behind the *Lion*, with Admiral Beatty at the head, followed by *Tiger* and *Princess Royal*, when we received a signal to send a seaplane aloft to reconnoitre. Lieutenant-Commander Robinson, our captain, got the unwieldly hangar door open. The crew got the machine on deck, spread its wings and hoisted it by derrick into the sea. It was twenty minutes before Flight Lieutenant Rutland and his observer, Assistant Paymaster Trewin, were airborne.

The plane had only been up about ten minutes when they sighted the enemy. As there was a low cloud base it was having to fly at about 900 feet. The Germans opened fire, but it circled around getting the disposition of the enemy and of our fleet. Unfortunately at about 3.35 the petrol pipe leading to the carburetter broke and so it had to land on the water near us. The pilot managed to repair the pipe and wanted to take off again, but he was told to come alongside, so we hoisted him in.

It was an historic flight though, because it was the first instance of a heavier-than-air machine being used in a fleet action. Her wireless reports had reached the *Engadine* but we were unable to pass them to the *Lion*. Then, at about 3.25, we heard the bugle sound for 'Action Stations'. Our lads were noting the flashes and fall of shot and one called out that the *Queen Mary* had gone up. I didn't know how he knew because he didn't have any binoculars, but she went down about 4.30.

At 5 pm we got another signal to return to base. They weren't going to use our aircraft again and we had *Onslow* and *Moresby* looking after us so we turned to go back. We hadn't been sailing long when we saw a cruiser on her own. We didn't know if she was one of ours or theirs. As we only had one six-pounder and two 4-inch guns on the *Engadine* we were a bit worried. However, it turned out to be one of our own, the *Warrior*. She signalled us and ordered us to take a line astern to accompany her back to Rosyth. But she was in a sorry state. She had been hit fifteen times and had about a hundred killed and wounded. So at 9 pm we took her in tow.

Unfortunately during the night the weather worsened and her stern sank low in the water. By the morning it was obvious she wouldn't make port and we received a signal that she was going to order 'Abandon Ship'. The sea was quite choppy and disturbed but the *Engadine* had a huge rubbing strake so that we could go alongside. Without that we could never have stayed long enough to take off the crew who numbered about 900. I was one of the inboard men on a hawser while the others grabbed each man as he came across. The ships were really working hard and the noise of the rending steel was terrific. *Engadine* was holed in a number of places.

The wounded were passed over on stretchers. As the last was being passed there was a big swell and the poor lad slipped off the stretcher and fell between the ships. Lieutenant Rutland came up to me and asked what had happened. We could see below that the lad had fetched up on the remains of a fender. A lot of men wanted to go down and try and bring him up, but the captain wouldn't allow anyone to go over the side. A bit later, he was seen to have drifted in the water. Lieutenant Rutland grabbed a rope which some men were using to try and lasso the lad, and went down on it. He put the bowline round the man and got hold of him in his arms. He ordered those on deck to pull him up.

Unfortunately the poor lad, a handsome lad too he was, no more than eighteen, died of his wounds. Lieutenant Rutland got an Albert Medal for his bravery in trying to save him and because of his flight over the German fleet, he was from then on known as Rutland of Jutland!

Later the captain of the *Warrior* stood with his men and gave three cheers to his sinking ship. It was a sad sight. The following day we buried the young lad at sea with another of his mates.

Boy First-Class Charles Morris

My first action was Jutland, and *Marlborough* was part of the First Battle Squadron. As far as we knew it was just an ordinary cruise round, but we got the news that we were to engage the enemy. We really knew something was up when we started to make full speed. That got us going. We wanted to see what was happening, so we went up on deck, which we shouldn't have done. We couldn't see anything, but we could hear the guns. Then we were called to action stations and everything was closed down.

My station was a 6-inch gun. I was a loader. On the 6-inch gun you had nine men, a gun layer who fired it, another trained it on to the target, then there was the breach loader, four loaders and one on the voice pipe taking orders. As the breach was opened the shell would be rammed home. We could load up pretty quickly when we had to. Each shell came up on a tray in a mechanical loader.

When all five guns went off the whole ship vibrated. They then began just firing two or three at a time. It was very exciting especially as we were at the head of the fleet as the Flagship of the

First Battle Squadron with Admiral Sir Cecil Burney on board: he was second-in-command to Beatty. The *Marlborough* first opened fire at about 6.15 pm at a range of 13,000 yards. I heard later that we got a hit on the *König*, and the *Grosser Kurfürst*. We never fired our gun because we were facing in the opposite direction. So it was a bit frustrating. But there was a lot of enthusiasm as the battle went on. Of course we didn't know how we were doing or how the battle was going. We had been in action for about an hour when we were hit by a torpedo on the starboard side. The ship almost came out of the water.

We carried a diesel engine on board in a special compartment. That compartment took the brunt of the explosion and two stokers were killed. As water filled the hull we had to slow down, and then disengage from the battle. Admiral Burney was transferred to a light cruiser.

There was a lot of talk on the way home about the battle and how much leave we might get. Somehow everything went back to routine – to normal; that was the best way. When we docked we were given leave and I went down on the train to my parents in Tooting. I think they'd been a bit worried about me. I was not yet eighteen, but they were really proud of me. My father shook my hand, which he'd never done before.

Boy First-Class Harold Bryce

In February 1915, when I was sixteen, all the young men were joining up because the poster of Lord Kitchener was everywhere, pointing his finger at you and saying 'Your Country Needs You'. So I volunteered. A few days later a recruiting officer came down from Oxford and brought documents for my father to sign. He said, 'Give it to his mother to sign first'. But she said, 'I'm not going to sign that'. She was upset, you see. Eventually my dad signed. I then went down from Witney with another boy to Whitehall in London. (I had never left home before except for a day trip to

Portsmouth which cost five shillings.) We stayed the night there wrapped in an old army blanket. In the morning we fell in with some more boys. Every boy in those days had their best suit for special occasions, but some of the ragamuffins who turned up had bare feet. I'd never seen anything like them before.

We were sent down to Devonport, to HMS *Powerful*. As soon as we got aboard a Petty Officer said, 'If you've got a watch or any money, hand it over'. The next morning we were sent to the barber who cut every bit of hair off our heads with clippers. We all looked like criminals wearing white duck suits. Later that day we were put into different classes, and the instructors were very hard on us. One boy couldn't answer a question so the instructor hit him about the face as hard as he could and knocked him from one side of the deck to the other. If a boy got caught smoking, he got six cuts with a cane. That never happened to me; I was too afraid.

But I was only on the ship for a week before I caught scarlet fever, and sent to hospital in Devonport and put on a milk diet. After I got better I was sent on leave and then drafted to Scapa Flow. It took ages on the train to get there. At Thurso we slept on the floor in a hotel and the next morning we caught the steamer to the Grand Fleet. I've never seen ships like it in my life; they were great big battleships.

I was sent aboard HMS *Blanche*, a light cruiser, as a sight-setter on one of the ship's eight 4-inch guns. I'd had a week's training for that. In the turret I wore a telepad on my head in the shape of a hood with a flexible pipe to my mouth and earpieces so that I could hear the orders. At sea I did four hours on and four hours off in two watches, night and day. The gun's crew all wore duffel coats, but because I was a boy, I wasn't given any protective clothing. After I'd been on that gun for about a fortnight, sticking it out through the cold weather without even a pair of gloves, one of the old sailors brought me a pair of duffel trousers. Then another brought me a duffel coat. The first morning at sea an officer looked at me and said, 'When was the last time you had a shave?' I replied, 'I've never shaved, sir'. So he swore at me and I was sent below. In those days there were no safety razors so I had to use a cut-throat razor and shave while the ship was rolling about!

On New Years' Eve 1915/16 we were moored on the Cromarty Firth. Across the other side, at Invergordon, was the cruiser *Natal*.

I came up on the quarterdeck about 3.30. I was quietly standing there alone until the Chief Stoker came on deck. All of a sudden there was this thunderous explosion on the *Natal*. The chief said, 'Christ, her boiler's gone up'. But it was her magazine. We just stood there and watched her keel over. There was a terrible loss of life, over 360. Among those killed were several naval wives and nurses from the hospital ship *Plassey* which was close by. They had been invited to a party aboard the *Natal*. Most of the crew were below deck on a 'make and mend day'. They never had a chance.

Before the First World War, any boy who got sent before the magistrates used to be offered the choice of going to prison or joining the Navy. There were lots of boys who didn't fancy prison on ship and we volunteers got fed up with being treated like them, as if we were criminals. I was made to feel like one once, just before the battle of Jutland. It was my first leave. I had my liberty ticket with the date on for when I was to return. When we fell in, my mate, who had a girlfriend in Witney, started chattering to me about her and I didn't hear the Petty Officer telling us when to get back. Two weeks later when I walked through the dock yard gates the guard said, 'Do you know you're adrift off leave?' I said, 'I'm not, it's the twenty-fourth today. It's on my ticket.' He didn't seem to care about what was on my ticket, he took me to the officer of the watch. Eventually I was sent before Captain Casement who said, 'There's no excuse. All you boys were told what day to come back and what train to catch from London'. Fourteen days pay and leave stopped! Which meant I fought in the battle of Jutland at no cost to his Majesty!

The morning of the day of the battle was beautiful. The North Sea was like a lake, no movement in the water at all. The first time we saw the enemy was when a Zeppelin passed over us. As we steamed ahead an officer came along and said we would be at the scene of action at 6.00 p.m. He told us that the battle-cruiser fleet had already been in action that afternoon. As we got closer there was a slight mist in front of the German fleet, so we could only see one or two ships now and again as the mist cleared. Even though the action was on the starboard side we positioned ourselves on the port side of the *Iron Duke*. We had a large signal staff on the *Blanche*, and our job was to relay signals to Admiral Jellicoe on the *Iron Duke*. We could see her in action, this 25,000-ton super dreadnought. She had five twin 13.5-inch turrets and twelve 6-inch guns. She was quite a sight with all the black smoke coming out of the funnels and noise of the guns. I was on P4 gun when, at about 6.30 that evening, sailors from the starboard side shouted out, 'Come and have a look, quickly, there's a ship going down'. It was the battle-cruiser *Invincible*. Only six men were saved.

On another occasion the commander came running along the upper deck shouting, 'Has anyone seen a torpedo?' No one had, but it planted a suspicion in our minds that there might be U-boats about.

We were never hit. But later that night I saw a number of our destroyers on fire — red flames lighting up the night sky. The destroyer *Munster* came alongside and took on medical supplies to deal with the casualties. One of these was 'Boy' Cornwall. He was a sight-setter on the *Chester* and, like me, was sixteen. Although he was mortally wounded early in the battle he stood by his gun awaiting orders until the end of the action with the rest of his gun's crew dead or wounded. He deserved his Victoria Cross.

One strange thing happened during the action, while all the firing was going on. A tall sailing ship passed down between the German and British lines. Someone thought it must have been Swedish. It was in full sail as if from another age, another time.

All the way through the battle the *Blanche* never fired her guns, nor did we know if we were winning or losing. It was just excitement all the time, one thing after another, though by 9.00 pm that evening the main action was over. By dawn we had withdrawn.

Then it was back to normal routine.

Midshipman Frank Layard

HMS *Indomitable* was part of the Third Battle-Cruiser Squadron consisting of *Invincible*, the Flagship of Rear Admiral the Hon. Horace Hood, *Indomitable* and *Inflexible*. We had arrived at Scapa

Flow from Rosyth on 23 May 1916 to carry out gunnery and torpedo exercises. The gunnery exercises were of particular importance for us as it was the first opportunity we had had to test out, and get acquainted with, the new Director system which had just been installed.

At about 6.30 pm on the evening of 30 May, a signal was received to raise steam for 22 knots and at 9.30 the squadron sailed, followed by the whole of the Grand Fleet. We had no idea why we had been ordered out, but there was a feeling of suppressed excitement on board as we passed through the Hoxa gate in the fading light. On more than one occasion we had set out at high speed to intercept enemy ships which had been reported at sea, but each time we had returned without making contact. This time, however, I had a strong feeling that something was really afoot. In fact some of us junior midshipmen were pacing up and down the quarterdeck discussing among ourselves whether a midshipman had any chance of distinguishing himself in a modern fleet action and deciding probably not!

At eight o'clock next morning, I went up to the foretop to keep the forenoon watch as submarine lookout. There seemed to be no sign of any urgency and the previous night's feeling of excitement ebbed away. I decided that this must be just another routine sweep into the North Sea.

This atmosphere of calm was suddenly shattered when, at about 2.30 pm, we intercepted HMS *Galatea*'s first sighting report. From then on excitement steadily mounted as further signals came in with the news that the First and Second British Cruiser Squadrons (BCS) were engaging the enemy battle-cruisers, and then that the Fifth BCS had joined in. The *Invincible* hoisted BJI G 25 (assume First degree readiness: speed 25 knots) shortly to be followed by BJ (Action Stations). As we pushed on southwards, working up to our maximum speed, the thought uppermost in everyone's mind was, 'Are we going to get there in time?' I felt some slight apprehension at the thought of going into action, but the prevailing sensation was one of intense excitement. My action station was in the foretop as dumaresq worker* and of course I had a grandstand view. We were given no idea of what was happening, only that we were doing our utmost

* See above, page 63.

to join Sir David Beatty in the *Lion* and take our place in the battle-cruiser line.

Soon after five o'clock the sound of distant gunfire was heard and half an hour later the *Chester*, on our starboard, opened fire. The *Invincible* immediately swung round to starboard and led the squadron towards her. Then three German cruisers came into sight, broad on the port bow, and we opened up on them with our main armament at 10,000 yards and they quickly turned away and vanished from sight. When they turned they must have fired torpedoes at us, because I saw a torpedo, with its red warhead and propellers slowly revolving, passing slowly down our port side on the surface not more than ten yards from us. It was obviously at the end of its run, but it was a very near miss. At the same time I saw *Invincible* haul out to starboard, and stop with all her safety valves lifting and a tremendous roar of steam and with the 'Disregard' flag flying. I thought, 'Oh God, she has been torpedoed'. But the next minute she hoisted Flag One (line ahead) and hauled down 'Disregard'. She then led off to the westward again in the direction of heavy gunfire and we followed, falling in behind *Inflexible*.

Just after six o'clock I could see flashes of gunfire ahead. Then the *Lion* appeared almost right ahead and steering towards us, with her guns firing to starboard. As the *Invincible* led round to port, to bring the squadron into station ahead of the *Lion*, all of a sudden the dim outline of four enemy ships loomed up out of the haze. They were difficult to identify but we took them to be battle-cruisers. As we turned to bring the enemy ships on our starboard beam at about 10,000 yards, the squadron opened up with all its main armament guns. Our fire was quickly returned and soon shots were falling all round us.

We had done only one test firing with our new firing system a day or two before leaving Scapa. The Gunnery Officer therefore had a difficult decision to make. Should he use the new system which, though more efficient, was virtually untried, or should he revert to the old less accurate but well tested system of gunlayers firing? He decided not to risk using the new Director system and so, throughout the action, guns and turrets were individually laid and trained. For about twenty minutes we were hotly engaged but I was too busy with my dumaresq to feel frightened. We sent out a continuous ripple of flashes all along the enemy line but, in the poor visibility, I couldn't tell where our shots were falling although

I found the noise of our guns most heartening and welcome. It helped to drown the rumbling noise made by the shells passing over us and the crack of those falling short. But the enormous columns of water thrown up were only too visible and sometimes uncomfortably close. We must have been constantly straddled but not once were we or *Inflexible* hit. A number of shell splinters did however come on board which indicated that the enemy's shells which fell short had burst on impact with the sea.

It was during this phase of the action at about 6.35 pm that *Invincible* was hit by two salvoes in quick succession from the *Lützow* and *Derfflinger*. She was hit aft and on 'Q' turret amidships, between the guns. The turret blew up and the flash went down into the magazine. The explosion must have touched off the other magazines and she blew in half with the loss of over a thousand lives. Although only separated from her by the *Inflexible* nobody in the foretop saw the explosion or realised what had happened as we were all fully occupied with our fire control duties. The first we knew of it was when, close to starboard, we passed the bows and stern of a ship sticking up about thirty feet out of the water with some half a dozen figures clinging to some wreckage. It was a grim and very sad moment for us when we saw the name *Invincible* on the stern portion and realised we were passing all that remained of our Flagship.

Shortly after this the enemy ships turned away and were lost to sight and, although we altered course, we could not regain contact. Then on orders from the *Lion* we turned round and took station astern of the other battle-cruisers. It was only then that we realised the *Queen Mary* and the *Indefatigable* were missing, leaving only *Lion*, *Princess Royal*, *Tiger* and *New Zealand*. At this point the disabled and motionless German cruiser *Wiesbaden* appeared dimly in the direction in which the German Fleet had disappeared and received a broadside from each battle-cruiser as the line passed and then faded from sight astern.

Some minutes later we saw the Grand Fleet coming into action astern. We could not distinguish the ships but through the haze and smoke we could see what appeared to be one continuous line of flame from the flashes of their guns extending over an arc of about 60°, a truly tremendous sight. However we did not have the time to admire this display for enemy ships appeared again briefly and we engaged them again. At the same time we saw a flotilla of German destroyers approaching on the starboard bow and, as the big ships disappeared from sight again, we shifted our fire to the destroyers and forced them to turn away under the cover of smoke.

At about 8.15, as the light was failing, we had our last brief sighting and short burst of fire but we lost touch again and that was the end of the battle for us. We steamed southward throughout the night in company with Admiral Beatty and the rest of the battle-cruisers, remaining at action stations all the time. I was able to nip down to the gunroom for a few minutes to get a little food, but spent the rest of the night in the foretop feeling very cold, but too excited and worked up to sleep.

Early in the morning Admiral Beatty signalled to the battle-cruisers, 'The losses on both sides have been heavy but we hope to cut off and annihilate the whole German fleet today. It is up to every man to do his utmost.' Unknown to us at the time the German fleet had slipped through astern of the Grand Fleet in the night and had regained the safety of its own waters. When this became known later in the day we turned for home. On the afternoon watch we passed through a large patch of oil and wreckage in which was floating a lot of dead fish and a number of dead bodies. We could not identify the uniforms and we hoped we were passing over the graveyard of some German ship, but in all probability it was the spot where one of our own battle-cruisers had blown up.

We reached harbour early on the morning of 2 June and immediately started to take in 1,400 tons of coal.

After the battle there was much speculation about the German losses (2,551). From all reports it was generally believed that they must have been as heavy, if not heavier, than ours. This proved to be wishful thinking and so, when some time later the true facts became known (6,097), we felt bitterly disappointed. Somehow we had missed our opportunity. We had allowed the German fleet to slip through our fingers and instead of winning an overwhelming victory we had only achieved a partial success and in all probability we would never be given another chance.

Looking back it would seem that for the battle-cruiser force, at any rate, the war at sea in 1915/16 was fought at a very leisurely tempo. During the eight months from the time I joined *Indomitable* to the battle of Jutland, we only did 33 days at sea, and moreover, because at the time the submarine threat in the North Sea was slight and the air threat non-existent, it was possible, when at sea, to maintain a very easy three-watch defence organisation. It was only necessary to assume a higher state of readiness on the rare occasions when contact with enemy surface ships was expected. Since no practice facilities were available in the Firth of Forth, firings had to be carried out either from Invergordon or Scapa Flow. The result was that, during those eight months, we only fired our main armament four times and our secondary armament once. In the circumstances it is hardly surprising that the gunnery of the battle-cruisers fleet at Jutland was poor.

Midshipman Jack Lumby

I was born in 1897 in Sidcup and educated at St Paul's School in Barnes, London, where the High Master was a most severe disciplinarian. The school had a strong music bias, but my strongest subject was mathematics. By public school standards St Paul's was not a large school, yet during that war we were to lose 592 boys.

When the war started I volunteered for the Navy and joined HMS *Keyham* in Devonport which meant a long train journey on the Great Western Railway from Paddington. Like St Paul's, the discipline on board was tough. I was a public school entry and didn't go to Dartmouth. In fact I went to HMS *Shannon* in 1915 as the only midshipman. *Shannon* was an armoured cruiser, built in 1908. She had the disadvantage of a high forecastle, four funnels which made first-class aiming points for the enemy and only a thin, one-and-a-half-inch deck armour; nor was she very fast. But there was a good atmosphere on board – the skipper used to wave to me. There was great respect at all levels. It was a happy ship. Because I was older than most snotties I was well received by the other officers.

Jutland was my first action. We steamed out of Scapa Flow as part of the Second Battle-Cruiser Squadron, accompanied by the *Minotaur* and *Defence*. We were sailing at full speed towards the enemy in the late afternoon and passed one of our battleships which seemed to outrage her skipper because he flung his cap on the ground and jumped on it! When we went into attack at about 5.45 pm I was in one of the gun turrets. We opened fire at a range of 16,000 yards. We couldn't see the enemy, but at least we were firing. The enemy salvoes were dropping very short. In fact the *Shannon* wasn't hit during the battle, she was weaving around all the time. We were more lucky than the *Defence*. She was heavily shelled at about 6.20 pm from no more than 8,000 yards, blew up, and disintegrated with the loss of 856 hands. Our other cruiser *Warrior* was also badly hit and sank later.

During the battle *Minotaur* was only about 400 yards from us and we seemed to work in tandem because she wasn't hit either. We fired broadside throughout the battle and by the end of the day were all rather weary. We had no idea of the tactics of the battle, we simply stayed in the turret and fired when instructed. I saw no ships sink – or any of the casualties of the battle. At dawn we did take a break.

Things come back to me from the battle: how good 'Guns' was, our Gunnery officer – really first-rate; the noise of battle, the extraordinary amount of shouting amidst the din of the guns and smoke. But even in all that noise people were very controlled, very determined: it never occurred to us that we might lose the battle or be sunk. There also was a lot of good humour. I think that came from our confidence. Of course we had no protection for our ears, it's a wonder I'm not deaf. When the enemy finally moved off we hadn't fired for some while. We couldn't see them, not even their smoke.

The next morning no one talked about the battle, not even among the midshipmen.

We simply went back to our regular duties. I suppose Naval people of that time didn't talk about things, whether in or out of battle, we simply got on with the job. Perhaps it had something to do with the watch system – it gave us a framework. I had a great respect for Jellicoe and wasn't surprised that the Germans steamed off. He was not only skilful, but cunning. He was not in the same world as Beatty, who I thought was a nasty bit of work. Jellicoe won the psychological battle. There was no need to attack any further than we did, because we would have lost more ships and I think Jellicoe must have had a rough idea as to how many men and ships he'd lost already. No, he did the right thing, we could well have lost the battle had we continued.

After Jutland we went out on patrols, full of confidence, because we knew damned well that the enemy was not coming out again. And they never really did. To gain more experience I went next into submarines which, by contrast to the *Shannon*, was a quiet, serene world.

We did patrolling in the North Sea. I saw out the war and, on Armistice Day 1918, we all celebrated with a few tots of rum. By the time the war was over, though, we were all utterly weary, we'd had enough. I had lost two good family friends both on the Western Front, but I never came in contact with death: I lost no one on the *Shannon*, nor in submarines. All death for me was at a distance. When the German U-boats were scuttled I went on board and removed a clock which I still have in my room. The clock is inscribed with the name of Franz Happe Keil, 1849. It had obviously been taken from a sailing ship and handed down. Little would the clockmakers have thought it would finish up in the hands of a British Naval officer!

Able Seaman Arthur Sawyer

My dad was a farm labourer and lived to be a hundred, but my mum died when she was forty-three and left six of us kids. So I went off and joined the Navy when I was fifteen and nine months. I was sent to Shotley and, after training, I joined the *Iron Duke*, the flagship of the Grand Fleet.

I was based in the seamanship department. You kept the ship clean, the boats crewed, worked on the upper deck, and learned to steer and navigate. We knew where our place was for Action Stations and where to 'abandon ship' if we had to, though I couldn't imagine having to abandon the *Iron Duke*.

In the afternoon of 30 May 1916 Jellicoe was ordered to concentrate his fleet in the 'Long Forties', about a hundred miles east of Aberdeen. We knew something was up and began to get excited. I was in the torpedo-room between the decks. It was a bit nerve-racking, all those alarm bells. We thought we saw submarines, then a mine. It was like living on your nerves.

We just concentrated on the work we had to do which was to get the torpedoes ready in the tubes. No one told us what was happening. We just knew we were going into battle against the High Seas Fleet. We went into attack late the next day.

When the five turrets fired at the same time the ship just stood still and shook. You wondered what the hell was happening. We did get radio messages but no one asked us to fire our torpedo. We did hear that our 13.5-inch guns had scored seven hits on the *König* and we sank a torpedo-boat.

Later I was ordered on deck to be part of a searchlight crew for the night action. That was something else. The searchlight had a long beam and we could pick out the enemy. It was all bangs and flashes and a lot of action, like a fireworks show with all those bombs dropping in the water with big splashes. You'd see our guns fire away at the flashes and then the ship they were firing at wouldn't be there any more – just blackness in its place.

I always think it was a miracle that the ships didn't collide with each other. We never used our navigational lights, only our port and starboard lights. This made the ship really dark to move around in and difficult for us to see other ships.

The battle for us finished in the early hours of the morning. But as the darkness went on we could see spasmodic flashes from the cruisers who were still engaging the enemy. Jellicoe was a very clever man. The enemy thought they could draw him into their minefields, but he wasn't going to risk his ships. After all, we'd lost three battle-cruisers, *Invincible, Indefatigable* and the *Queen Mary* as well as other ships. That was a lot of men lost.

When we got back the first thing we did was to coal and rearm the ship which meant pretty well twenty-four hours non-stop work. The next day we mostly slept. A month later I got some leave, the first time for fifteen months.

I didn't read about the battle for some time after. As we were never hit on the *Iron Duke* I thought we'd done well. But the numbers killed were very upsetting.

All the time I was on the *Iron Duke* I found Admiral Jellicoe a very nice gentleman. We never really saw much of him for months on end though sometimes you would see him exercising on the upper deck. If you were working on the upper deck you would stand to attention when he passed and he would say, 'Carry on'. He was only a little man, but we liked him. His wife sent us all Christmas cards in 1915 and I've still got it. He left the Fleet in November 1916.

Admiral Beatty was next. He was more of the old bulldog soldier. We didn't see a lot of him and he didn't have much to say to us when we did. But he was a very brave man – a proper 'let's get at 'em' sort of chap. The *Lion* was the right name of ship for him to command. And it got knocked about a bit too like him. But he shook it off and kept going to search for the prey. He was afraid of nothing.

In our world between decks we got to know each other. We were together for so long and we were very young. We never seemed to see the sun – it was so bleak up in the Orkneys, barren and bleak – just bloody heather everywhere and cold grey seas. You never saw a girl. You had to make your own enjoyment. The officers had their deck hockey and we used to run around the upper deck and do exercises. Then in the evening we'd play cards and housey-housey (bingo). And we had concert parties. My best friend was from Aberdeen and my two other special friends came from Manchester and London. It was really marvellous just to sit on deck and talk and learn about other people's lives. Their lives became important to you.

After the war the Fleet was hit with the 'flu epidemic. Having survived the war we lost six men on my ship. One minute they were all right and the next they were down and out. We were given inoculations and vaccinations, but a lot of us reacted badly to them.

After that it was the Mediterranean to keep the Turks and Greeks apart and then the Russian revolution. I wouldn't have missed a minute of it.

Midshipman Bill Fell

At the time of Jutland I was eighteen and a junior midshipman on the *Warspite*, part of Fifth Battle Squadron. Within forty-eight hours of arriving at Rosyth we were all under way, battle-cruisers steaming out ahead of us. May 31 was a gloriously fine and calm day. As the morning went on, our speed was increased from 18 to 20 knots and then to full speed at 24 knots. The battle-cruisers ahead of us were *Lion, Tiger, Princess Royal, Queen Mary*, with others closer to us.

I'd had forenoon watch on the bridge and, at about 12.30, I went down below and cut and made some sandwiches. I then ran off to my action station, the transmitting station, right in the bowels of the ship, five decks down. Three heavy armoured hatches rang shut above us. We then got orders that the enemy were in sight. Then 'ranges' and 'elevations and bearings' began to come in. My job was on a bearing plot, a very simple device on which I had to plot the rate of change of bearing so that the guns could follow it. The senior midshipman down below was plotting the mean of the ranges that were coming down to him from the range finders. Shortly after 4 pm we opened fire at 18,000 yards (just over ten miles) on the battle-cruiser *Von Der Tann*. There were corrections straightaway because we were short: we went up 800 yards. Then all of a sudden there was a monumental crump which sounded as if all the tea trays in the world, full of crockery, had been dropped on our heads; the whole ship rattled and shook. We realised we'd been hit by something pretty big. We were only just recovering from that when there was an even worse crash which knocked us off our stools. I was dazed and when I sat up I was in water. Apart from one stuttering light in the corner it was pitch dark. Worst of all was the complete silence. No sound of the engines, no sound of the action, no sound except for swishing water.

After a moment, I noticed that down all the voice pipes was

spurting a good old sluice of water – so we were slowly flooding. I think we all began to come to about the same time and two young midshipmen, who had only been on the ship a couple of weeks, began to whimper a bit. The senior midshipman went across and banged their two heads together and dropped them back into the water. Well, that solved that problem.

We then went back to trying to do our job, but of course no information was coming down. Then, reassuringly, the engines started and we found a few lamps and got them going. But we were still anxious about our situation. The senior midshipman found his way to the voice pipe and called up 'Foretop? Foretop?' He then paused. 'What another one gone up? Splendid!' He was in fact speaking to a mythical Foretop through a wrecked voicepipe. Of course we didn't realize that, and so our morale shot up. After that we waited and waited for about an hour and a half. Then we heard banging on the hatches and someone let us out.

I didn't recognise the ship when I got up on deck. She was a shambles, every single boat had gone, splinters everywhere, funnels were riddled or falling down. She was a hell of a mess. Thirty dead and wounded. A cordite fire had broken out in the starboard 6-inch battery and many had been burnt. She was right down in the water with the quarterdeck nearly awash. I went up on the bridge and Captain Philpotts turned to me and said, 'How did you like that, boy?' I said, 'Not much, sir'.

We were now out of the action and on our own. We had suffered a jammed helm probably from being put hard over at 24 knots and we'd done an unrehearsed complete circle within 10,000 yards of *Scheer*'s line around the sinking *Warrior*. We'd become an irresistible target and we'd been hit eighty-seven times, thirteen of which had been big calibre hits. Everyone else had disappeared and we were ordered back to Rosyth. The constructor came up on the bridge and told the captain that we could not exceed 8 knots otherwise we'd sink. The captain rang down to the engine room '12 knots'.

We were attacked the following morning by a U-boat. A torpedo was fired at us and we all watched as it ran from the stem parallel with us about 40 feet away to disappear ahead. The U-boat broke surface very close and we nearly rammed her. In fact people were throwing wreckage at her, from the upper deck. She had lost buoyancy and so was too close to fire. We were very lucky! Then two little torpedo boats came out to join us and we were very relieved to see them.

I don't think we gave any thought to how we would be received at home. But as we passed up the Firth of Forth and under the bridge, all the railway people were lined along it. To our dismay they shouted 'Cowards! Cowards, you ran away!' and chucked lumps of coal at us. We were received at Rosyth with very, very great disapproval by the local people. They were all in mourning black hats and black arm-bands. They all felt the Grand Fleet had suffered complete defeat and that some ships, like the *Warspite*, had run away. That was the news that had reached Scotland and it was twenty-four hours before things got better, when the other ships returned and more facts were known.

The *Warspite* had proved to be a wonderful ship, apart from her steering mechanism, and we remained in fighting order.

Leading Stoker Mechanic Jack Cotterell

On 31 May 1916, as far as I knew, *Gloucester* was just on another patrol. We went into action in the middle of the afternoon and the fight was on. We could hear the sound of the gunfire above the boilers. As the guns went off you could feel the ships go down and rise up, which would shake the dust out of the crevices, creating clouds of smoke. Of course we were in the stokehole, the lowest part of the ship, and in battle that's a very vulnerable position. Our Petty Officer would get all his orders from the bridge. We were kept pretty busy and, when we came off watch, we helped in the magazine with the shells. We wouldn't normally do that, but as the battle went on we all pulled together. For us it seemed a long battle and a hard one. But there was a good feeling on the ship as we made our way back to Rosyth. We had no casualties and had no idea of the losses. When we got back we saw the state of the *Lion* and the *Tiger*. The *Lion* had a big hole in her. As soon as we came into port we coaled and went straight out again. When we reached where we had fought the battle, the debris of battle still floating around. It was a mournful sight. We saw the nose of a ship sticking out of the water, but we couldn't tell whether it was one of theirs or ours. While we were there a Zeppelin flew quietly over.

When we got back to Rosyth again we had a chance to talk to other sailors from the battle and slowly began to piece the events of Jutland together. There was great sadness, though, because of the losses.

Midshipman Henry St John Fancourt

When I was sixteen I joined the *Princess Royal*, sister ship of the *Lion*, the Flagship of the First Battle-Cruiser Squadron. She was armed with eight 13.5-inch guns on the centre line, two turrets forward, one aft and one in 'Q' position amidships, and was part of Beatty's 'Cat Squad' along with *Tiger* and *Queen Mary*, all based at Rosyth. I was, along with the other midshipmen, very keen to fight the Germans who had been quite active for the previous four months under their new C-in-C, Admiral Scheer.

On the afternoon watch of 31 May I was on submarine lookout. I was in a small cubby hole which you put your head into and looked along bearing 000 to 095. I thought we were on another flap, another stunt, and didn't expect to go into action. I had just finished my watch and was going down to the gunroom to order myself a boiled egg for my tea when they sounded off 'Action at the double', so I never got my boiled egg. Apparently Beatty had ordered his battle-cruisers to form a line of bearing 110° and was steaming to the south-east for a better position to close the enemy. The Germans also turned and were on a line of bearing when they ordered 'fire straightaway' at 1548. Not that I knew it, but we were firing on the *Lützow*.

I was sitting on a little stool in the turret with my fire control instrument, a dumaresq. We were on standby in case we went

Royal Naval College, Dartmouth, 1908. Cadet Harry Hodgson sitting on the immediate right of the tutor.

In a skit on *Pirates of Penzance*, the same cadet, holding the fan, plays Belinda.

HMS *Cumberland*

Gunroom of HMS *Cumberland* with two midshipmen.

Auctioning of a dead man's kit on HMS *Cumberland*.

Coaling aboard HMAS *Australia*. Note the unusual clothes and headgear.

Admiral Sir John Jellicoe on board his flagship, HMS *Iron Duke*.

Admiral Sir David Beatty.

Stern view of HMS *Bellerophon* at Sheerness.

Destruction of HMS *Invincible* at the battle of Jutland, 6.48pm, 31 May 1916.

The wreck of HMS *Invincible*. The bows and stern standing above the water. HMS *Badger* is seen approaching to pick up the six survivors.

HMS *Chester* after the battle of Jutland in which one of its youngest crewmen, Boy First Class Cornwell, received the Victoria Cross.

Converted seaplane-carrier, HMS *Engadine*, prior to the battle of Jutland
sent up her short 184 piloted by Flt.Lt. Rutland RNAS and later took on
crew of the crippled HMS *Warrior*.

K22 (ex K13) under way at speed during trial in the Firth of Forth.

into local control. I was glued to this instrument. Only the turret officer who had a little hole to look through could see anything. The *Queen Mary*, astern of us, was firing well, she was a good gunnery ship, but she was hit badly and sank about 16.20 with a loss of 1,200 men. We continued firing. All the time I could hear the lieutenant calling, 'Battleship, battleship bearing so and so': I had to estimate the position from those details and shout up to him 'rate is opening' or 'rate is closing'. The control officer then had to try and spot his fall of shot. We were firing at about 16,000 yards. There was a hell of a lot of firing going on and everyone had really to concentrate. 'X' turret was hit in its barbette, and 'A' turret got off about thirty rounds. But we always had the feeling we were winning. The strongest units are the people that keep their spirits up longest. I think we had something like 28–30 dead and 70 wounded, that is about ten per cent casualties.

The *Lion* however, only two cables from us, was hit very severely so we took over their wireless which had been damaged. The third shell which hit *Lion* almost sank her. It struck and penetrated 'Q' turret; everyone there was either killed or wounded. One of the guns was loaded when the shell struck and the turret system was fully charged with cordite. Major Harvey ordered the magazine doors to be closed and the magazine to be flooded. Almost as soon as this was completed an explosion occurred in the turret trunking. The magazine doors, which were not fully flash-tight, were bulged inwards by the force of the explosion. If they had not been flooded, the ship would have blown up.

When the Fleet was trying to form into some form of night organisation the general signal made from the *Iron Duke* said, 'Fleet will proceed into the German Bight at dawn and annihilate the Germans completely'. We were all pretty weary by now and I thought we had done enough annihilating for one day. But of course there was something of a lull before the night action at about 8.28 when we opened fire on the *Seydlitz*, quite close at 12,000 yards, and scored a couple of hits. But of course we didn't know then what we were hitting or what was hitting us. Jellicoe had not got into the action until after six o'clock, so his chaps were still fresh.

We didn't fire again after nine o'clock. I don't think we did well in the night action. We had never been trained to fight a night action, nor had we ever fired our guns before at night. The

Germans were much better trained for night action. Our policy was that you didn't fight at night.

I remember seeing a Zeppelin on the horizon at dawn and one of the battle-cruisers fired some armour-piercing shell at it. By now the ship looked a bit messy so we began to put her right. I was asked to draw sketches to record the damage. We held a funeral service on the quarterdeck and delivered to the sea the lads who had given up their lives.

In those days communications were much slower, and it was some time before we heard of casualties. It was a different way of living, a different war.

As we came into Rosyth in the morning, the colliers were waiting ready to come alongside to coal the squadron the moment we dropped anchor. Someone said, 'Look, there's the collier for the *Queen Mary*', but of course she had no ship to coal, so she moved off. It was rather a sad sight. As soon as we docked we coaled ship.

When we got ashore there was an awful lot of badly handled propaganda. The Admiralty did as usual and said everything was gloomy and that rather took the heart out of us because we thought we had done rather well. But then that's war and I don't think we conduct the aftermath of war very well. We patched up at Rosyth, saw what a mess the enemy had made of the *Lion*, then sailed down to Portsmouth to refit.

There was no great excitement about the Battle of Jutland, we hadn't decimated the Germans – it was not Trafalgar. People didn't throw their arms around you and say wonderful things about you. It really wasn't a satisfactory battle. A lot of things went wrong and needed to be rejigged.

After that I was involved when the High Seas Fleet came out on 19 August 1916 to attack East Coast towns. We got down there in time and they withdrew but the *Nottingham* was sunk by a U-boat. Again, on 17 November 1917 off Heligoland, we had a bit of a tussle with the enemy but that really was the last time the High Seas Fleet came out.

So the poor old Grand Fleet worked very hard, tried very hard, but it didn't succeed in the sense that we would have liked.

Ordinary Seaman Stan Smith

While I was at Chatham Barracks a notice went up asking for volunteers for Q-ships. These were the Royal Navy's first answer to the menace of the submarine. They were dilapidated old merchant ships taken from the scrap heap and fitted up with concealed guns. They were so old and decrepit that a submarine would not waste a torpedo on them, relying on gunfire to intimidate their crews into abandoning ship. The theory was that when they had done this, the submarine would gradually circle the Q-ship and eventually come alongside to loot the vessel for provisions.

I was chosen, and after passing a medical, we volunteers were kitted out with civilian clothing, although we had to pass the things around to get a decent fit. We were then sent by train to West Hartlepool to join our ship, Q-12, which quickly went on to disprove the optimistic theory of the strategy.

She was a rough old vessel, eaten up with rust. But she had two 4-inch guns concealed under the bridge behind flaps which dropped down. On no. 3 hatch a coil of manila rope would fall back at the pull of a lever to reveal a 12-pounder gun. The control tower was located in a hawser reel on the fo'c'sle. She was also fitted with bell pushes around the upper deck so that if you saw a periscope you could press it with your foot, sending everybody, unseen, to action stations. Then you would light a fag and stroll away casually to your own.

Q-12's mess decks were in a filthy condition so we turned to and scrubbed out, gathered up all the fish and chip papers, lunch bags, bits of bread and butter and other litter until she was fairly shipshape. But this didn't half get us into trouble. It caused a dockyard strike. Apparently women were employed to clean the ships behind the dockyard people and we had done them out of a job. After some fuss our commanding officer managed to square things up and they got back to work.

When she was completed in the dockyard, Q-12 had to go out to sea to swing compasses. The accuracy of these instruments is always affected by riveting or any changes in the ship's metalwork.

On 30 April, with one or two dockyard people still on board, we were steaming 200 miles west of Ireland getting on quite well when 'Whoof!', a torpedo hit us amidships. She didn't take more than two or three minutes to sink. I was quickly picked up by one of our lifeboats. That was the end of the Q-12 without a shot fired in anger and with no opportunity to test the Navy's Q-ship strategy.

We went back to barracks and it wasn't long before I got another Q-ship, again from West Hartlepool. The *Pargust*, a collier was fitted out almost the same as the Q-12, except that instead of a 12-pounder being under the hawser reel, it was in an upturned boat which was cut away in sections which fell away at the pull of a lever.

While in West Hartlepool, waiting for the ship to be completed, we would go ashore, although there was not much pleasure in it. The girls, seeing us in 'civilians' and knowing we were of military age, would stick white feathers in our coats. In the public houses we were invariably caught up in an argument about why we weren't in the forces. Three of us went to the cinema one night and during the show the place was raided by the civilian and military police, looking for men of military age. We were taken to the police station and, since we were sworn to secrecy, our commanding officer had to come and bail us out.

When the ship was completed, we finished with the dockyard and went to sea. Having swung compasses and carried out gun trials – this time uneventfully – we were on our own. The unwieldy old vessel would plough up and down the length of England in the trade routes. Her screw and rudder were only one-third in the water, and although she had a ballast, she would spin and yaw all over the place in a strong wind and a decent sea.

The food was not so good either. We only carried fresh provisions for five days and after that we would be on corned beef and biscuits. We used to dish the corned beef up in various different ways to break the monotony. The biscuits were so hard we had to soak them overnight, strain them off and mix in a tin of suet. Then we'd add a few currants and a little sugar and bake the mixture until it was quite palatable.

The routine had us doing about ten to twelve days at sea at a stretch before going in to coal and water. Coaling was quite easy because we would go under the chute.

The events of our second patrol demonstrated how the Q-ship strategy was supposed to work, with the enemy running true to form. One of the chaps spotted a periscope, put his foot on the alarm and sent us all off to our action stations. The submarine cruised around the ship – which was quite easy since we were only doing about four knots – and had a good look at us.

Part of the ploy involved one of the seamen dressing as a woman. His duty was to go up and hang out some washing on the fo'c'sle line. He would then come down and join his action station. The submarine surfaced about a mile away and opened fire. Then another of our schemes came into play. We had containers scattered around the ship which were electrically operated from the control tower. These could be activated to cause a miniature explosion, showering fire, sparks and smoke all over the show. If the submarine sent a shell over the ship, its crew could be confused into thinking they had scored a hit. Being low in the water, they wouldn't be able to spot an 'over' if it was in line with the ship.

Her first couple of shells fell short, then she scored an 'over' which we immediately gave her as a hit. She carried on firing for some ten or fifteen minutes and did manage to knock the mast down and the derricks over the forward hold, but they didn't put the gun, hidden in the boat, out of action. Next we stopped the ship and sent away the 'panic boats' with all the men who were not manning the guns or the control. They dashed up on deck, lowered the boat haphazardly (showing every sign of panic), jumped in and pulled away as fast as they could.

The submarine stopped firing and began to circle the ship, coming closer each time. When she was about a hundred yards off the port beam and we could get two guns to bear on her – the 4-inch and the 12-pounder – we opened fire. After the third or fourth salvo we sank her and the panic boat crew went over. There were only two survivors to take on board.

When we returned to port, the Navy confirmed our claim. Unfortunately our reign on board didn't last very long. We were continually having engine trouble and could barely keep steerage way on at times. Eventually, one day as we were coming into harbour to coal and water, against wind and tide, we hit the jetty and tore a large gash in the port side. We hoped this would give us a few days leave but instead they paid her off and we returned to Chatham Barracks.

My next ship was HMS *Montbretia* which was totally different from the other two Q-ships. She was a 17-knot sloop which had been converted to look like a merchantman. She had two 4.7-inch guns concealed under the bridge and a 12-pounder in an upturned boat, but she was fitted with all the latest controls. She had a listening device, the only snag being that you had to stop the ship to listen. There were two depth-charge throwers, one on each side of the quarter-deck. Each was like a mortar and had a cradle into which the depth-charges were lashed. I should imagine the depth-charges weighed over a hundredweight [112lb. or 50.8 kilograms] and were about the size of a large oil drum. They could be set to explode at a depth of 50 feet to 250 feet but, being a new invention, they didn't always operate as we should have liked. They would often explode on hitting the water, showering the ship with lumps of cradle and causing quite a bit of damage.

We didn't have a lot of success with submarines, although we claimed to have sunk one by depth-charges. Oil and debris came to the surface but the Navy would not confirm our claim. Apparently the submarines could tell we were not what we seemed because the beat of our screw was much faster than that of a merchant ship. So we were put on convoy duty where we could fly the White Ensign, get back into uniform and show all the guns.

We were next transferred to Northern Patrol which was right up in the Shetland Isles and based at Lerwick. This was a real one-horse town at the time, where the monotony was relieved only by the monthly visit of the beer boat. It was quite a job to get a drink, but a crowd of us used to buy a small barrel and take it up into the hills.

Patrols were pretty arduous and used to last from ten to twelve days. We not only had to contend with a lack of fresh provisions half the time, but also ice; tons of it. Huge icicles hung from the rigging and upper works. We had to chop them off in the mornings to avoid carrying too much top weight. She carried quite a lot as it was and could roll like the very devil.

Look-outs were posted around the clock for we were in the 'Land of the Midnight Sun'. It used to be daylight almost all night long which made it easier for a look-out to spot anything unusual. One night the masthead look-out spotted a submarine on the port bow. We were all sent to action stations and the ship turned full speed ahead to ram. We hit the vessel just as what appeared to be the bow lifted from a large swell. We immediately wished we hadn't as the contents of the thing shot all over the ship, showering us as far aft as the funnel, and oh boy! What a stink! It turned out to be a huge bloated dead whale left by the whaling fleet. Goodness knows how long it had been floating around for it was white with seagull droppings. The smell was atrocious. We couldn't get rid of it. It went down through the ventilators into the mess decks so we were eating it as well as smelling it. It took us days to clear the smell and wash the ship clean of the blubber that was flung all over it. It was the closest I ever came to getting sea-sick.

Wren Ada Bassett

I didn't like school so I left as soon as I could in 1910 when I was thirteen years old. I was taught to drive by a young man who had been at school with me. I found it very easy. He'd just turn up and change seats and off we'd go. No licence, no 'L' plates and very few cars. Wonderful time to learn. We used to drive up to London and all around. Petrol was so cheap and I could get out and get under the car because the young man taught me how to change a tyre and sort out the engine.

I had five brothers who were all older, and an older sister, and all we seemed to do was laugh. They even laughed when I had a boyfriend. I don't think they wanted to lose me. All my brothers joined up in the Army. I missed them all at home so, in 1917, I joined the Women's Royal Naval Service (WRNS) because I thought it would open up something new for me.

When I joined the WRNS some of the other girls came from posh homes, and myself and my friend, who I shared a house with, used to irritate them. They were from another world, but

I used to laugh at them because they had to have lessons to drive whereas I could drive anything, including lorries, and I'd only had an elementary education!

Of course in a lorry you seemed high up off the ground, and they weren't very good in bad weather. You had to wear lots of warm clothes. They weren't easy to start either – we had to crank it up by hand. In those days too the brakes were not very good so the back wheels were covered in metal studs which worked all right on wet roads but on wooden paving the wheels just went on and on spinning.

Lord Jellicoe could have had any of those snooty girls, one of whom was a lord's daughter, but he chose me to drive him everywhere. We went all over England. He was a very quiet man. I used to salute him every time I met him: but I didn't see Lady Jellicoe very much. I was based at Albany Street while he was at the Admiralty. I used to meet him at Waterloo Station every morning, then wait on him all day, and return him in the evening. He always had lots of appointments and meetings. He was very thoughtful and considerate to me, not patronising; he seemed to trust me – he was truly a dying breed. I did also meet Lord Beatty, but I didn't take to him; Lord Jellicoe was more dignified.

As I joined up when the WRNS were just starting I had the number G.5. I think the 'G' stood for 'Garage' where I did my extra training as a driver for officers. I never expected to get to drive the most famous naval officer of them all! 'Ginger' Smith, who taught me, was over the moon when he heard. You see, I was only small, but I was a very experienced driver when I joined at twenty. Most drivers would only drive what they were used to or had learnt on, but I even learnt to drive a motor cycle and a three-wheeler – that was like a large box arrangement which had been commandeered from a milliner's who used it for delivering the large hats.

I remember the night (2/3 September 1916) when Leefe Robinson shot down the Zeppelin. It lit up the whole sky over London; but when I drove out to the field in Cuffley those guarding it wouldn't let me in. I was very sad when Leefe Robinson died after the war. He'd come all the way through, and then died during the terrible 'flu epidemic.

And I remember too Armistice Day in 1918. But we didn't celebrate it. We were just glad it was all over.

Boy First-Class Alfred Sprinkett

I was fifteen and a half when I joined the Royal Navy in July 1916. That was the minimum age. I was the only one in my family who ever went to sea. I was sent to the training establishment, *HMS Ganges*, at Shotley. We had to spend time in the gym doing physical jerks and we had lessons as well, but it wasn't any tougher than school.

When I finished my training I was sent to the Second Cruiser Squadron based in Scapa Flow. I was supposed to go on the *Duke of Edinburgh* but as she was out on patrol, I had to spend my first week on the flagship, *Minotaur*.

Originally we were out patrolling north of the Shetlands. We then changed to escorting convoys across the Atlantic from Liverpool to Halifax, Nova Scotia, and sometimes to New York. On one trip, when we were in New York, I was transferred to another heavy cruiser, the *Berwick*, because they needed a boy telegrapher. She was one of the coal-driven county-class cruisers.

I was discharged from the *Berwick* in November 1916 because I had pneumonia. I was in a naval hospital which was the old Admiralty house overlooking Halifax dockyard. At nine o'clock on the morning of 6 December 1917 the French steamer *Mont Blanc*, which was loaded with 3,000 tons of TNT, collided with the Norwegian freighter *Imo*. They were blown to pieces in the explosion.

The first thing we heard was like a repeated roll of thunder, and the whole of the sky became dark. From the windows we could see objects going by through the air. The nurse had just been by and I was sitting back in an armchair with a thermometer in my mouth waiting for the doctor to come around. The chair I was sitting in moved away from underneath me and I got to my feet. It was a most peculiar sensation. All the time large fragments came flying through the open wall of the ward, so we quickly tried to get out of the place. As I crossed the ward to get to the doors which led into the grounds I got hit in the right side of my head in the thick part of the cheek just below the eye. It left a heavy scar.

I lost my slippers in the rush so I was standing in the grounds in about two inches of snow with nothing on but my pyjamas. Which wasn't going to help my pneumonia! When I got back to England I was telling an old Scots lady that I had been hit in the head and was bleeding like a pig. She said, 'Ah yes! It was the blood-letting which cured the pneumonia'. It was an old-fashioned idea which they still believed in those days.

The explosions subsided fairly quickly. Since nobody knew the cause one old salt in the hospital ward said, 'Oh, it's a Zeppelin raid'. Another one replied, 'Don't be a fool. The Zeppelins can't get over as far as this'.

It was very frightening. It was the biggest man-made explosion ever, razing two square miles of the north end of the city. The *Mont Blanc* also had a deck cargo of barrels of benzine which caught fire. She was ablaze. There were a number of factories, one of which made maple syrup. There was a crowd of women looking out of the window at the burning ship so when the explosion happened the windows took the full force of it. Any number of women were injured. The hospital was in a very good neighbourhood. On one side was the harbour and on the other a residential road. I walked through the snow but I knew I had to do something because I was bleeding like a pig. When I stopped to cross the road I saw a two-horse dray dashing like mad along the road with no driver. The horses had gone mad with fright. They were all good Victorian houses with three or four storeys. The door of one of the houses had been burst open so I went in and up to a bedroom on the first floor. I saw that part of the ceiling had come down and the coverlet over the bed was covered with plaster. I pulled all that back and hopped into the bed. Being young, I'd got the idea into my head that if I lay down flat all the blood would flow to the brain. I thought I ought to sit bolt upright. Presently a woman came in with two or three pillow cases to clamp on to the side of my face to stop the blood. I sat there for a while and then I heard voices so I called out. Some Canadian soldiers came up the stairs. They looked at me and then opened a wardrobe and took out a woman's lovely, dark brown fur coat — a pretty valuable one as it turned out — and put it on me. They couldn't find any shoes to fit me because they were all women's shoes but I could get my toes in. They took me down below, put me in a car and drove me to hospital.

By then I'd lost quite a lot of blood. I was in a very big ward with two rows of beds. I was fortunate enough to get a bed. A woman came in with two teenaged daughters. They'd all been looking out of the window watching the ship on fire and when the explosion happened the glass had blown in on them. The woman was not badly injured but one of her daughters had glass in her face. She and her mother slept in the next bed and the daughter who was uninjured laid on my bed with me. Before very long, all the spaces between the rows of beds were filled up with people lying down. We later heard that about 1,600 people had died and another 4,000 were injured. The next day a blizzard struck.

After some days there I was put into another civilian hospital. Everybody was questioned and when they found out that I was a Naval person I was sent to the Canadian depot ship, which was really a hulk moored permanently along the quay. I was there for some time. After New Year I was feeling pretty well so I was transferred to an armed merchant liner, one of the Royal Mail boats which used to run to South America. I was brought home to Chatham Barracks.

When I got back the doctor examined the place on my cheekbone and he said 'Well, I think it's all right now'. Then I was sent home on sick leave. I discovered that the nurse in Halifax had written a letter telling my people that I was getting on all right and not to worry. From there I was sent up to the Second Cruiser Squadron who were based in the north Shetlands. We were patrolling between the Shetlands and Iceland, but didn't see any fighting. That continued until the summer of 1917. Then we were engaged again in escorting convoys across to New York and Halifax.

In those days convoys were quite slow. They only did about seven or eight knots, so they took about twenty-one days to get across the Atlantic and the same to come back. They weren't like ships nowadays. There was a big refrigerator on board which you could put fresh meat and fish in when you were in port, but that would only last us three days at the most. The rest of the time we had salt-pork one day and salt-beef the next. There were no fresh vegetables at all. They made bread on the ship and there was plenty of tea. I was too young for a noggin of rum.

I spent 1918 on the destroyer *HMS Victor* escorting ingoing convoys as far as Dover and outgoing convoys to the Bay of Biscay. The *Victor* was one of the first oil-burners. The *Duke of Edinburgh* and the *Berwick* were coal-burners, but as I was a telegrapher in the radio department I was excused from taking part in the coaling because the authorities thought that we would get coal dust in our ears and wouldn't be able to hear. The convoys were liable to attack by U-boats. We were escorting a convoy outward bound, somewhere in the middle of the Channel between Dover and Portsmouth when one of the ships, the *Knight Templar*, was hit by a torpedo. Most of the crew took to the boats. We went alongside to try to pick up the rest of the crew but there was a bit of a heavy sea blowing which bumped us up against the side of the *Knight Templar*. Our captain decided to abandon this idea and let the men take their chances in their own lifeboats. We went around and picked them up. Most of the men survived and the *Knight Templar* went down. It's a terrible sight to see a ship go down.

I remember that incident well. When we went alongside, some of our crew went aboard the *Knight Templar*. They went inside the saloon and seamen's quarters and found they'd been playing cards and gambling because there were cards and money lying on the table.

By 1919 I'd had enough of the Navy so, as I had a very bad scar and they were cutting down the personnel after the war, I was invalided out. The scar is barely noticeable now.

Wren Marie Scott

I was born in Leicester on Boxing Day 1897 and started work in a Jewish tailor's at the age of thirteen. I worked there for three years and at sixteen was earning thirteen shillings and sevenpence a week. When my brother joined the Royal Flying Corps, I decided I'd join up as well. I went down to Cecil Hotel in the Strand in

London and told them I wanted to sign on in the VAD (Voluntary Aid Detachment). They told me they needed drivers so I was sent back to Leicester to learn how to drive.

Not only was I taught to drive but to do running repairs as well. One of the things I learnt was how to use carborundum, under-paste, on the valves. Once I learnt how to drive the car they sent me to Doncaster to learn to drive heavy vehicles. When I arrived there all on my own I met all these rough-looking soldiers, but they were very nice to me. I was the only woman on the camp and it was my first time away from home, so I was rather lonely. I took my test on a Crossley tender, a great big thing that was a devil to drive, especially uphill. You almost needed two hands on the gear stick! Somehow I managed to pass the test and then I went home to wait to be called up.

After I passed I joined the VADs. In fact we were called the Forage Corps – which involved anything to do with the country, farms, grass, and feeding horses – at King's Lynn and put in charge of a squad of women: Lady Ogilvy-Grant was one of them. We had to guard the docks – well not so much guard as look after the tons of hay that were stacked on the dockside. The hay was for the horses of the Expeditionary Force in France and Belgium. We had to guard it in case it tumbled over, or ignited – spontaneous combustion.

I did that for a long time: so all my driving and the other glamorous things I'd envisaged didn't come into it. All I can remember from then is the taste of the horrible soup they used to give us when we came off duty. We were billeted in St Margaret's House in King's Lynn where there were about fourteen of us. We worked very long hours so I tried to cheer everyone up by playing the piano. I used to play the popular songs like 'Have you any dirty washing, Mother, dear?' and 'I've got sixpence,' but on one occasion I played a couple of love songs and a few of the girls began to cry. I couldn't understand why until one of the older girls told me that some of them had lost sweethearts and brothers.

I was then seconded to the Coastal Defence Station at Lowestoft as the driver for Egbert ('Bertie') Cadbury of the RNAS. He was a pilot and flew a Sopwith seaplane. This was a new world for me, a lot more glamorous and really what I'd joined for. I used to drive him from our depot to the beach and back again. The seaplanes were flying anti-submarine patrols and watching out for Zeppelins which seemed to come over in droves to attack the East coast. I used to watch the men, sometimes up to their armpits, dragging the seaplanes down into the sea; in the winter they were frozen stiff. We also had lots of women called civilian subordinates who used to clean the wings of the seaplanes. One night in October 1916 ten Zeppelins launched an attack and dropped a bomb nearby where I was sleeping and blew me out of bed. Bertie Cadbury and two other pilots attacked one of them from underneath. Even though he was under fire himself from the Zeppelin he fired off two trays of ammunition without any effect; then he fired his last two trays into the stern which didn't seem to have any effect either. But a few minutes later flames appeared where he'd hit it in the stern. One of the other pilots continued firing until it burst into flames. That was a great day for us and the camp was all excited that evening with the success. One pilot got the DSO, and Bertie Cadbury and the other pilot got a DFC.

Bertie Cadbury was always very busy. He was in charge of all the transport and all the aircraft as well as instructing the new pilots. So life was very busy for me too. But every week or so he'd receive a parcel from the Cadbury factory and I knew it was full of chocolates. He was a very nice man. On one occasion he nearly cost me my boyfriend. I drove him early one evening to the ward-room. He told me he'd be out at eight o'clock. A bit after 8 pm I went and inquired from a steward as to what was happening. The officers must have been celebrating because he came out and said, 'Miss Scott, I meant 8 am!'

In late 1917 I transferred across to the newly formed WRNS. When the RNAS merged with the RFC, we remained as WRNS. Bertie got another Zeppelin in August 1918. He was watching a concert where his wife was singing when he was told about three Zeppelins over Yarmouth. He raced off in his Ford and, with his observer Captain Leekie, attacked and shot down in flames L70 which was the finest airship that Germany had. On board was the Chief of the German Airship Service. They announced at the concert what he'd done and everyone cheered. He was carried shoulder-high through the streets when he came back. It was all very exciting.

In the September edition of our camp magazine 'The Bat' (our seaplanes were called Bat boats) Major Cadbury was congratulated along with Captain Leekie for getting the DFC, and the concert was recorded as a great success. On the next page, under the headline 'Great Scott', it read: 'Another Station Romance – another "WREN" driver as the heroine! Norman Scott, one of the most popular of drivers, is, we understand, engaged to Miss Marie Scott, also an "at the wheel" girl. Best of luck to both!'

Marie Northwood, née Scott, died in the summer of 1995. For the last forty years of her life, among her many activities, she regularly played the piano at the Hammer and Pincer in Barrow upon Soar, Leicestershire.

Midshipman Brian de Courcy-Ireland

On 9 July 1917 *Vanguard*, anchored in the next line to us at Scapa Flow, blew up just before midnight. The explosion was terrific, all magazines going up almost simultaneously; the cause was probably the same as the *Natal*. Such was the force of the explosion that a large chunk of metal from the interior of one of her boilers landed on top of my turret and a packet of pound notes from the ship's safe fell outside a crofter's cottage on Flotta Island a mile away. Out of approximately eight hundred men on board there were only two survivors: a Royal Marine and a stoker. They were several decks down and went right up before pitching in the sea. The tragic sequel for the marine was that he was killed in a bombing raid on Chatham a fortnight later while on survival leave.

As for me, I was one of those who walked along that dreadful mile of beach on Flotta with buckets. I will leave the description of it to Rudyard Kipling who, in his poem *The Scholars* referring to us, wrote:

They have touched a knowledge outreaching speech—
as when the cutters were sent

To harvest the dreadful mile of beach
after the *Vanguard* went.

I believe our sickberth staff pieced together over a score
of bodies.

At the end of July 1917 I was sent to a destroyer called *Relentless*,
a fine ship, oil-fired and capable of 40 knots, for what was called
a fortnight's training. She was mainly on convoy work and the
captain made the excuse to keep me for three months. Towards
the end of this period I was taking my turn as Officer of the Watch;
which officially I was not entitled to do. He was then ordered to
return me to *Bellerophon* and I was transferred to another destroyer,
the *Pellew*, for return to Scapa. But we were whisked away and
it was another two months before I finally got back, just in time
to sit and pass my exam in Seamanship and ship my first stripe as
Sub-Lieutenant. I had missed an attack on a convoy in which her
consort *Partridge* was sunk. I was immediately reappointed to the
Pellew whose captain had asked for me back.

In *Bellerophon*, with more than eight hundred men, life was very
impersonal and you were a bit of a dogsbody: in destroyers it was
heaven to me. There was a tremendous camaraderie on board;
you knew everyone; it was to a certain extent a picked ship's
company. You were doing a man's work and you were treated
as a man. Of course it was a hard life. On the slow convoys to
Norway, for example, at an unbelievable 4 knots, we averaged
six and a half days at sea and eighteen hours in port refueling etc,
week after week. For six months I was 'Watch and Watch' – four
hours on four hours off. I never took my clothes off at sea. And
in bad weather you often got wet and turned in wet. It was an
unwritten law in destroyers that the only time you turned back in
bad weather was if you lost a funnel or your bridge. I remember
well one of my term at Osborne losing his bridge and being saved;
he had tied himself to the wheel trunk.

We lost a number of merchant ships due to U-boat attacks. We
were able to depth-charge them if we were close by – but in the
end the Germans got us. On 19 July 1917 we were escorting
mine-layers across the top end of the North Sea, which was not
a job I cared for very much. I had kept the morning watch (4 to
7.30), and after breakfast was resting in my bunk when there was
a heavy crash and I found myself on the cabin floor. I think the

German U-boat had been trying to torpedo one of the mine-layers but instead hit us. The torpedo had struck just aft of my cabin and also set off one of the depth-charges which made a mess of the stern and trapped myself and the chief engineer in the cabin flat. The hatch was jammed, the ship was settling and oil, fuel and water were coming in, but we could hear them shoring up the bulkhead and were pleased that the water level wasn't rising any more. Eventually some of the crew smashed their way in to where the hatch had been and got us out. I was slightly relieved! I ran to report to the captain and at the bottom of the ladder up to the bridge I fell over a crate of Plymouth Gin which had been blown from the stern to the foot of the ladder and had arrived intact. Absolute godsend!

We were about a hundred miles off Aberdeen, so the Navy sent six tugs out and we got what was left of the ship in. The men were put up in a drill-hall and the four officers and myself were taken in a taxi to the Palace Hotel. When we arrived at the hotel, covered in oil and stinking to heaven, it was a Sunday. We were met by this grim looking female who said, no luggage, no room. So we went down to a Naval store in Aberdeen and they gave us a couple of packing cases which had had soap in them. We dumped them down in the foyer and said, 'There's our luggage'. Without batting an eyelid she then took us up to our rooms. I'd lost everything including my kit, but the outfitters were very good and dished me out a new kit which I had to pay for, but I did eventually get the money back.

During the incident I must have swallowed some oil fuel. Nobody asked me if I wanted a doctor, they just gave me a week's leave. I'd only been home a short while, which I spent kitting out, when the Admiralty contacted me and told me there was a war on, and that I was appointed to a new destroyer, HMS Westcott. I had a poor start on her. I believe I had delayed shock because I had a couple of blackouts, which was worrying at the time, but eventually things got better. Because she was brand new Westcott was heaven after the Pellew. We had one or two scrapes in her and on one occasion went into Heligoland Bight to pick up an airman who had been attacking Zeppelins. He had been shot off the end of a ship, and of course had no way of returning to it, so he ditched. We had to go right into the Bight to pick him up. We also managed to pick up part of his aircraft because we wanted the petrol out of his tank for our motorboat. In exchange, we filled him up with Plymouth Gin.

Sub-Lieutenant Bill Fell

In 1917, having passed my 'Subs' exams, I joined the Dover Patrol. We were under Admiral Roger Keyes. I was on a P-boat, P11, which had one low funnel cut off diagonally across the top, hopefully to resemble a U-boat. They were frightfully bad sea boats, low in the water but capable of 24 knots. We spent our nights sitting over the tops of minefields with hundreds of trawlers milling around us. Every few minutes a 3,000,000 candle-power flare would be set off. Because of the mines U-boats had to come up and it was hoped that they would be illuminated and then hunted by us. This method certainly kept the U-boats down though one or two got through. The others had to go around the minefield which meant a much longer journey for them. When occasional raids took place, and the Germans came down fast in their destroyers on a black south-westerly night, our job was to shepherd the trawlers out of the way. We couldn't get mixed up in the action as we only had one miserable 4-inch gun and a couple of pom-pom guns.

While I had been on the *Warspite* I had applied to join submarines. To my joy and delight, at the beginning of 1918 I was selected. After three months training I was sent to *Titania*, a submarine depot ship, as a spare hand longing to get out on patrol. At last I did get out on G.2. The G-boats were double hulled, slow to dive, but excellent sea boats. We had four 18-inch torpedoes and one little 3-inch gun, and our captain was Neville Lake. On my first trip we went out in a hurricane. I was sick for the first few hours. Then at noon, when we were on the surface, out of a rain squall appeared a British cruiser and two destroyers. They immediately turned towards us. We could see little black figures rushing fore and aft manning guns. I was on the bridge and fired the recognition signal, a grenade fired from a rifle, but inadvertently I'd forgotten to take out the pin and it did not go off. I then began anxiously searching for another in all the water that was slopping about in the conning tower. At last I got my hands on one, but when I pulled the trigger it misfired. By this time the destroyers were practically on top of us. I got a third one off and the navigator and myself were waving everything we had. I then fired another but realised the signal had changed at noon! However I think they had realised we were not the enemy and turned away into the squall.

The weather moderated later that afternoon and towards evening we saw a U-boat (U-78) way ahead of us. We lowered a hand on a bearing line down over the conning tower to the gun and then lowered a projectile to him which he pushed into the bridge of the gun. He went to one side and trained the gun then round to the other side and layed the gun. While he was doing this, waves were repeatedly washing him off, and we would pull him up on the end of the line. When he finished, without any instruction, he suddenly fired and we saw the fall of shot right alongside Fritz. We hastily got some more shots to him but we never saw any of these fall. Of course, Fritz dived. Being ahead of us he was in a perfect position to attack so we dived as well. We spent the rest of that evening in the Dogger Light Vessel area stooging around listening with the hydrophone.

Our orders were to surface at 2 am and recharge until daylight. At 1.30 am I went over to the radio operator who was listening on the hydrophone and had taken the phones off because the noise was so intense. He said it was 'Fasendend' (the underwater communication system used by the Germans). I called the captain who was fast asleep in his bunk and told him what I had heard. He said, very irritatedly, 'Go to bed. Go away. I don't care what it is.' But I kept on saying that it was very loud and reluctantly he agreed to get out of his warm bunk. When he arrived he had a pair of long woolly drawers on and nothing else. He listened and then told us to surface, but not to go to diving stations. So with a very sleepy crew we surfaced. We opened the lower lid, the Captain went up and opened the top conning tower and there was a silence. Then an almighty shout from him: 'Hard starboard! Full ahead! Gun action stations! Flood the tubes!' All yelled down the conning tower. The voice pipes were full of water so a lot of the crew who were still pretty fat-headed, having been down for some time, didn't hear a thing

The engine-room, in blissful ignorance of what was happening, assumed we had come up to charge our batteries. So they took the starboard engine clutch out and put the tail clutch in which effectively meant you couldn't go forward on your starboard side either on your motors or engine. As they'd heard there was a bit of a flap on for'ard they thought they had better go ahead port. With the helm hard over the other way all the submarine did was steam slowly away from a large U-boat which was steaming across our bows on the surface, as large as life, two or three hundred yards away. At that moment a half-moon came out, just shone for a moment silhouetting the U-boat, making it a sitting target. Down below the navigator and myself got the clutches changed over and the right screw going ahead on the motor.

The First Lieutenant, who was particularly fat-headed and asleep, got hold of the Lewis gun, put the pan on and was starting to go up the conning tower hatch when he unfortunately let it off! Well, bullets were whizzing around the control rooms hitting everything. He even shot the giro compass dead and that went spinning around as well. On top of this, there was a chain of men up the conning tower trying to get ammunition up to the gun, when the top one dropped his shell down on the others!

However, we were slowly turning. We had no night sight on the bridge in those days, but the Captain held his hand to his eye and was shouting down instructions. As we were swinging under full outside screw and under full helm he yelled 'Fire'. This instruction trickled down the conning tower and eventually reached the fore ends. In this time I should think we had swung an additional ten degrees before the torpedo gunners responded and sent off a 'fish'.

By this time Fritz had disappeared, the moon had gone in and we couldn't see a thing. We were disappointed and were just about to go below to clear up the mess when there was an enormous crump and crash and up went Fritz sky high. It was the luckiest shot of the war!

We went over to the pool of oil and wreckage and saw a lot of chaps all floating with their faces down in the water, with their bottoms up, all dead. We did pick up two and put them on our saddle tanks. The Captain then realised that Fritz had been talking to someone pretty close by, so he ordered us to dive.

At the end of the war as a result of us sinking the U-boat and one or two other incidents I received about £200 in blood money which was rather a lot of money in those days. I also had the pleasure of serving in submarines until 1945 and wouldn't have changed a minute of my time.

Sub-Lieutenant Gordon Hyams

Royal Naval Air Service

I went to Charterhouse School when I was fourteen in 1912. In the holidays I used to cycle from my home near Watford to Hendon Aerodrome. I had always been mad keen on aeroplanes and used to make models all the time. I called them flying sticks because that is what they looked like. I made a model of the Caudron and another which had a six-foot wingspan and fitted it with a compressed air engine which I had to pump up with a bicycle pump. At Hendon I saw all the early planes and flyers, including the famous Warren Marrian. The Germans were impressive, too, especially Dietrich, their ace looper. I also used to see Graham White who owned Hendon. The pilots would race flat out around pylons and sometimes they'd crash or fall out of the aircraft. There were big cash prizes on offer in those days.

Even though I was reading of the terrible casualties in the war, I wanted so much to become a pilot that I joined the Royal Naval Air Service (RNAS) in 1916 straight from school. My first posting was to Ponders End, near Chingford in Essex, where my flying instructor was Ben Travers. He later went on to make a name for himself writing farces for the Aldwych Company such as *Rookery Nook* and *Cuckoo in the Nest*. He taught one how to fly a Maurice Farman Longhorn. He was a very patient instructor, a quiet man, who had also been at Charterhouse. Most of the other trainees were flying Henri Farmans. On 18 March 1917 I flew my first solo for nineteen minutes after four hours of dual control. I flew some other aircraft, like the Avro 504K and the Curtiss JM4, and then went on to Cranwell, where I piloted a BE2 (Bleriot

Experimental 2), nicknamed 'Fokker fodder' because of its high casualty rate against the German Air Force.

I was then posted as a Flight Sub-Lieutenant to Calshot on the Solent to fly seaplanes. Arthur (later Lord) Tedder was an instructor there. We flew FBAs (Franco-British Association) which were not very good machines. The engine was in the middle on the back of the wing above and in front of my head. To start it, I had to stand on my seat and crank the starter handle. If the engine caught fire, you opened the throttle which blew it out. One of the observers at Calshot under training was Wedgwood Benn (later Lord Stansgate). He was much older than all of us but mucked in, particularly on the day the coal barge arrived. After completing my training I was posted to Westgate, near Margate, for our first crack at anti-submarine patrols. Each day we'd go out well prepared for the cold with heavy leather coat and helmet, plus a pigeon and Horlicks tablets which were very sustaining.

On one of my early take-offs, downwind, I managed to turn a cartwheel in a Sopwith Schneider and finished upside down in the sea. I escaped from the cockpit and swam ashore, but the aircraft was a write-off. From Westgate I went up to Hornsea Mere, a sub-station of Killingholme. It was the ideal place to take off from because it was a lake and so had no tide. We patrolled out from there along the shipping lanes between the Humber and the Tees. In March 1918 I spotted a U-boat on the surface off Scarborough. It was probably recharging its batteries, but as soon as it saw me it dived very quickly and, as the weather was very rough, it did not leave a wake. I dropped a 65lb bomb which went straight to the bottom.

On another occasion I was returning from a patrol when I saw a ditched H12 American flying-boat. As I descended it suddenly split in half and burst into flames. Somehow the crew of four managed to get into their dinghy. They seemed all right, but I thought I should drop them my life belt which I found out later, landed in their dinghy. I then flew back to Hornsea Mere to let them know of the situation, refuelled and flew back out to circle the dinghy. Later a Short came out, but for some unknown reason didn't see them and returned. I signalled to the now rather anxious crew below that I would seek further assistance. I flew for quite some while before I found two trawlers. I attempted to indicate the problem by Very Light, but they didn't seem to understand.

I tried to find other ships but by now was getting low in fuel so I returned to the trawlers and fired off several rounds from my Lewis gun, which seemed to alert them! They made their way to where I was circling and picked up the rather wet and cold crew.

While I was at Hornsea Mere, in the winter, some boys were playing on the frozen lake when one fell through the ice. I grabbed a ladder and ran across the ice until almost touching distance when the ice gave way and I fell in. Fortunately I came straight up and could claw my way out, but the boy had gone under the ice so I was unable to reach him and he drowned. It was a sad day.

On 28 February 1918 our senior pilot, Lemmon, was flying our Commanding Officer, Flight Commander Robertson, in a Short. He had taken off on one of the narrower parts of the mere and then made a sharp turn and plunged nose first into marshy ground. Robertson jumped clear, but the pilot was trapped inside the aircraft which had burst into flames. The ammunition on board was likely to explode, but Robertson tried to rescue Lemmon and only gave up when he was severely burnt in the face, hands and legs. I saw him later in hospital; his face was badly scarred and he'd lost an eye. However, he was awarded the Albert Medal and continued in the RAF right through the Second World War.

In the spring of 1918 I was looking forward to a bit of leave. I got home and was just beginning to relax when I received a telegram ordering me to report back to Hornsea immediately. I was cross about losing my leave, but my anger evaporated when the CO told me I'd been awarded the Humane Society Award for attempting to save the boy under the ice.

When the RNAS merged with the RFC to become the RAF, it meant that we had left the senior service to join the most junior service. We were first issued a khaki uniform and given Army ranks, then uniforms of various shades of blue and the new RAF rankings. We didn't welcome the so-called unification at all.

Later, in the early summer of 1918, I was posted to Egypt and based first at Alexandria, then Port Said. On one occasion I was told to recce the swept channel to see if there were any mines that had been missed: this was for a convoy setting out from Alexandria to Salonika. About half way through this task my engine gave out and I had to ditch. I instructed my passenger to stand on the front of the floats to keep the back out of the water. Unfortunately we were there for some time and the sea became very rough. Suddenly the aircraft went down tail first and we were thrown into the air. We managed to scramble on to the upturned floats and had to stay in that precarious position all night. It was my twentieth birthday and I thought I was going to die. The next day we spotted the convoy that we were supposed to have escorted after our recce. They had apparently left late and, fortunately, one of their zigzags coincided with our position. We were picked up by the Australian destroyer *Swan*.

As if that was not enough, a few days later I was taking off in a Short in Alexandria harbour when I found the engine responding very sluggishly. While I was trying to get her into the air I could see we were approaching a large breakwater at the entrance to the harbour. I tried to climb over it and went head first into the water. Had I continued, I would have collided with the statue of Ferdinand de Lesseps!

Aircraftsman Bert Adams

Royal Naval Air Service

When the Great War came I was seventeen and an apprentice printer. I volunteered for the Army but failed my medical because of the three months I'd had of rheumatic fever. So I decided to try the Navy and was accepted as a Medical Orderly for work in sickbays. I had the lowest possible medical grading of C3. They said I'd be all right for emptying the buckets or cleaning up. I was sent initially to Crystal Palace and slept on the top floor of that amazing building in a hammock under all the glass. I used to sleep in fear of a Zeppelin raid, especially when the moon was up because we glistened like a beacon.

The Navy seemed to forget about my medical training because I was posted in 1915 to Pulham in Norfolk, near Bungay in Suffolk, which was to become a base for the airships of the RNAS. At the start we had to work as navvies and clear the ground of trees and hedges and mix the concrete for the bases of the hangars. These hangars were to house the non-rigid, hydrogen-filled airships which patrolled the North Sea in search of German submarines. Airships were known by us as 'lighter-than-air ships'. It was the most hazardous way of travelling because the hydrogen was so inflammable.

In those early days at Pulham we had a Sea Scout non-rigid airship and three other small craft called Beta, Gamma and Delta which had previously been operated by the Royal Engineers. We used to sleep in a tent and start the day about 7 am. We'd sometimes have a wash in a five-gallon petrol can which was heated over a coal burner. When the airship was approaching for docking about a hundred of us would run out to wait for its arrival overhead. When it was about 500 feet above us, the airship's crew threw out a landing line. We caught hold of it and started to pull it down. As it got lower there was more rope to get hold of, so more men could pull it down. The rope had wooden toggles so that you could get both hands on it and pull. There would perhaps be fifty men on the starboard side and fifty on port, all pulling down. Well, sometimes the wind would catch the airship and if the pulling was not greater than the lift, then you'd find yourself hanging on going up and up. People would panic and drop off. But of course the more who dropped off the higher it would go, with others hanging on for dear life. In one case one of our men held on too long, drifted off and was killed when he could hang on no longer.

When the airship was down we would attach it to a Burrell Steam Engine which would, with us hanging on to the ropes, be directed into the hangar and guided into position by the shed-master. When it was finally in position the ropes would be tethered to concrete blocks. When deflated the envelope would hang suspended from the roof by wide canvas straps – hence the word hangar. The massive doors of the hangar would be opened and closed by the type of tank used at the battle of Cambrai.

Part of my job was to go up in the airship and act as ballast. There were probably about eight of us up there. We just drifted around the airfield while the crew made adjustments.

It was really a simple life. When it was undocking we walked the airship out and tried to keep it steady. Then Warrant Officer Evason would hold up his handkerchief (no windsocks at Pulham!) to see which way the wind was blowing. We'd then be told 'bow to starboard' or 'bow to port' to head it into the wind! When we got it right the airship became like a caged animal straining to be released. You see, the hydrogen was trying to pull her up and the engines were trying to take her forward, the wind was trying to take her back and we were trying to hang on! The engines would rev up and off it would go, heading towards Yarmouth for its patrol.

If the airship saw a submarine it could drop small hand-held bombs from about 1,000 feet. It could also come down above the submarine where its propellers would cause considerable turbulence around the sub. It also had a primitive wireless on board, so it could also let nearby destroyers know where the sub was. One of the experiments carried out at Pulham in June 1918 was to attach a Sopwith Camel beneath the belly of His Majesty's Airship (HMA) No.23. When it got over a sparsely populated area the Camel's motor was speeded up and the release gear activated and the fighter flew off. In the last week of the war they actually released two Camels which landed back at Pulham, both from 212 Squadron. HMA No.23 was an enormous airship built by Vickers. It was 535 feet long, had swivelling propeller mounts which could be angled downwards to push her upwards, and was constructed of metal covered by two layers of rubber-coated cotton fabric cemented together with a third layer of rubber. It had four Rolls-Royce Eagle engines, a top speed of 52 mph and could reach 3,000 feet. There was a crew of seventeen and it held four 100-lb. bombs.

The hydrogen needed for the airships was either brought in giant cylinders weighing seven hundredweight apiece or it was produced from our silicol gun plant which could produce 10,000 cubic feet an hour. HMA No.23, for example, needed 942,000 cubic feet of hydrogen in its 18 cells. Great care was needed in the manufacture of hydrogen. While I was at Pulham there was a bad explosion and two men who were working in the plant were killed. Even to this day there is not a blade of grass where the gasworks were. Nothing will grow there, nor do you ever see birds.

Sometimes the airship would be disabled and have to alight in a field, often miles from Pulham. But the local residents seemed to have an affection for the 'pigs', as they were called. They'd all down tools and whole villages of sometimes two or three hundred people would hold on to the trail ropes and restrain and guide it back to us. It was quite a sight seeing it floating along being carried over ditches, hedges and trees. People would have torn clothes and bruises, but they enjoyed the task – they had a common purpose, they were doing something for the war effort.

Of course, with airships so vulnerable, there were always going to be accidents. Our first was the loss of C.17 with all five of its crew. It was shot down by a seaplane while on patrol and this occurred in the same week as the gas explosion. The next loss for us meant a lot to me. Three German floatplanes shot down C.27 on 11 December 1917. The crew of five all perished. I knew them all, in particular J.E. Martin and Jack Collett, and it cast a gloom over the whole station. Then C.26 went out to look for it but ran out of fuel and came down over Holland where the crew was interned for the rest of the war. After that they stopped patrols until HMA No.23 came along.

HMA 23 was also used as a guinea pig, or workhorse. At one point a 2-pounder, quick-firing gun was attached and mounted on top of the hull. The airship had almost to stand up before it was fired. Conducting the trials was a young man from Vickers named Barnes Neville Wallis. But unlike his remarkable experiments later, this one proved a failure.

Throughout my time at Pulham we were constantly reading about or hearing of Zeppelin raids. They really were feared by the people on the east coast. In these raids over 500 people were killed. The last raid was in August 1918 when Major Cadbury's DH4, operating from Great Yarmouth, shot it down. When the Armistice came along in November 1918, like everyone else I got very drunk and thought about those who had fought far harder wars in other lands. Never did I think that twenty years later I'd be back in uniform again.

Leading Mechanic Bill Argent

Royal Naval Air Service

I left school at the age of fifteen and got a job in an office, but I couldn't stand it. The war had only just started and you only saw the spectacular side of it, the glory. I saw this glossy advert about the Royal Naval Air Service wanting boys to train in wireless telegraphy so I joined up in November 1915 at South Kensington in London where the RNAS had taken over a factory. I had only been there a day when I wished I hadn't joined. The discipline was really tough, you had to run everywhere. The Petty Officers kept calling it a ship, we even slept in hammocks. At six o'clock it was 'Wakey, Wakey' from the Master-at-Arms.

One of the first things I saw was a beating. A boy had been caught smoking. He was stripped to the waist and spread-eagled over a vaulting horse and really flayed. It didn't make any difference because a few days later I saw him smoking again.

When I moved to Cranwell, then known as HMS *Daedalus*, the discipline was just as harsh and the pay was seven shillings a week. The huts were so cold that, at one point, I had to get a hammer to my boots to get them out of the ice. We had to leave them outside to ensure the floor stayed shiny. We wore a square rig: jackets, patch pockets, open neck, grey flannel shirt and a peak cap with the RNAS insignia on it. Sunday mornings was the great treat because we had bacon and eggs. Traditionally tea was served in a bowl, not a cup, but I was put off tea because one day I saw a mess cook having a bath in one of the big wooden vats in which it was made.

I spent a year training at Cranwell and only had one leave – when I got home I was horrified by the effect rationing was having on the family. Our training was very thorough; it was mostly on wireless, which was still in a very crude state, and the other traditions of morse and flag-signalling. To pass out we had to signal to manoeuvre the Fleet. The other boys played the ships on the parade square. They weren't very happy if they collided because you'd cocked up your signals.

Rather than waste the public's money training a boy to be a pilot or observer only to find he became airsick, they used to take us up first in a balloon to 1,000 feet and then to the more rarefied position at 2,000 feet. Directly anyone was sick they were bundled off the station or found another job.

On my eighteenth birthday in January 1917 I became a 'man' and was posted to the gunnery school at Eastchurch on the Isle of Sheppey. I was waiting for my first flight in a Maurice Farman when I saw the lad in front of me go up and, with his Lewis gun, shoot away one of the struts! To simulate bombing we used to sit up on a gantry about the height of two houses. Below there was a moving artificial pictorial landscape. We would drop a dummy bomb down on the target and, if it hit, a light came on. You didn't actually drop the bomb, you pulled a lever. Very ingenious.

After training I was posted to Calshot, as an observer/wireless operator. We flew H12s and F2A flying boats on anti-submarine patrols. At last I was in the war. My first attack on a U-boat was on 21 June 1917. We dived as quickly as possible but the U-boat submerged rapidly, so we dropped four 100-lb. bombs with two-second delayed fuses which sink some way before they explode. Nothing happened, and no oil appeared on the surface, so we dropped calcium flares to indicate its probable whereabouts, so that ships could drop depth charges.

On the next occasion, 26 June, we caught a U-boat on the surface. The captain obviously panicked because he gave the order to 'down hatch' and abandoned some of the crew on the deck.

A few days before that we had a report of a U-boat operating in our area. When we arrived we saw a tanker had been torpedoed, and there were all these men swimming in flaming oil. That was my first experience of death. I take my hat off to the Merchant Navy; they go through all that, lose mates, get picked up, and then sign on again. At least we had the chance of hitting back, but those poor devils never did.

On other patrols we would fly in support of a convoy. On one occasion we accompanied *SS Olympic* which was acting as a troopship carrying thousands of Americans. The troops seemed grateful to have us along and would wave to us all the time. I suppose we gave a certain security. On 12 May 1918 we escorted fifty ships and the *Olympic* rammed and sank *U-103* off the Lizard. Once we had to force-land and came down at Budleigh Salterton. The Home Guard turned out and managed to drag the aircraft up the beach. A real old Colonel Blimp came over and told us to stay with him. We had a hell of a party most of the night. The next morning when we arrived on the beach the locals had covered the aircraft with flowers. That was a very moving sight. Many of course had never seen an aircraft up close. The fitters came and put the engine right. Then all the locals pulled and pushed the aircraft into the water. The mechanics who wore long waders then piggy-backed us out to the aircraft. I think they were sad to see us go. We came back later that day with presents of chocolates and preserved fruits. Up to then we'd had no idea how much we were appreciated.

I ditched with various pilots eight times. The first time was in a Short 855 piloted by Lieutenant-Commander Waugh when we came down off Portland Bill. We were picked up by a drifter, which towed the machine back. On the second occasion in a Wright seaplane, we were rescued by the armed yacht *Lorna* which towed us to Poole. A month later we had to be picked up by a torpedo boat. But the worst moment was when Lieutenant Jarman had to ditch our Short 1085 twenty miles south of Lyme Regis in very rough weather. The engine simply packed up in mid-flight. I thought we were for it. There was one hell of a sea running as the pilot brought us down, so as we landed the floats were pushed in and the propeller caught them and ripped them off the front. I was sending out wireless messages giving our position and fired off a Very light to attract attention. I then sent off the two pigeons as the aircraft began to disintegrate. We were in the water for four hours which made us realise the wireless messages had not got through. We were depending on one of the pigeons getting back to base. I had scribbled the two messages and placed them inside the small aluminium canister that was attached to the pigeons' leg. One, thank God, got through. She had actually been shot and as the poor thing arrived she collapsed and died. She certainly saved our lives. The Commanding Officer himself flew out and located us. He could see our aircraft was practically submerged by now and we were hanging on grimly. He signalled down to us to inflate our life belts and swim for it. Unfortunately mine had been punctured. As he was flying overhead and we were struggling in the sea we saw a torpedo boat heading our way – I've never been so pleased to see a ship. They took us on board and then tried to tow the aircraft, but it finally sank in Lyme Regis harbour. That incident really shook us both up. If it hadn't been for that pigeon we'd have had a watery grave. That's why I've never touched pigeon pie in my life, and whenever I look at a pigeon now I thank God.

Seven weeks later down we went in the sea again, but it was a much less dramatic rescue this time because they picked up our wireless message. My final ditching was in a Companion seaplane I259 in the summer of 1918, when a destroyer picked us up and treated us royally.

We certainly worked hard, especially when I was posted to Portland. It was patrol after patrol. Flying in the winter was a miserable experience. We were absolutely frozen to the bone – I've never experienced cold like that since. We had lambswool leggings and leather coats, fleece-lined helmets and gloves, but they were never enough.

When we were out on patrol we were given a recognition signal for the day. Many of our submarines were bombed because they didn't answer the recognition signal – which was either a colour flare or two letters to be flashed with the Aldiss Lamp. If the sub didn't flash, I'd drop a bomb on it.

On 25 March 1918 we saw an enemy sub fully blown on the surface. I dropped two 100-lb. bombs from 600 feet – both missed by a hundred feet. I dropped two more, one of which fell directly on the deck but failed to detonate. The sub went straight down. I dropped the usual marker flares. Depth charges were dropped, but no one reported back to us.

Years later I read a book which gave the locations of all U-boats sunk in the Channel and there was one on that very spot. But I'll never know. We did celebrate, yet as Naval men we also realised that probably fifty men had been sent to the bottom. But that is war and those U-boats were destroying our convoys without any warnings.

Lieutenant Leslie Kemp

Royal Naval Air Service

Like many a good lad I obeyed Lord Kitchener's call and joined the Army at the age of sixteen. I served for about eighteen months and then transferred to the Navy, in fact the Royal Naval Air Service, as a midshipman. My first appointment was to the sea plane base at Great Yarmouth where the RNAS had commandeered a big hotel on the sea front. I spent three weeks there before I went to Eastchurch to train as an observer and I carried out all the usual training of map reading, aerial photography, bombing, navigation, cross-country flying and recognition of ships. It was very thorough training. We were flying in some of the first aircraft such as a BE2E, a Bleriot experimental, a DH4, a DH6 and an American aircraft, a Curtiss. I always remember the DH6 didn't have rounded edges on its wings, they were square. Looking back I wish I had trained as a pilot because all you have to do is learn how to fly. It was hard work being an observer!

I then went to Greenwich for officer training. That was a wonderful experience because you learned naval history, customs, as well as ship recognition – not only our warships, but those of other nations too. Hour after hour there was a Petty Officer putting up models that you had to identify and record. On top of this you had map reading and meteorology. It was all lectures, swatting, lectures, swatting, lectures all the time; and we started at 6.00 in the morning doing PT in shorts, summer or winter.

It was wonderful, the experience of Greenwich, a place full of dignity. We dined every night in the hall with the painted ceiling, in full mess kit, wing collar and bow tie. Many would have thought that crazy in war time, but we did it nevertheless because it was the tradition. We had all the famous ornaments out on the tables, including a lovely silver model of Nelson's Column and another of HMS *Victory*. I was just eighteen and, I think, a little overwhelmed.

After Greenwich I was sent on leave to await my first appointment. Eventually I got a telegram to report to the Admiralty. I was told to go to Mudros. Well, I didn't know where Mudros was or what was going on there. In the Army we either went as a battalion or as a party, but in the Navy apparently you went on your own. I went down to Dover, got aboard a ship and asked if it was going to Ostend. No, they weren't. I asked in a number of others and at last I finished up on a sea-going tug. We left Dover at midnight with no navigation lights at all, and it was so cold. It was a terrible crossing which took over eleven hours to reach Cherbourg. I simply sat on deck with my arms around the funnel trying to keep warm. I saw a Railway Transport Officer and asked him if there was a ship going to Taranto. But there wasn't, so I stayed a week outside Bordeaux. I then went by train across France and all the way down to the east coast of Italy. It took ages. There was always a row between the French and Italians as to when they were going to get their carriages back. The Italians used to poke us into sidings, I think for the fun of it. It took me three weeks to get to Taranto! Then, once there, it was the old retort, 'No, we don't know anything about you'. Nobody knew anything. Then I found out that there was an air station close by, so I reported there. The CO said, 'Oh, no, we don't know anything about you, but you better wait here until we find out'. At last they found out that I was due to go to Limnos, one of the Greek islands. Eventually I got there and they did know about me and wondered where I'd been all this time!

We had DH9s, which were light bombers, on the island and shared the aerodrome with the Greek Air Force. I'm sorry to say it, but the Greeks were terrible pilots. They had some of our machines, but they didn't know how to fly them. Instead of coming down to land as we did, they used to come down in steps. On one occasion they 'missed a step' and came down on top of one of our machines! The DH9a, though, was not an easy aircraft to handle. It had an improved cockpit layout to the DH4, and radio equipment, but it had a low operational ceiling which made it vulnerable to attack, and its unreliable engine caused more casualties than enemy action. Its maximum speed was 112 mph. What the Greeks lacked in aeronautical skills, however, they made up with friendship. We celebrated Christmas 1916 with them. They'd filled a great metal container with all the alcohol on the island and set light to the top of it. We were plastered, crawling home on our hands and knees.

We had a hard winter in Greece, where our main target was Turkish shipping, but it was the attack on the battle-cruisers *Goeben* and *Breslau*, in Constantinople on 9 July 1917, which comes back to me most vividly. Each of our DH9s carried about twelve 16-lb. bombs on each wing and 200-lb. ones on the under-carriage. We came in low enough to get an accurate position on both ships. I don't think they opened fire because I didn't see any flashes. In fact I think they went below, closed the hatches and waited until we'd left. I don't know how much damage we did, but they certainly didn't go to sea again.

We continued right up until the armistice to patrol and attack enemy shipping. We chased a number of submarines up the Albanian coast, but even if we hit any we never saw any oil on the surface. When the armistice came I was in Salonika. Everyone went crazy, firing pistols from tram cars, really enjoying the fact that the war was over. I thought we were coming home, but instead we were sent to Russia.

Petty Officer Jimmy Jeffs

Royal Naval Air Service

I went into the Royal Naval Air Service when I was sixteen, just after the first battle of the Somme. I was kitted out at Crystal Palace and then sent straight to Cranwell. We had quite a smart looking uniform in those days, cut a bit different to the average Able Seaman. I didn't want a commission straightaway, so I went into the ranks with the hope of getting somewhere later on. At sixteen it was all such an excitement.

At Cranwell I met all sorts of chaps of my own age. We slept in hammocks in freezing cold huts. Hut number 1, Cranwell. The intake was about 25 to 30 men every four or six months. Six months after my arrival at Cranwell, there was an outbreak of the strongest known form of influenza and we were all sent home. I didn't come back for six months. Before I went home I'd been in training to become a pilot and was taught by Hinchcliffe, the famous naval pilot with one eye, in a BE2 (Bleriot Experimental 2).

At Cranwell at the same time was Prince Albert (later King George VI). He had been serving in the *Collingwood* at Jutland and, although he suffered from a stammer, he was a very fine fellow, a gentleman. He was five years older than me, and at the time what we called Jimmy the One – that is the First Lieutenant – and Jimmy the One is the chap who really runs the ship. You were taught from day one that you were not on a station, you were on a ship. There were several departments at Cranwell, teaching engineers, welding, every trade you care to mention. But we were flyers and Prince Albert ran our little ship of flyers, although he wasn't a flyer himself. Three of us decided that we wanted to understand how difficult it was for someone who stammered. We got hold of some ordinary steel knitting needles and put them in our mouths. The knack was to get the three together, so that you found yourself almost talking like Prince Albert. I think he appreciated that. I know he made a commendation on our passing-out papers. I remember meeting the very attractive Miss Elizabeth Bowes-Lyon who asked me where Prince Albert lived as they were playing tennis together that day.

Cranwell gave you a hell of a training. Wherever you went afterwards, you were Cranwell trained and felt you were the cream of the ship. But punishment was hard. I was once punished for smoking under the age of eighteen. I got what they call 10 days 10A, punishment confined to the ship. I did see people get the tawse now and then. If there was any punishing to be done it was with the whole section present at the boxing ring. If it was a serious crime, then you would be bent over a table and you'd get so many cuts across the backside.

When I started learning to fly they had put me straight into a BE2 as the pilot behind the real pilot. My first flight was in mid-summer 1917. I'd always wanted to fly. At the age of eleven I saw Graham White at an airshow and got a kick up the behind by a policeman for getting too close – White was a bit of a God to us. And the smell of castor oil! Once you got it on your nostrils it was intoxicating, like so many smells of war they remain in your memory bank.

When I returned to Cranwell after the 'flu epidemic I was told the RNAS wanted navigators, so I had to give up my ambition to be a pilot and begin a new training.

After I finished at Cranwell I went to Eastchurch (on the Isle of Sheppey) and from there I was posted to the Royal Naval seaplane base at Westgate-on-sea, near Margate. On my birthday, 27 January 1918, we had a bad landing in a Shorts 184 seaplane north of Westgate near the lightship. The aircraft broke up but we stayed with it. We were picked up by the destroyer *Fervent* and taken to Margate pier suffering from hypothermia. From there we were taken to Kingsgate Castle where we were were covered with Colman's mustard, in fact positively plastered with it. Then we were put into a hot bath, and after about two hours of that went straight into a hammock wrapped in blankets. After eighteen hours we were feeling much better. A colleague said we ought to go to church, firstly to thank God for saving us and second because it was the warmest place in the borough. We arrived in the middle of a funeral! As we tried to back out the verger beckoned us up near to the front. We felt very uncomfortable because we'd only come to keep warm and thank God. There couldn't have been more than a dozen mourners but there was one girl in front. I could only see the back of her until she passed the hymn books. As the mourners were leaving she dropped her handkerchief. I picked it up, and three years later we were married and lived happily together for seventy-two years.

Most of our flying at 19 Naval Squadron was over the North Sea looking for submarines and mines, floating mines. We didn't have a lot of success, but sometimes we'd see a porpoise leading a school with his tail up, and think it was a submarine. We'd attack, and within a matter of moments the sea was all red. We recorded one or two successes, however, against Gotha bombers who made regular and heavy attacks on London and the east coast.

The Germans were much superior to us in seaplanes because they had the Brandenburg which surpassed us for speed, climbing, everything. Our job was to protect the mouth of the Thames and up as far as the south-east channel, to the eastward of Lowestoft, an area which also included Westgate, Felixstowe, Yarmouth and

Dover. We flew Shorts 184s, made by Short Brothers of Rochester, and later the American F2A flying-boats. We had lofts at Westgate full of pigeons. On each flight I had to take two pigeons in separate compartments (to stop them fighting) of a wicker basket. This was strapped inside my cockpit. They used to sit there cooing away. On one occasion we came down with engine failure in the North Sea. I immediately despatched both birds with a message and rough grid reference attached to a leg. Well, the first bird found a mate and set up house on the Kentish Knock Life vessel, but the other, although he'd had his eye shot out, got back to Westgate. A seaplane came out to find two very relieved flyers. If nothing happened on a patrol, as we turned for home we would release the pigeons who invariably got home before us, which showed how fast the seaplane flew!

Because of the speed of the German seaplanes and fighters we often got attacked. To them we must have seemed like a beached whale. Although we had two Lewis guns which we could swing round, we'd often come back peppered. The best thing to do was to get down as quick as we could because the plane was only made of cotton fabric which would simply tear away. So in that respect the Short was a safe aircraft, with a big wingspan but it suffered from having a Sunbeam Maori engine which sometimes gave the impression of seizing up. We'd panic and get it down on the water at Westgate as fast as possible only to be inspected by the mechanic who would find no fault at all!

My most frightening experience was running out of gas and coming down on the edge of a known minefield. We let off the pigeons and prepared to wait but the sea had quite a roll on it so we were both as sick as hell. Then the next minute the turret of a submarine appeared. I can see it now, *H 16*. We shouted to the skipper that we wanted a tow. He said he wanted the 'colour' of the day (the identifying code) which, needless to say, we couldn't remember. This was greeted with some pretty foul language from the skipper who dispatched a kayak, took us off the aircraft and then, amidst much protest that it was brand new, set fire to the aircraft. God only knows who he thought we were.

On an earlier occasion I was woken out of my hammock to be told I was to be part of the crew of the airship *R27*, a 'lighter-than-air' machine. It was a strange experience being in the air and not in a cockpit. It was large enough for us to walk around in the compartment under the airship. I also saw them lower an observer in a basket in which there was a telephone link to the airship. We'd stay, wherever possible, in the clouds while he was lowered beneath the clouds to spot the enemy. It felt very eerie, and the skipper of the *R27* said to me, 'We are waiting for death!' After three long trips I was glad to be back on the squadron.

On 1 April 1918 the RNAS merged with the RFC and became the RAF. Most aircrew retained their own uniform, the RFC their khaki and we the Navy blue with leather boots. One chap wore a pale blue uniform, but he soon discarded that because we used to pull his leg and tell him he looked like the commissionaire from the local fleapit cinema.

On Armistice Day we decided to paint the town red, in particular to plaster the house of the most famous RNAS pilot, Wing Commander Charles Samson, who was commanding at Felixstowe. His house was white so we took all the brown lavatory paper we could find and decorated the outside. Civilian paper was 4″ × 4″ but Navy was 5″ × 4″ to allow for the roll of the ship. Not shiny, just rough and the cheapest brown. Samson, alas, didn't see the joke and in the forenoon of Armistice Day we were placed under arrest. But our skipper had a word with him and his humour returned.

And that was the end of my war.

Jimmy Jeffs later became the first Air Traffic Controller at Heathrow.

Private Alfred Hutchinson

Royal Marine Light Infantry

I was a printer's assistant when the war broke out. I had a friend who lived about four doors away from me and we both decided to join up. We went along to the Recruiting Office where I was told at 17 that I was too old for boy service in the Navy, but I could join the Marines. I asked if I would be with my friend and they told me I would. I didn't see him again for three years!

I went first to Deal in November 1914 and joined the Royal Marines Light Infantry and then went on to Chatham for small arms training. After this I joined *Lowestoft*. On my first voyage we delivered gold to Halifax in Nova Scotia. All I can remember is lying on deck being sick for the whole seven day trip. After that we did patrols of the North Sea. On 19 August 1916 we were part of the screen for the Grand Fleet as it went south to intercept the High Seas Fleet. This was their main sortie after Jutland. It had intended to bomb Sunderland. I don't think there was ever a real risk that we'd engage them, but we lost the light cruiser *Nottingham* and the *Yarmouth* which were sunk by U-boats. Overhead, Zeppelins were scouting which were quite a sight. I was the sight setter on the gun but we didn't hit anything. The main danger was from planes – that was really frightening. The German fleet never really came out again, but their U-boats continued to be a success, especially against Merchant Ships. They really were a menace because from January to the end of April 1917 they sank 380 merchantmen and we were getting anxious about supplies, especially to the troops in France. It was around that time that the convoys were brought in to accompany these ships. We also had air support from aircraft and balloons and that turned the tide.

We then moved to the Mediterranean, mostly around Mudros and Malta. I was working then as a decoder. It was all very quiet – it was as if we were out of the war. Towards the end of 1917, having been paid off *Lowestoft* at Alexandria, we returned to England.

In the early part of 1918 I returned to Deal to undergo training for a secret raid. We didn't learn what it was until we set sail. The aim of the raid was to block the Bruges Canal by sinking a number of ships at the point where it entered the harbour and at the same time to destroy the port installation at Zeebrugge. There was also to be a raid on the canal at Ostend. It was known that U-boats were coming out of the canals and were still menacing our shipping. If we could block their exit, we'd save some ships. The main problem at Zeebrugge was the Mole. It was made of stone and well guarded. It was impossible to sail our blockships through Zeebrugge harbour and into the canal entrance unless the guns on the Mole were put out of action or diverted. That was to be our task.

Most of our training was done at night. We had a mock-up of the Mole and we trained each day with bayonet practise, and strangleholds. We even did it in gas masks with smoke screens and starshells going off everywhere. When we weren't training at night we were doing twelve mile route marches. We were also told, because of tidal conditions, we would only be there for about two and a half hours. A lot of us couldn't understand why they were sending about 1,000 Marines when we had all those troops already in France.

On 2 April we had a full rehearsal at 9 pm. Fireworks, starshells, the lot. Three days later the 4th Battalion got its marching orders, gas masks, barbed-wire pliers, sixty rounds, waterproof sheet, muffler and gloves and overcoats. The three companies from Chatham, Portsmouth and Plymouth all fell in and the band ahead of us played 'Auld Lang Syne' and other sing-songs like 'Britons Never shall Be slaves' and 'Good Bye Dolly Grey'. We embarked on the *Iris II* at Dover. The *Iris* along with the *Daffodil* were to accompany the *Vindictive* and storm the Mole. The *Iris* and the *Daffodil* were ferry steamers that used to ply their trade on the River Mersey. They both had a very shallow draught which would enable us to ride over and clear any mines. The people of Liverpool were not best pleased to lose them, but when they heard later what we'd done they were really proud of their two ships.

On 10 April we were alerted for the attack but the winds became unfavourable for the smoke attack so we turned back. Morale was a bit low. We were told the next morning we were to attack at 2 am. Time hung heavily. We fell in on deck at 1 am, and could see the searchlights on the Mole and starshells going up. We were going in. Then they called it off! We then stayed on board for 12 days playing cards, arranging concert parties, generally filling in time. Gambling is a very serious offence in the Navy, but a blind eye was turned and we played a lot of Crown and Anchor.

It was a beautiful morning, 22 April, but reality hit us when the No. 1 ordered us to cover the top deck with sand to soak up the blood! Later that afternoon we watched the sunset, everyone was very quiet. I think we were wondering if we would see it rise in the morning. We were to be alongside the Mole at midnight. The old and ugly *Vindictive* was ahead. It looked like a giant beetle with fourteen legs. The legs were the landing brows to be used in the Mole. Behind us was *Daffodil* and the three blockships, *Thetis*, *Intrepid* and *Iphigenia*. At 11 o'clock we had a tot of rum which for many was to be their last. Close to midnight we were about 300 yards from the Mole and all was going well, when the wind turned completely around from the shore this time and there we were lit up like daylight caused by the starshells. It was very frightening. The German battery opened up and hit the *Vindictive* smashing her bridge. The flashes seemed to be coming from the wrong place. This was because the Germans had cunningly shifted their guns from the Mole to the pier. The *Vindictive* had during exercises practised how fast she could stop right under the guns on the Mole. She still had to get to where she had planned to come alongside and to do this she had to pass the guns on the pier. The German guns had really damaged *Vindictive* so that she only had two brows serviceable. It was bad. The *Daffodil* and *Iris* came in close to the Mole clearing our way with machine guns. The starboard anchor was dropped and we went astern on it to get in close. The hook we used on the derrick wouldn't hold and the Germans were opening fire on us with machine guns. It was hopeless. Lieutenant-Commander Bradford realised how bad our position was and climbed up the derrick. But he was cut down. Then the second-in-command tried and he was also killed. We had to abandon our position or we'd all have been killed. It was decided we could come alongside *Vindictive* and land over her deck. As we ran alongside her there was all this noise and smoke. The *Vindictive* being the biggest ship was really taking it, but it was fighting back.

Then all of a sudden a starshell burst overhead and made the night day. We were immediately ordered below. The German 5.9s opened up and we were hit fourteen times and twice from their eleven inch. One of the shells hit the bridge and killed the Captain and the Major of Marines and a lot more. Then another came through the upper deck and burst on the main deck where 56 Marines were waiting to go up the gangplank. Forty-nine were killed. There was just one big heap of arms and legs. My friend, he had his head blown off. He'd only got married on the weekend before we left. We heard that blockship had entered the harbour and so we were told to get the hell out of the place because the main objective had been achieved. We waited about a quarter of an hour for those who had got ashore to return. What did surprise me, when we were hit on the way out, was the sight of NCOs diving over the side. No one had given the order to abandon ship and never did. That shocked me. I couldn't believe my eyes to see them going over the side and swimming away.

There was nothing else we could do but scram. We put out all our lights and began to tend the wounded and the dead. Eventually destroyers arrived and escorted us back to Dover. Seeing the White Cliffs on that misty morning, and to be alive was quite something. As we came in and with only a young Lieutenant on the damaged bridge, steering by hand compass, the ships in harbour sounded their horns. We were greeted at Dover by Sir Roger Keyes.

We paid our last respects to our comrades. Then we had the grimmest of parades, 'The Roll Call'.

From Deal we went to Chatham. As we marched into the town we were surprised to be greeted by crowds of people lining the streets and cheering. We didn't know why, until we saw the newspaper reports. My feelings were that I was lucky to be alive and in one piece, and sorrow for the friends I had lost.

Sergeant Harry Wright

Royal Marine Light Infantry

After six weeks hard training at Deal, the 4th Battalion Royal Marines received orders to proceed to a certain destination. During this time we had been inspected by King George V, the First Lord of the Admiralty and the Adjutant-General of the RM Corps. The latter informed us that what we were going to do would live in history and he hoped that each man would do his duty and uphold the honour of the Royal Marines. Any man who did not want to go had the privilege of falling out, but no one moved.

At 6am on 6 April 1918 the battalion fell in and was inspected by our colonel, and with the band leading, we marched off through the town to the station. The people of Deal turned out to give us a good send-off. We were all singing, laughing or joking, and as we passed our old bayonet instructor, who had given us a stiff training, we gave him a rousing cheer. There was a special train in the station and the whole battalion of some 850 officers and men were entrained in less than ten minutes. When we arrived at Dover station there was a steamer waiting which convinced us that we were going to France. However our first port was Sheerness. When we arrived there we were rather surprised to read a signal from one of the ships which said that 'A' and 'B' Companies will proceed to HMS *Hindustan* and 'C' Company to HMS *Vindictive*. On getting alongside *Vindictive* we were surprised to see how she was fitted up. There was a special deck built on the port side with ramps leading from the lower deck on the starboard side up to the special deck. On the port side there were fourteen huge gangways pointing out to sea and triced up with pulleys ready for dropping. She carried two 11-inch howitzers, one forward, one aft, numerous Stokes guns and a pom-pom in the crow's nest halfway up the mast, the majority of her armament being on the port side. Sandbag revetments were built around the forebridge and other vital parts. In addition there were two very powerful flame-throwers and machine-guns. The ship was a floating arsenal for there were shells already fused everywhere. Apart from her proper complement for sea and with 'C' Company comprising some 270 men, we were rather overcrowded; but we were all men used to roughing it in all parts of the world.

Next day Captain Carpenter had everybody aft on the quarter-deck and told us for the first time what we were going to do. 'We are going,' he said, 'on a very dangerous errand, and any hitch in the operation might mean a naval disaster, so it is everyone's duty to do his best. The *Vindictive* is going through the enemy's minefields and alongside the mole at Zeebrugge. On getting there the 4th Battalion will storm the mole and engage the enemy while at the same time, three blockships filled with concrete will go round the other side of the mole and sink themselves in the mouth of the canal. A bridge connects the mole with Zeebrugge and during the operation a submarine with ten tons of high explosive will be set under the bridge and so cut off reinforcements from Zeebrugge. While this is going on two other ships will proceed to Ostend and sink themselves in the mouth of the canal there, and by this means close up the hornet's nest of submarines so that none can come out and those that are out cannot go back to refit. It may so happen,' he continued, 'that some of you may have the misfortune to be captured; if so, bear in mind you must not give any information to the enemy, especially about our fleet, but on the other hand there is certain information we would like you to pass on. In the first place, tell them that we are capturing their submarines, taking them to England, putting English crews on board and sending them to sea again as decoys. Secondly, tell them that on every merchant ship there is fitted an instrument which can detect a submarine at a two-mile radius. This information must be tactfully passed on, but let the enemy bring the subject up first.' Captain Carpenter finished by saying, 'The success of this whole operation depends on two things, namely secrecy, and the wind, which must be blowing towards the enemy so that destroyers can use their smoke screens effectually.'

We were then shown a clay model of the mole and given its dimensions, which were 1,800 yards long and 80 yards wide. It was built in peacetime to enable ships to land their passengers as the water was too shallow inshore. The passengers could be landed either side according to the tide. There was a railway running the whole length of the mole to take passengers to Zeebrugge. On the sea end of the mole was a lighthouse. Since it had been taken over by the Germans the mole had been fortified, being one mass of concrete shelters. In the centre was a huge seaplane shed with six powerful machine-guns. On the sea end of the mole and about fifty yards from the lighthouse was a strong concrete shelter with four 5-inch guns, and machine-guns were hidden in various places along the mole. *Vindictive* would go alongside the mole on the northern side. Grappling irons would then be lowered on to the concrete wall, and on a given signal, the first Company would land.

We had previously drawn lots to see who should land first and 'C' Company, all Plymouth marines, won that honour. Each company had four platoons, Plymouth Company being numbered 9, 10, 11 and 12. Some sailors, as a demolition party, would accompany the leading company. On the advance being sounded no. 9 and my platoon would land first, turn to the right on getting ashore and capture the first objective, a strongpoint 200 yards along the mole. Almost immediately afterwards no. 11 and no. 12 platoons and seamen would land, turn to the left and advance towards the four guns and capture them. At the same time, if the enemy extinguished the lighthouse, they would burn a flare so that the blockships could get their bearings; the operation was to be carried out at midnight. On reaching their positions the platoon sergeants of the leading platoons would fire red flares into the air as a signal for the other company to come onshore. They would land, come through our line, carrying objectives to a depth of 800 yards and then, on firing their red flares, nos. 1, 2, 3 and 4 platoons of the Chatham marines would come through the others already in position on the mole and carry objectives to a depth of one mile.

Each platoon was armed with a Lewis gun and a flame-thrower. There was also a special platoon of machine-gunners and a special signal platoon with telephones, etc. There were also demolition parties for blowing up the concrete shelters and sheds. Each man carried Mills grenades and every NCO had a stunning mallet for close fighting. The officers carried revolvers and walking out canes weighted with lead on the handle end. Each platoon had two ladders and four ropes for, on landing, there was a drop of twenty feet, hence the use of ladders and ropes. The demolition parties, chiefly sailors, carried ammanol gun-cotton, safety and instantaneous fuses and detonators. The Howitzer and pom-pom guns were manned by the Royal Marine Artillery and the Stokes guns and machine-guns, manned by marine infantry, would keep up a covering fire while we were ashore. Each platoon had a specially trained bombing section to deal with dugouts etc. Each man wore a rubber swimming belt in case he fell into the sea. The signal to retire would be a succession of short blasts on *Vindictive's* siren.

The monitors out at sea would assist us by trying to silence the batteries at Zeebrugge. The enemy, thinking this an attempt to take Zeebrugge, would concentrate their fire on to the mole and so give the blockships a chance to get in. Aeroplane photographs were handed round to the officers and NCOs and some of us drew a sketch from the photograph marking off positions. By the time we had seen the model and drawn the sketch, the officers and NCOs at least could have walked from one end of the mole to the other blindfolded and every man knew exactly what to do and where to go.

All day Sunday we were busy detonating grenades and unloading tugs which came alongside with extra sandbags and shells. The men stripped to the waist and worked with a will, finishing late that night with everyone dead tired. We had a good supper and turned into our hammocks for the night.

On Monday 8 April during the forenoon, it was reported by wireless from the Belgian coast that the wind was favourable and it was decided to do the 'stunt' at midnight. The two companies of marines left the *Hindustan*, some coming on board *Vindictive* and others going aboard *Iris* and *Daffodil*, two smaller ships. The destroyer *Warwick* with Vice Admiral Sir Roger Keyes aboard came out from Dover and gave orders for our little fleet to proceed to Zeebrugge. At 11am we got under way towing the *Iris* and *Daffodil*. Our fleet consisted of *Vindictive*, *Warwick* and five obsolete cruisers, *Intrepid*, *Brilliant*, *Iphigenia*, *Thetis* and *Sirius* filled with concrete. In addition there were a number of motorboats and the submarine filled with high explosives. We also had an escort of destroyers and overhead were a few aeroplanes.

It was a beautiful day and everyone was in the best of spirits. As we left harbour, the *Hindustan* and other ships gave us a rousing cheer. We reached our destination late that night and lay just off Zeebrugge. The monitors and aeroplanes were already engaging the enemy. It was a very dark night and we could see the flashes of the guns onshore as they replied, and as we watched and listened the bombardment got more intense, until it seemed to us that nothing could land there and live. They certainly knew we were coming. A few quick flashes on the morse lamps, just a single letter code, and our little fleet turned back without being seen by the enemy. The men were very disappointed but we could not hope to effect a surprise if the enemy were prepared for us.

We arrived back at Sheerness during the forenoon and the *Hindustan* detachments were sent over to her. Admiral Keyes came onboard *Vindictive* and we all fell in on the quarterdeck. He mounted a bollard and explained that at the last moment the wind had changed, but told us to have patience because we would go again. We gave him a rousing cheer as he left the ship.

On Sunday 21 April the parson gave us a very interesting sermon on what became of us when we died. Little did we think then that within a few hours so many brave lads would have laid down their lives. The next day we were drilling on the quarterdeck when the signal came to prepare for the stunt. We went below, labelled our kitbags and other things we did not want, and handed them over to the ship's steward. A tug was already alongside to take us to the *Vindictive* and Colonel Elliot watched us as we clambered over the side. If anyone was downhearted and looked at our colonel, they would at once feel happy and confident. There he stood, wearing his DSO and a smile on his face. The men loved him for he had a kind word for everyone.

We crowded on board *Vindictive* and at 3pm we once again left for Zeebrugge with the *Iris* and *Daffodil*. Something seemed to tell us that we were going in that night. At midnight it would be St George's Day, and when at sea, the admiral made the signal which will always be remembered, 'St George For England', to which the captain replied, 'May we give the dragon's tail a damned good twist'. It was a beautiful day and one could see miles out to sea, which was as calm as a mill pond. The wind again seemed likely to change but we kept steadily on course. We rendezvoused halfway, where the fleet divided with three ships going to Ostend. The daily ration of rum was issued to the men about 8pm. Right up to the last the men were in good humour, laughing, joking and playing cards, just as if they were on leave. Some were boasting of what Jerry would get when they got on the mole.

The order was then passed; everyone fell in on the upper deck fully rigged. In our Sergeants' Mess we hastily shook hands and went out to get our men made up, and then on to the upper deck in the darkness and quiet. Rifles were loaded and bayonets fixed. There was a bit of a sea running as the ship made its way slowly through the water. The destroyers went ahead and put up a dense smoke screen. There were no lights showing and everyone talked in whispers. Our nerves were taut. Would we get alongside the mole without the enemy knowing? There we stood, rifles in our hands ready for the dash forward; not a movement, hardly a whisper and only the noise of the propellers broke the silence. Would we never get there? A starshell floated just above the ship, lighting it up as though it were day. I could see the men's white, drawn faces ready for the spring forward. No sooner had that light gone down than another went up. 'They've seen us,' someone whispered, for the lights had been fired from the mole.

We were crowded together, shoulder to shoulder as thick as bees, when the silence was broken by a terrific bang followed by a crash as the fragments of shell fire fell amongst us, killing and maiming many as they stood to their arms. The mole was in sight – we could see it off our port quarter, but too late. Our gunners replied to their fire, but they could not silence that terrible battery of 5-inch guns, now firing into the ship at a range of only 100 yards and from behind concrete walls. A very powerful searchlight was turned on us from Zeebrugge and their batteries also opened fired upon us. The slaughter was terrible, Colonel Elliot and Major Cordner were killed by the same shell whilst on the bridge waiting to give the order 'advance'. The shells came on board thick and fast but our brave fellows stuck to their post. Men were hopping about on one leg, shouting in their frenzy. Some of the bodies were intermingled with the decks, and our ranks got thinner every moment. They were taking every bit of cover they could.

Captain Carpenter stood on the forebridge calmly and steadily giving orders to the engine room staff as if he was taking it alongside the mole in peacetime. The gun crews of the *Vindictive* fired away. The pom-pom in the crow's nest had three crews wiped out but luckily Sergeant Finch, in charge, was only wounded and remained at his post and kept going all the time. (Sergeant Finch got the VC and richly deserved it.) At last we came alongside and by this time we were only thirty yards from the muzzles of the German guns. The grappling irons were dropped and officers tried to get ashore to make them fast, but as each one attempted it he was killed by machine-gun fire. The *Iris* now came up on our starboard side and rammed *Vindictive* to the mole, and the gangways, only two left out of the fourteen, were lowered on to the mole.

No sooner had this been done than the order to 'Advance' was given by Major Weller who had assumed command, so the remnants of nos. 9 and 10 Platoons led the way up the ramp. The Officer in Charge of my platoons, Lieutenant Stanton, had been fatally wounded, so I, as Platoon Sergeant, led 10 Platoon on shore. Up the ramp we dashed carrying our ladders and ropes. We passed over dead bodies lying everywhere and over big gaps made in the ship's decks by shellfire, finally crossing the remaining two gangways which were only just hanging together, and then jumping on to the concrete wall, only to find it swept with machine-gun fire. Our casualties were so great that out of a platoon of 45 only 12 of us landed, and 9 Platoon had about the same. We quickly lowered our ladders and dropped on to the lower part of the mole and two men at once got down the twenty-foot drop and rushed across to the shed on the far side. Everyone was anxious to get down as the machine-guns were mowing our lads down. As some of us were getting down the ladders and ropes a few Germans rushed across the mole with bombs, but we made sure not one of them got halfway across.

We rallied the men, now reduced to no more than 14 in the two platoons, and charged our position. We dashed forward, our rifles in a terrible grip, a fearful hatred on our faces, and ready to plunge our bayonets into the first living creature that opposed us and so revenge our comrades lying dead on the *Vindictive*. But on reaching our position we found the enemy had retreated to their concrete shelters further up the mole. Disgusted, we now turned our attention to the concrete dugouts on our right and left and gave them a good bombing. We also bombed a German destroyer lying alongside the mole. Sergeant Bailey and myself now fired our red Very lights to let the others know we had reached our position, but the *Iris*, after pushing *Vindictive* in, went alongside the mole to land her marines. There were 56 on board but the batteries ashore got a direct hit amongst them and 49 were killed and the others wounded. The casualties were so great amongst nos. 11 and 12 platoons, and with nearly all the sailors being killed, there were only a few to deal with the German guns, but what there were dashed for the guns only to be killed, Commander Brock amongst them. What few were left on the *Vindictive* came through our lines. These brave fellows, headed by their officers, came on walking in extended line as if they were on parade, but only a few of them reached their positions.

The Germans, in their excitement, had forgotten to extinguish the lighthouse so the blockships, taking a bearing from the light, went round the other side of the mole, sank the German dredger on their way in, passed under the muzzles of the batteries ashore and sank themselves obliquely in the entrance of the canal; the crews, what were left, got away in their boats. The submarine C3 went under the bridge and blew herself up. The explosion was so great that the whole concrete mole shook from end to end. A shell struck *Vindictive*'s siren so that she could not make the 'retire' signal, but another ship was ordered to make it. The signal was made to retire after the *Vindictive* had been alongside for one hour, but instead of making a succession of short blasts, she made a succession of long and short blasts. We took it, however, as the order to retire and commenced doing so when, as order was passed that it was not the signal to retire, we were ordered back to our position. We obeyed the order and very shortly afterwards we had the nightmare of seeing our only means of escape slowly move away. The *Vindictive* had left, the officers thinking everyone was aboard. We were two hundred yards from the ship when she left and we still had the twenty foot wall to climb.

We were now stranded, left to the tender mercy of the Germans, our only hope now gone. How hard, it seemed to us, to think we had come through the terrible slaughter, to be alive and well and with no means of escape. Shells were now falling fast on the mole. How long would it be before death relieved us of this terrible agony of suspense? We thought motorboats would be sent in to our assistance and with this faint hope we crossed the mole and climbed the twenty-foot wall, took off our equipment, blew up our swimming belts and waited, lying stiff and pretending to be dead. Some of us looked over the wall occasionally but not a vestige of anything was in sight. To remind us that we must not look over the wall, a machine-gun only thirty yards away was turned on us, but lying close to the concrete wall, it was not so effective as it might have been. For two hours we lay there and listened, with starshells floating over us, some falling and burning us. Two men were badly wounded but lay still for the sake of the others.

Shells from our own ships were now striking the mole and we could hear them whistling overhead. The firing now eased down and a German officer and two privates came to us, shone a torch on us, and thinking we were a heap of dead, went away. It would have been useless to have killed them so we lay still. About half an hour after this the firing ceased and the Germans came out no doubt to search the dead, when one man moved and then another. Nerves being highly strung, they jumped back shouting and gesticulating, and made ready with their bayonets. We had not relinquished our rifles and got ready to fight to a finish and if need be, to die fighting. A German officer shouted in quite good English

'The game's up, lads,' and seeing that we still hesitated he continued, 'Play the game and we will play the game with you. Lay down your arms and put your hands up and we will not harm you.'

We obeyed this order and were made prisoners-of-war.

Lieutenant Leslie Kemp

Royal Naval Air Service

En route to Russia, we packed two DH9s on the metal deck of an old cargo ship, *John Sanderson,* and were about to leave when a large consignment of BP diesel arrived. It was too late to be put in the holds so it was left on deck. We were the first ship through the Dardanelles after the war. As there were mines everywhere the captain issued us .303 rifles and as many rounds as we wanted to fire at mines. Not an easy task in a rough sea, but we managed to hit the nipple of three, so the skipper got some sort of bonus. For us it passed the time. Once we were through the Dardanelles the ship hit heavy weather and the seas were monstrous. We were rolling and pitching and twisting and everything was coming up to meet us. I was really ill. With all the rolling some barrels of oil split and smothered the metal deck with oil. You simply couldn't stand up. At one point the oil got under the wooden support of a pilot boat we had on board and it slid right across the deck and took a lump of the ship with it. My skipper, who was ill too, told me to take charge of the troops. They came to me and asked if I would give them permission to sleep in one of the two lorries we had on deck because it was too bad to sleep below. That night, to my horror, I saw one of the lorries slide across the deck and crash into the icy seas and disappear. Thank God it was the one which contained our luggage.

When we arrived at our harbour in the Black Sea we were ordered to anchor outside. That night was the worst of my life. We lost our anchor and we were drifting about, it was an awful night, a terrible night. Eventually we tied up in the harbour and somebody put a hawser round one of the supports of the railway bridge. In the morning when we woke we were rolling about in the harbour and the railway bridge was down! We were put up in a hotel and, just when we thought all was well, we were summoned in front of our Wing Commander, a strict disciplinarian who threatened to court-martial us all for destroying the railway link. He was also particularly fierce with one chap because he didn't have a coat on! It was not a great introduction to Russia.

We were based in Petrovsk at the edge of the Caspian Sea and billeted in a school. We had no hangar for our aircraft, so we got Russian labour to build a wooden screen and we wheeled the aircraft around it according to the weather. The snow was terrible. When we went on patrol we had to scrape about an inch of snow and ice off the wings. For protection against the cold we wore a Silcott suit and gloves, which were useless when you came to fire your gun. We were up against the Bolsheviks and supporting a White Russian naval flotilla on the Caspian. We also flew 250 miles over enemy territory to drop two 240lb. bombs on the Bolsheviks in their stronghold in Astrakhan.

We saw a lot of the Cossacks who would strut about the place. They came on to the aerodrome and gave us a wonderful display of bareback riding. They seemed to be able to do anything on a horse, including going underneath the horses's stomach while firing a rifle, and pig-sticking with a sword. On one occasion we were invited to the local Russian Air Force mess. On the table there was a sturgeon, a beautiful fish, we had never tasted anything like it before, and of course the only drink was vodka which had to be drunk in one gulp. As the evening went on I danced with the Russian women, and was enjoying myself with one in particular until I saw a revolver drop out of her skirt! Next day it was back to being fired at as we flew over their villages! But of course some of the peasants had never seen a plane before.

I was never really sure why we were in Russia. To us

the real war was over. Eventually public feeling back home was becoming firmly set against further foreign involvement, so in August 1919 we were sent home on the SS *Trent*. We were glad to leave because by then the Russians were sticking cotton wool down our exhaust pipes and trying to steal petrol.

When I got to Dover I was demobbed. It was all over. Until the next time.

Ordinary Seaman Tom Spurgeon

When the Russian Army withdrew from the war in 1917 the Western Allies thought that the Germans would walk through Russia. We had much to lose, so the Navy was sent to Murmansk and Archangel. By now I was in the *Cochrane* which had been at Jutland. We sailed out and reached Murmansk in March 1918 and landed a party of Marines.

While I was there I met a Russian officer who could speak better English than I could. I suppose he was about thirty and he had been a solicitor in Moscow before the Revolution. One day he asked me if I could get ashore the following morning. I managed this and met him. We walked together, talking away as we always did about the Western way of life. Without noticing too much we strolled into a park where there were a number of soldiers and dissidents, including women and children. When the soldiers saw us approach the civilians were all lined up. Then, as calm as anything, this officer I had been talking to walked down the line and shot every one of them through the back. He then went back down the line and if any were breathing he shot them through the head. To him it was like having breakfast. There were women and small children but it didn't seem to worry him at all. I remember clearly some of the bodies quivering on the ground. I can never forget it. I am haunted by it even now.

Able Seaman Fred Pedelty

From *Engadine*, I volunteered for submarines. I did six months training at Haslar before joining *K22* in Rosyth. Lieutenant-Commander de Burgh was the captain, there were four other officers and 54 ratings. She was over 300 feet long, driven by steam turbine, and carried sixteen torpedoes.

In contrast to the *Engadine* everything was steel. It was a ship within a ship. I don't think we ever stayed below for more than two hours when we would surface to recharge our batteries. I slept in a hammock, but some of the others slept on the deck. There really wasn't very much for me to do, so I played a lot of cards.

K22 had previously been *K13* which had failed to surface while undergoing trials in the Clyde in January 1917. She had been down 57 hours before any of the crew were released. Over thirty died on her. She had been brought up and refitted. On the day of his diving trials Lieutenant-Commander de Burgh dived *K22* in exactly the same spot where *K13* had gone down, and the crowd watching held its breath as the periscope disappeared under the surface. Ten minutes later she surfaced and the trial was over. Two weeks later her four-hour acceptance trial also went without a hitch. I can't say all that affected us, but we were aware of her history.

On Armistice Day we were out on patrol in the Skaggerak area. I was on the conning tower when I thought I saw a mine right ahead. I informed the captain who said, 'That's not a mine, it's a fisherman's pallet'. 'Well,' I said. 'It's got horns on.' He looked at me and gave a wry smile. For us the war was over.

The old 'K' boat was a prison, but it wasn't a bad prison. It had its own smells, its own camaraderie.

Lieutenant Brian de Courcy-Ireland

In July 1914, just before the outbreak of war, I saw the Royal Review of the Grand Fleet at Spithead. Now, ten days after the armistice and the end of the war, I was to witness, on 21 November 1918, the surrender of the German High Seas Fleet at sea.

We in HMS *Westcott* went out to meet them halfway, fully manned and ready. We were rather uncertain about what was going to happen, though we understood they had removed their ammunition. Out of the mist on that sunny day it really was quite a sight to see them coming towards us. Beatty had made a general signal: 'The German flag will be hauled down at sunset'. As they did so to the sound of the bugle 'Making sunset', Beatty was given a round of cheers by all of us in the Grand Fleet. I heard later on this remarkable occasion that he had raised his cap and said, 'I always told you they would have to come out'. We escorted them first to Rosyth and then later round to Scapa Flow. Then we spent a lot of time as guard destroyer in Gutter Sound looking after their destroyers and smaller ships.

That whole period was really rather dicey for us. You weren't allowed to fraternise in any way; you had to keep a pretty good watch on what they were trying to do, and we understood their morale was very poor. I remember going slowly past a German destroyer, whose crew as always was trying to barter with us to get some food. I saw a German sailor go up to an officer and pluck the Iron Cross off his coat and offer it to us for some cigarettes. The officer could do nothing.

On 21 June 1919 we were lying in Gutter Sound doing our turn, having a gin before lunch, when the senior Sub-Lieutenant came running into the wardroom and said 'The Germans are abandoning ship'. We thought at first he was being funny. However we rushed up on deck and indeed they were abandoning ship, every ship. In fact they were scuttling them. They were flying various signals and laying boats, but there was nothing that we could do. There was no way we could prevent seventy ships from being scuttled. Our C-in-C had rather foolishly taken the rest of the Fleet out on exercise and we were the only warship left on duty. We were some way from the bigger ships but we could see them keel over and sink lower in the water. So we went at full speed towards them to try and stop the crews of the battleships or cruisers from abandoning ship. They took no notice of our words, so we fired a few rounds close to one of the cruisers and of course, quite naturally, the whole lot just jumped straight over the side! There was nothing you could do. We just stood there and watched this giant cruiser go down in front of our eyes.

The *Hindenburg*, one of the biggest ones, was not far away, in fact she was in the entrance to the Flow. She looked to us as if she wasn't going down as fast as any of the others, she was upright. So, the First Lieutenant, myself and about twenty men, which was all we could spare, got on board her. The crew had abandoned ship and reached one of the nearby islands. Before they left they had opened all the watertight doors and everything else needed to sink a ship. The ship by now was already in a bad state, full of rust, and all power had been disconnected so we had to work in the dark to try and close the hatches. We realised pretty soon that she was gradually going down and of course, as she was sinking, the water pressure just blew the hatches. By now we were beginning to feel a shade anxious and scurried up to the bridge. When the water got up to well over the upper deck we began to get pretty worked up and were thinking seriously of jumping over the side. We had no idea of the depth of water she was in, but fortunately she hit the bottom and settled upright. One of our whaling boats came and picked us off the bridge: it was all rather fun really, but then it usually is with hindsight!

Everywhere we looked we saw mast after mast sticking out from the water, it was an awesome sight. An entire fleet of 71 ships, ships that had fought at Jutland, all scuttled. We were the only warship to witness this extraordinary event and this made things a bit complicated.

We gathered up the German crews from all the ships on to one island. However, one stupid German went and climbed up on a bell buoy which rang every time it swayed so we left him there for the day. We were then left with these Germans as prisoners, but they weren't really prisoners. Eventually they were taken down south.

While the High Seas Fleet had been based at Scapa Flow its crews were serviced by a mail ship which used to come over from Germany with provisions once a fortnight. The German Navy was pretty clever because they would get rid of all their malcontents and difficult people and have them sent home on this mailship. Our powers-that-be were frightened that, when she arrived and saw nothing but a pile of masts, she would go and sink herself at the entrance. So we were sent off to intercept her. We had to come alongside and board her, you know, fixed bayonets; they all thought we were going to shoot them. This German Petty officer came on deck with a cat o' nine tails which he'd obviously used on the boys on the ship; when he found himself looking down the end of a bayonet he agreed to let me borrow it and I still have it.

To relieve us after guarding the High Seas Fleet we were sent to Hamburg in July 1919. The Navy had taken over the docks and had the cruiser *Coventry* there with a party of experts on board. We were sent to lie alongside *Coventry* because of the difficulties she had with her draft. We simply went out there for six weeks with nothing to do but lie alongside her. To get there we made our way up the Elbe to Hamburg which was an utterly demoralised place. We had to be very careful when we went ashore because of the German Workers Party and we allowed no one into the dockyard. Money was scarce so we could buy a German sentry's rifle for about five shillings and if we bartered with two penny bars of Pusser's soap, we got five bob too for them. We did very well while we were there. It was a very interesting time, for I really did see the repercussions of war on land. We made a visit to Hagenbeck zoo and, as we walked around, a chap came up who spoke very good English and offered to take us on a tour. He was in fact the owner and, surprisingly, had done very well during the war. He told us that some of his elephants were used to haul heavy guns out of the mud near Verdun, but were withdrawn after two had been killed. His family, however, had not gone short of meat because he had a thriving herd of buffalo.

We then moved to Heligoland, where we anchored outside the harbour because none of the minefields had been swept. One evening we were walking on deck after supper when we heard a voice hail, 'Warship ahoy, permission to come on board'. Four men clambered aboard led by a great burly chap in a seaman's jersey who saluted and said, 'My name is Nicholls and I'm the Head of the Elders of the citizens of Heligoland and we have a petition. May we see your captain?' So we took him below and he presented our captain with their petition. He said, 'We Heligolanders in our little island in the middle of the sea used to belong to Britain and we want to belong to Britain again'. At the outbreak of war the islanders had been rounded up and interned in Germany. He went on to say, 'My wife just had time to burn my service certificate and hide my medals before we were taken away'. They had returned to find most of their houses had been wrecked by the Germans who occupied them. They were now looking for some form of security. As he was talking our captain suddenly said, 'What was your last ship, Nicholls?' 'The *Glory*, sir,' he replied proudly. 'I was the Master-at-Arms (Senior Rating) and I remember now, sir, you were a midshipman in her.' He had joined the Royal Navy as a boy in 1887 when Heligoland belonged to Britain, and after serving his time for pension, returned to his birthplace to find it had been sold to Germany in 1890 in exchange for Zanzibar.

After Heligoland we were sent to join the 2nd Flotilla at Byorko in Finland but were ordered to call in at a port called (in those days) Libau, in Latvia, and report what state it was in.

The little port lay still and almost deserted as we approached. The long breakwater protecting it from the sea was intact, but as we cautiously made our way in, the rusting upper works of two steamers and masts of a wooden schooner protruding above the water told their story. On the quay a line of cranes, their jibs leaning drunkenly at odd angles, and the roofless warehouses completed the picture.

The town had fared no better; along the front facing the harbour the houses bore tragic witness to the havoc of war. The road was potted and cluttered with mounds of debris and wrecked vehicles. A few people picked their way through the litter, their features grey and drawn; and added to the air of despair and death that hung over the place like some dreadful miasma.

We were still feeling our way cautiously, but we secured alongside the pier and, after an interval, a small group of men appeared and contact was established. They had brought an interpreter who spoke English, and he explained the situation. He spoke in a voice devoid of expression, drained of emotion, the voice of a man who had seen so much and been through such experiences that no spark of hope or feeling was left. He told us, 'When the Germans first came in there was some resistance; but there was little we could do. Nearly all the younger men were away fighting, and we that were left had few weapons. But those that could, sold their lives dearly. For the first two days after the fighting stopped they did little and we began to hope. Then came the order. All women between the ages of fifteen and forty were to parade on this pier. The houses were searched and those found hiding or trying to escape were dragged here and shot. The German soldiers formed a line, and two by two the women were taken into a hut and raped. Their particulars were all written in a book: oh yes, the Germans are thorough. If a child was born it was taken from its mother after six weeks and sent to Germany.'

The terrible recital went on. As we were listening a woman in ragged skirt and black shawl drawn close about her face drifted aimlessly by with a vacant, haunting stare. The interpreter paused. 'That was one,' he said. 'Two children she had.' 'How old?' I asked. 'About eighteen,' he replied. I began to feel sick with the horror of it. So did the rest of the men with me.

When I returned on board a two-badge Able Seaman called Maddox was cleaning the shield of 'Y' gun on the quarterdeck. As the gunlayer he held himself responsible for the cleanliness and proper working order of the gun and mounting. And woe betide anyone who laid a hand on it without his permission; not that anyone was particularly anxious to be on the receiving end of Maddox's opinion of his ability, efficiency or ancestry. As I passed he looked up. 'Any chance, Sir, of having a go at the swines that did that?' he asked, nodding shorewards. I looked at him in some surprise. Maddox wasn't given to opening any conversation; he kept himself to himself and seldom spoke unless riled. 'A slight hope,' I replied. 'They say ashore that the Huns are advancing up the coast again. Why do you feel strongly about it?' 'I got what you might call a special interest,' he answered and relapsed into silence. I knew he would not be drawn any further.

It was a few days later when the captain spoke to the ship's company. 'I need not remind you,' he said, 'of what we saw and

143

heard at Libau; few of us will ever forget it. The German army force, or whatever you call it, has been located on the shore road south of our present position. It consists of an estimated 4,000 men under the command of a Prussian officer. It is not in any sense a regular formation and lives off the land, and is reported to be moving northwards again. An ultimatum was delivered to the commander. He was to evacuate the area within forty-eight hours and return to German territory, otherwise punitive action would be taken against him by HM Ships. I understand the German commander replied "You would not dare; I will blow your little ships out of the water. I will go where I like." The time limit has now expired. The 4th Sub-Division led by *Westcott* will carry out the punitive action.

'We are now proceeding to a position close inshore,' the captain continued. 'When the enemy is located fire will be opened and will continue for fifteen minutes and I expect rigid fire discipline and self-control. There may be opposition, the rest of the flotilla will remain in support to seaward. We shall close up at Action Stations in two hours time.'

The low shoreline with its flat sand dunes was clearly visible now. The gun crews were standing alert and tense around their mountings. The layers and trainers had their eyes glued to their telescopes. The rangefinders' crew were calling out the ranges as we closed in. A puff of smoke came from near a sand dune followed by another and a couple of shells from field-guns came ricocheting across the water and passed between us and our consort. The captain turned to me and ordered, 'Open Fire'. As we did so the ship shuddered and shook to the crash of the guns. I fired two salvos to get the range and then changed into independent firing, with the foremost guns concentrating on the field-gun battery. The crews were working like demons, sticking rigidly to their drill. I could clearly see the terrible carnage on shore. The field-guns were silenced under a hail of fire; tents and vehicles were burning, ammunition exploding, men running blindly in every direction; a few even plunged into the sea. Our consort was plastering the road in and out. There was no escape; they were trapped.

We got the order to cease firing.

Our ears were singing from the crash of the guns, the smell of blistered paint was in our nostrils, the canvas screen around the bridge rail hung in tatters. The gun crews stood panting with exertion, sweat streaking their faces. Some of the loading numbers had stripped to the waist, and as they began the task of sponging out and stacking the empty cartridge cases their bodies glistened in the sun. I made my way from gun to gun receiving the reports from each in turn.

When I reached the quarterdeck the crew of 'Y' gun were still sponging out. AB Maddox was squinting carefully up the barrel from the breech end. 'One more with the clean rag, lads,' he said, 'and she'll do.' He looked up. 'Forty-nine rounds, sir,' he reported, 'and I had good targets for them all'. 'That's three more than anyone else,' I said. He grunted with satisfaction and gazed at the receding shore.

'I've waited four years for this,' he said quietly; 'and when the war was over I never thought as 'ow I'd get another chance.' He turned and looked at me, his eyes burning. 'I 'ad a kid brother,' he said. 'Cabin boy in the Merchant service, just turned fifteen. His ship was torpedoed by a U-boat. They managed to get away in the boats before she sank, but the bastards surfaced and opened fire on them. He was hit in the face and he died slowly before they was picked up two days later. It broke our mother up.' He jerked his head to the shore. 'I paid some of that off today.'

I went up forward again to my cabin at the break of the fo'c'sle to file the reports. It was in a bit of a shambles. I began to clear up and, as I picked up a book of verse written by a soldier in France, I remembered the verse that echoed the feelings of the Tommy who had seen his mate killed by a sniper:

> There's some as fights for freedom
> And there's some as fights for fun
> But me my lad I fight for bleedin' hate
> You may damn the war and blast it, but
> I 'opes it won't be done
> Till I've got the bloomin' blood price for my mate.

Is that where it ends? I wondered. As I stepped outside we were taking up our position with the Flotilla again. As we passed them in line, they were quietly manning the rails. 'What's that signal Captain D. is flying?' I asked the signalman. He replied, 'To *Westcott*, thank you from us all'.

We then steamed towards our original destination, Byorko in

Finland. As we approached the harbour the sound opened up and we could see into the anchorage and the two lines of destroyers at the far end. The Leading Signalman started making our pennant number and asking for an anchor berth with his signal lamp. When he had a reply he came up on the bridge and read out what was on his pad. He seemed slightly embarrassed. 'Anchor in position five cables, 268° from Niki Point, end of B line. Behave yourselves and eyes down for LELKA.' The Captain asked him to repeat the message, which he did. 'Ah!' said the captain. 'Captain D. likes his little joke. I suppose we'll learn what he means soon enough.'

On the afternoon of the second day we were working ordinary 'part of ship' routine. I happened to be Officer of the Day, so was on deck more than I would normally have been. Gradually it dawned on me that a large number of men appeared to have discovered some work that required to be done on the port side of the ship, the side facing the shore only a few cables distant. I next observed the quartermaster on watch gazing through the trainers' telescope of 'Y' gun, which was trained on the shore.

'What the blazes are you doing?' I asked. The quartermaster emerged somewhat sheepishly, and murmured something about practising. I let it go at that and turned my own gaze shoreward. Immediately opposite the ship was a sandy beach, studded with a few large boulders. Sitting with her back against a rock, reading a book, was an elderly woman, clad in black and holding a parasol; while running up and down near the water's edge was a girl or, to be more accurate, a young woman, as naked as the day she was born!

Smugly I went down to the captain's cabin and knocked at the door. 'I beg your pardon, sir,' I said, 'but I have discovered who Lelka is: she is a young woman.' 'And what is remarkable about that?' replied the captain. 'Have you never seen a young woman before?' 'Oh yes, sir, of course, sir,' I said. 'But this one has no clothes on.' The Captain leapt to his feet. 'And what precisely is she doing without any clothes on, if it's not a rude question?' he demanded. 'I think she is swimming to the ship, sir,' I replied.

The situation on deck was rapidly assuming crisis proportions. Lelka was in fact swimming vigorously towards the ship, and obviously aiming for the accommodation ladder on the port quarter. Reaching the platform at the bottom of the ladder, she hoisted herself gracefully up on to it, and sat there like some beautiful mermaid. Wringing out her long fair hair, she coiled it skilfully on top of her head and, after a friendly wave, called out cheerfully, 'I speak little Inglish'.

Apparently it was quite normal etiquette in the Baltic seas in those earlier decades of the twentieth century for people of both sexes to bathe without costumes; it would in fact have been considered prudish to wear them. Lelka was thus only following the custom of her country; and it would never have occurred to her that it could cause embarrassment. Our First Lieutenant dispatched a midshipman to fetch a towel and to go down the ladder and wrap it around the uninvited guest. Carrying the towel, only too conscious of the number of eyes upon him and the advice being freely given, the midshipman advanced, his face scarlet with embarrassment. Lelka stood up, accepted the towel with a polite smile, spread it carefully over the platform, sat down again on one side and, patting the spare section, invited the midshipman to occupy it. The First Lieutenant called down, 'Perhaps you will be good enough to carry out your instructions. If she won't put the towel round her, tell her to go.' 'But she doesn't want to go,' pleaded the midshipman. 'Then push her in,' said the First Lieutenant. The midshipman stood up reluctantly. 'You must go,' he said desperately. 'Go, swim ashore.' 'Pardon,' said Lelka puzzled. 'Go,' said the midshipman. 'Swim.' Lelka stood up. 'You swim?' she asked. 'Yes,' said the midshipman, 'I mean no.' He gave her shoulder a nervous and half-hearted push. A mischievous look came into Lelka's face. 'Go,' she said. 'Swim.' And she gave the midshipman a hefty and most unmaidenlike push. The unfortunate midshipman, caught completely unawares, lost his balance, and clutching wildly at thin air and to the laughter of all aboard hit the water with a resounding splash. Lelka dived in and retrieved the midshipman's cap, which she perched jauntily on her head and waved gaily. In response to frantic calls from the elderly lady in black, she swam swiftly back to the beach leaving the midshipman floundering.

When he finally arrived back on the quarterdeck looking utterly bedraggled he was firmly rebuked by the First Lieutenant but bravely he stood his ground. 'Permission to go ashore and recover my cap,' he asked.

Later Captain D. ordered another berth for us and then said, 'By the way, I saw your midshipman ashore this afternoon, looking very smart. No doubt he was paying a social call. He'll go far.'

The situation was a strange and unreal one. Based on a not too neutral Finland, we were supposed to be giving moral and physical support to our gallant allies, the Estonians, with a composite army commanded by the 'White' General Yudenich who was supposed to be advancing on Petrograd through Estonia. The difficulty was that we seldom knew of the whereabouts, or the identity, of our 'allies'.

Admittedly if we steamed too close to the fort of Krasnaya Gorka the Reds would open up with their 12-inch guns. If we bombarded the shore further to the west, as we were sometimes invited to do, the chances were that we might hit a redshirt, a white shirt or even a green shirt; the latter being a mysterious body of men who were apparently fighting everybody. In truth, the chances of hitting anything but a number of trees in the seemingly limitless pine forests were extremely remote. Apart from the Russian Fleet at Kronstadt, the main hazards, other than Krasnaya Gorka, were the unreliability of our charts, the suspected presence of minefields, and the activities of a lone Russian aviator, known to all as 'Reckless Rupert', who would periodically fly over and drop a few bombs on the anchorage. Rumour had it that the Reds held his family hostage against his return from his bombing raid. We'd go ashore occasionally and on one memorable picnic when we were all relaxing, a sniper opened up on us which somewhat disconcerted our First Lieutenant, who, clad in his buff, was seen running ahead of us still clutching a frying pan with our precious sausages sizzling away. There was also a visit to the Tsar's holiday chalet at Bzorko. It was occupied by a rather pathetic pair of caretakers who had not heard of the assassination of the Tsar and his family and were still waiting for them to return that summer. In one room were the children's toys – including a small wooden toy submarine. It was all rather sad.

Officially Lummy – a bulldog – did not exist; but unofficially she was as much a member of the ship's Company of *HMS Verulam* as any officer or rating on board. Her great jaw and lumbering gait was a familiar sight to most of the destroyers in the 2nd Flotilla. She slept in a specially made and low slung hammock in the galley flat, had a fine repertoire of tricks, a somewhat regrettable taste for beer, and a passion for football. Sporting a jersey knitted in the ship's colours, white shorts and a uniform cap, she attended all the ship's matches. To us in the *Westcott* she was an old friend; for with *Verulam* we formed the 4th Sub-Division, and were 'chummy ships'. On 3 September the wardroom of the *Verulam* came over by boat to give us the local gen, and brought Lummy with them.

When the *Verulam*'s boat came for them after supper, the trouble started. Lummy refused to go down the gangway; and when they tried to carry her down she turned savage, broke away, and retreated underneath the torpedo tubes defying all attempts to dislodge her. Eventually it was decided to leave her alone; and as *Verulam* was due to go out on patrol the next morning we agreed to look after her until they returned. In the morning the dog emerged, and behaved normally. She went ashore for a run with the canteen manager, who was buying eggs, and returned in good spirits. But she was off her food, and as the day wore on became morose, lying for long periods with her head resting on her front paws. She remained on deck all evening and was lying in the same position when we came up for some air after supper. She seemed to be listening or waiting. It was, I remember, a calm warm night, very dark; and the scent from the pine forests along the shore line very strong. We were discussing what Lummy could be sickening for when a flash of light momentarily lit up the horizon to seaward. In the pause that followed we all turned instinctively, and the dog raised her head. A moment later an expanding arc of yellow shot skywards and in the midst of it the debris of a great explosion.

One reacts automatically on these occasions. Before the sound had reached us across the water, the First Lieutenant and the quartermaster were racing forward, the chief engineer making for the engine-room hatch and I was scrambling down the ladder to the captain's cabin to report. When I made my way up to the bridge a few minutes later the cable party was already on the fo'c'sle shortening in the cable; and the Leading Signalman was reading out the signals as they were made by the Leader's shaded lantern.

'D2 General. Following from *Walpole*. Immediate, *Verulam* mined or torpedoed, position 175 Niki Point 2 miles. After magazine blew up, ship sank in two minutes. Am searching survivors.

'D2 General. Raise steam with all dispatch and report when ready to proceed, cover *Walpole*. 2nd Division will take up patrol line 155 Niki Point. 1st Division remain at instant notice. Acknowledge.'

A dark shape slid by, heading for the entrance to the sound. It was the stand-by destroyer. We waited impatiently for the engine-room to report ready. The Parts of Ship were closing watertight doors, and securing for sea; the gun crews were clearing away their mountings.

I worked my way along the upper deck, checking as best I could in the dark that all was secure. Just about at the break of the fo'c'sle I bumped into a little procession. It was headed by the Mess Deck's Petty Officer, with Lummy next, and the ship's butcher bringing up the rear. They were coaxing the dog along and above the roar of the boiler room fans I could hear snatches, 'come on, old girl . . . got to get below . . . action stations . . . doing all we can,'. As they reached the black-out screen leading on to the mess decks the dog stopped and looked up into their faces. There was nothing to be said. Out of a crew of over a hundred only seventeen survived. It was a terrible end to our time in Finland.

Now, in the tail-end of September 1919 for me and my contemporaries in that back-of-beyond war zone, it all came to an end. A ship appeared from England with our reliefs. We had had no warning, no advance notice, we simply went home. I, along with others of my contemporaries, was to go to Cambridge University for six months – *in statu pupillari*. It all seemed rather strange and slightly unreal. For it was, for us, an end of an era. Of the eighty-odd of my term who went to sea in January 1916, nearly a dozen and a half were dead, mostly killed when they were barely sixteen. We were not the only youngsters to suffer, nor the last. Kipling had captured it so well in *The Scholars*:

They have touched a knowledge outreaching speech as when
    the cutters were sent
To harvest the dreadful mile of beach after the Vanguard went.
They have learned great faith and little fear and a high heart
    in distress
And how to suffer each sodden year of heaped-up weariness.
They have borne the bridle upon their lips and the yoke upon
    their neck,
Since they went down to the sea in ships to save the world
    from wreck—
Since the chests were slung down the College stair at Dartmouth
    in 'Fourteen,

And now they are quit of the sea-affair as though no war
    had been.
Far have they steamed and much have they known, and most
    would they fain forget;
But now they are come to their joyous own with all the
    world in their debt . . .
Hallowed River, most gracious Trees, Chapel beyond
    compare,
Here be gentlemen tired of the seas – take them into
    your care.
Far have they come, much have they braved. Give them their
    hour of play,
While the hidden things their hands have saved work for
    them day by day:
Till the grateful Past their youth redeemed return them their
    youth once more,
And the soul of the Child at last lets fall the unjust load
    that it bore!

PART TWO

The Interwar Years, 1919–1939

HISTORICAL NOTE

While their old enemies rusted at anchor at Scapa Flow, the Royal Navy was slowly demobilised. But the decision to intervene in the Russian civil war led to British warships seeing action from the Arctic Circle to the Black Sea and the Pacific. There was even a squadron of improvised warships on the land-locked Caspian Sea. Rear-Admiral Cowan presided over several unsung victories in the Baltic where British torpedo boats attacked the Bolshevik fleet at its Kronstadt anchorage, sinking two battleships in an epic raid that led to the covert award of a Victoria Cross to Commander Agar. There is a memorial at Brookwood Military Cemetery to those who died in Russia during the World Wars, and it includes the names of 127 naval personnel killed fighting the Bolsheviks, headed by Captain F. N. A. Cromie, CB, DSO who died, gun in hand, defending the British Embassy in Petrograd. Naval support helped sustain the White armies in southern Russia, but could not prevent the eventual Bolshevik victory. Allied forces were withdrawn in 1920 and the last sailors came home. When Admiral Beatty assembled the warships of the Grand Fleet to accept the surrender of the German High Seas Fleet, the Royal Navy was at the zenith of its power. Over 438,000 men were serving in 58 capital ships, 12 aircraft carriers, 103 cruisers, 122 submarines and over 450 destroyers and escorts. The Royal Navy's global commitment was soon emphasised by intervention against the Bolsheviks in Arctic waters, in the Baltic, the Black Sea and the Pacific. Warships on the China squadron would see action throughout the 1920s and 1930s as Britain defended her interests from the local warlords in classic applications of 'gunboat diplomacy'. The international community in Shanghai conducted its business behind the bayonets of the Royal Marines.

Between 1919 and 1923 the British Empire reached its greatest geographic extent as territories of the former Ottoman Empire came under Imperial control. The Royal Navy smoothly continued its traditional deployments, maintaining battle squadrons in the Mediterranean as well as home waters, with cruisers in the West Indies, off North America, South America, South Africa and the East Indies. Construction of a new naval base began at Singapore, Admiral Jellicoe planning to base 16 battleships, four aircraft carriers and powerful light forces there to counter the growing Japanese navy.

From 1923–4 HMS *Hood,* the largest and fastest battlecruiser in any navy, was dispatched on a world tour to show the flag. Yet *Hood* was the only major unit the Royal Navy had built since the hard lessons of Jutland. Despite her graceful lines and imposing size, her protection was no more than adequate. While the rest of the British fleet had been laid down before 1914, American yards supplied the US Navy with a dozen new 'super-dreadnoughts' by 1920. Japan now boasted eight equally powerful battleships. The majority of the Royal Navy's capital ships, armed with 12-inch or 13.5-inch guns, would be no match for them. The Admiralty understood what had to be done to maintain Britain's naval position: Beatty demanded eight modern battleships without delay.

The fearsome economic cost of winning the First World War had profound consequences for the Royal Navy, however. Britain simply could not afford to maintain the pre-war 'two-power standard' – a navy equal to the next two foreign fleets added together. In fact, it could not really sustain a 'one-power standard'. While it suited the USA to broker a succession of naval agreements that staved off another naval race, the American economy was growing as fast as the British economy was declining. In 1919 the British government instructed its armed forces to assume there would be no major war for ten years. There would be a ten-year hiatus in naval construction.

Naval wages had been seriously-eroded by the inflation of the war years. Ratings were keenly aware that workers in industry were receiving pay increases to match, while naval personnel were left to struggle. Fortunately the wartime British admirals enjoyed a closer relationship with the lower deck than their German opposite numbers. Disturbances in the Grand Fleet were nipped in the bud in 1917 and ratings received an extra 2d. a day. In 1918 a one-day strike by the Police secured them a major pay award and the example was not lost on the armed forces. It was obvious that a substantial increase in wages was essential, and in 1919 ABs' daily pay was increased from 1s.8d. to 4s. In 1920 ratings over twenty-five were made eligible for a marriage allowance.

A year later, First Lord Sir Eric Geddes took his celebrated axe to the naval budget. Spending on warships was being slashed, and spending on their people would not escape either. One captain in three was retired as the wartime fleet was reduced at a speed not witnessed since 1815. Rumours of pay cuts did nothing for service morale although when they came in 1925 only new personnel were affected, new ABs receiving only 3s. a day. Four years later the industrial world was struck by the great crash. From 1929–32 British steel production practically halved; more than half the workforce in Britain's shipyards was out of work. A yawning trade gap had opened. Social spending was already seven times that of 1913 and now accounted for the majority of government expenditure. On the eve of the Great War, the Royal Navy had enjoyed 25 per cent of government spending; but by 1932 it received just 6 per cent.

At the height of the crisis, in the summer of 1931, British ministers struggled to sustain the gold standard. Like the civil service, the Police and the other armed forces, the Navy was instructed to cut pay. The Admiralty more than obliged. It was announced that all men being paid on the 1919 scales would be placed on the lower 1925 scales. This would affect chief and petty officers almost to a man and three out of four other rates. And since the decision effectively cut all rates by a shilling, the burden fell disproportionately on the lower deck: ABs were losing 25 per cent of their wages, officers only 11 per cent. Meanwhile, the Army and Air Force were accepting only ten per cent cuts across the board.

Married ratings were especially hard hit: with family budgets already fully stretched to meet hire purchase agreements and pay the rent, this drastic loss of earnings raised the spectre of eviction – or the repossession of their furniture at the least. Unfortunately for the Royal Navy it seemed many officers, especially aboard the big ships, had little appreciation of the hardships their companies were facing. Worse, the lower deck discovered what was afoot before any official statement and the impression grew that sailors' welfare was of secondary interest to the Admiralty; other service chiefs had resisted more extensive cuts.

The Atlantic Fleet, at anchor at Invergordon, received official notice on Saturday, 12 September 1931. Rear-Admiral Tomkinson warned Whitehall of ominous signs, but in the absence of any response, he ordered the fleet to sea on the Tuesday. The crews of four battleships refused to raise steam. While the 'unrest', as Admiralty documents often refer to it, was largely confined to the big ships – officers and men clearly enjoyed a closer relationship aboard cruisers and destroyers – the Invergordon mutiny made headlines around the world. The pound plummeted on foreign exchanges, losing over a quarter of its dollar value during the week. The National government was compelled to abandon the gold standard, and to impose the same ten per cent pay cut on the Navy as the other services were to suffer. Within the Navy, a fund was created to assist married men, especially ratings less than 25 who did not receive the allowance. While 124 mutineers were drafted ashore without delay, and several dozen discharged, no less than seven captains were relieved of their commands. Aside from one, no admiral involved was employed again.

Within a couple of months of the Invergordon mutiny, Japan intervened in Manchuria, deaf to all the entreaties of the League of Nations. While, today, we are used to the fact that a ringing denunciation from the United Nations is probably the single most ineffective tool in international relations, the revelation of its predecessor's impotence came as a disagreeable surprise. So many statesmen had placed their faith in collective security that the naked aggression of the Japanese left them floundering for a response. In 1931 the British people had more pressing concerns than remote Asian wars, but the lesson was not lost on Germany's rising political star Hitler, nor the posturing Mussolini in Italy whose Fascist Party dreamed of a new Roman Empire.

British re-armament did not begin immediately, indeed did not begin for several years. With the conspicuous exception of Winston Churchill, consigned to the political wilderness, all three parties opposed a radical increase in defence expenditure. The Conservatives were acutely conscious that taxes or slashing welfare spending would lead to a massacre of their party at the next election. Liberal and Labour leaders still clung to the ideal of the League of Nations, unable or unwilling to accept that some nations – and some governments – had not lost their appetite for violence for all the slaughter of 1914–18.

British re-armament began just in time to avoid disaster. The Navy budget doubled between 1933 and 1938. The ten per cent pay cut was restored in 1934 and the grim business of Invergordon, if not forgotten, was firmly put aside. Discipline was restored: re-enlistment rates increased and instances of punishment declined. Yet a battlefleet could not be improvised any more than a modern army could be. Even after the introduction of conscription, the British Army of 1940 was outnumbered more than 5:1 by the Wehrmacht. And whereas the French army had shouldered the terrible burden of the western front from 1914–1916, the morose militia assembling behind the Maginot line did not inspire the same confidence. Having shed the bulk of its obsolete pre-First World War battleships, the Royal Navy deployed 12 battleships and battlecruisers in 1939; five extremely powerful 'King George V' class battleships were building and four 16-inch gunned battleships were planned. It boasted five aircraft carriers, 58 cruisers, 200 destroyers and escorts and 38 submarines. Since the German navy had just two battleships commissioned and two more under construction, the balance of power in the North Sea was far more favourable than that of 1914. However, Britain's vigorous opposition to Mussolini's invasion of Abyssinia transformed a hitherto neutral Italy into an almost certain enemy. Italy's new and powerful battlefleet dominated the central Mediterranean. The threat of Italian air power compelled the British fleet to transfer its main base from Malta to Alexandria.

Even after the government had given the orders, re-constituting British naval strength proved harder than anticipated. The 'naval holiday' had had fatal consequences for Britain's shipyards; many went out of business altogether, and the survivors were no longer world leaders in design and technology. Skilled labour was lost. The late 1930s witnessed a dramatic revival in warship construction, but British warships required many more man-hours to build than those taking shape in US, Japanese or German yards.

Seaman Gunner Stan Smith

When the Armistice was signed, I had no chance to celebrate. I was placed on immediate draft to HMS *Emperor of India*, a battleship of the *Iron Duke* class. She had ten 13.5-inch guns, twelve 6-inch guns, four 4-inch anti-aircraft guns and numerous smaller weapons. She was also equipped with submerged torpedo tubes. It was an emergency draft and almost as soon as the ship's company got on board we set sail for a secret destination. I was about to find out that the world was still full of people at war with one another. We stopped briefly at Gibraltar and Malta, for oiling, but neither provided us with any leave nor any clues to our ultimate destination. On we sailed through the Dardanelles to the entrance of the Bosphorus, where off Constantinople we dropped anchor. The reason for our journey became obvious for the Turks were massacring the Germans and Armenians. Murderous parties roamed the streets by night, stringing people up by their feet from lamp-posts, slitting them up the middle and putting their testicles in their mouths. I was eighteen at the time and it was a sight I can never forget, however hard I try.

Our task was to round up all the Germans who had scattered and were hiding in every corner of the city. Even when we found them we could not be sure that they would treat us with anything more than suspicion, since we had recently fought against them in the war to end all wars. We took them to a merchant ship which had been commandeered and anchored, for their own safety, in the middle of the Bosphorus.

Hunger, thirst and disease were as much a threat ashore as the night-time murderers, for there was very little food and even less water. Our bakers were making bread day and night while the engineers were kept busy around the clock distilling water. We had to form the starving into long queues to stop them from swamping us and collaring the bread. Large armed parties of our ship's companies had to maintain order. With the aid of our rifle butts and the occasional bayonet prod, we persuaded them to queue properly and distributed the food as fairly as we could.

After this we went back through the Bosphorus to the Dardanelles on a mission to help the Army to clear Gallipoli. This took us right into another big mess on shore. Ammunition and bodies – mostly skeletons – lay everywhere and we had the gruesome task of collecting up bones and skulls. Often we would shovel up one skull to every two of bones and cart them in boxes to the top of a hill where the Army had cleared a space for a cemetery. There lay many a soldier whose name was unknown and grave unmarked. We also had to dispose of ammunition, exploding it or dumping it at sea to clear the island.

Faced with the same job on the ANZAC beaches where the Australians had lost a lot of men, we spent about ten days helping to clear up the fearsome debris of war. It was a task which I wouldn't wish upon anyone; except, perhaps the politicians whose decisions usually cause it all in the first place. This is the side of war which makes many an old sailor wince when brave words are spoken about honour and freedom; the grim face of glory.

We returned from that terrible task and were given leave in Malta. While I was there a notice went up asking for volunteers for an expedition to Enzeli on the Caspian Sea. I ignored the old Service advice and put my name forward.

We were a motley crowd of twenty-nine volunteers, placed under the command of Commander Bruce Fraser who was later made an admiral and commanded the Home Fleet at the time of the sinking of the *Scharnhorst* during World War II. He was a very nice chap and we soon formed a great respect for him.

A destroyer took us back through the Dardanelles and the Bosphorus to the Black Sea port of Batumi where we transferred all our equipment for repairing guns and engines on to a train bound for the Caspian Sea. The train consisted of an engine and three wagons with sliding doors, similar to the covered goods trucks seen in England at that time. We set off and two days out from Batumi, in the foothills of the Caucasian Mountains, the train ground to a halt. There was a blockage on the line and we were on the receiving end of a very efficient ambush. Under fire from bandits in the hills we flung open the wagon doors, built barricades with our kitbags and hammocks, and returned the rifle fire. Firing intensified as they started on the other side of the track. The engine driver refused to go on even if we cleared the obstruction on the line. The only alternative was to go back to Batumi.

Our stores were loaded on another ship and we were taken back through the Black Sea and the Bosphorus to Izmir (Smyrna) on the Turkish coast. We took the train to Baghdad which was the end of the line. From there we had no choice but to start a long, long walk. Our stores and equipment were loaded on to camels and we began to footslog our way across Persia, a prospect which held little appeal for a chap like me with a plate in his leg from the battle of Jutland. We could see ten to fifteen miles across open country during the day, but there was never a soul in sight. At night we were pestered by camp thieves who would creep in and steal whatever they could lay their hands on, no matter how many sentries were posted. We were a pushover for them until the Gurkhas arrived on the scene. They were the boys for the camp thieves; we were never pestered again.

Eventually we arrived at Enzeli to find just a few old huts, a couple of houses and a pier sticking out into the Caspian Sea. The huts, which had been used by nomads, were in a terrible state, so we did some temporary repairs, patching up the roofs of two of the buildings with anything we could salvage from the others. After our stores had been unloaded, the camels and the Gurkhas turned back. We were on our own.

It was my twenty-first birthday but I had no chance to celebrate and nothing to celebrate with. Twenty-one years old and I'd never been kissed.

We spent some time at Enzeli. Our job was to build up fortifications in case the Bolsheviks beat Denikin's men and advanced on Persia. We had to transfer guns from ships left by the Royal Navy and set up seashore fortifications. We were also supposed to repair ships for Denikin's men but a boat arrived with a message that these ships were still in Baku and in such a state they couldn't be moved to Enzeli. So we loaded up our stores and went to Baku where the ships were in a really sorry state of repair. I don't think the guns had been moved since the Navy left. They hadn't been elevated or trained and were thick with rust.

I was part of the team which tackled guns while other men worked on the engines and other machinery. I was partnered off with a chap called Dart to repair a recoil cylinder on one of the guns when – 'crunch' – the Bolsheviks entered the town bringing work to a halt quicker than a wildcat strike. Denikin's men fell back in some disorder. I was quietly working away when 'bang', I knew no more. I had been fairly effectively bashed over the head and when I woke up I was trussed up like a chicken with both hands behind my back and my feet lashed tightly together.

The Bolsheviks, who seemed like fearsome fighting men, eventually untied our legs and herded us on to the quayside. We were all roped together and marched away under escort to a grim, bleak room where our hands were untied and we were told to strip naked. Our clothing was searched and returned to us, but they had emptied all the pockets so we were left with nothing but the remnants of what we stood up in.

Commander Fraser argued our case with Astare Nasarate, the head prison guard, but to no avail. We were roped together and marched off to the prison of Byrloft Chyrma. It was a humiliating experience because there were jeering crowds on either side of us, giving every impression that they had won a great victory.

On arrival at the prison we were split into two groups and placed in two adjoining cells. With bare walls, no furniture and an earth floor, each cell measured about sixteen foot square at the most and into our cell sixteen men were crammed. We endured our first night as prisoners of war huddled together for warmth as there were no blankets or bedding of any kind. We were hungry too, but we weren't given any food until about noon the following day. I think it was noon, but our watches had been taken and we had no means of telling the time. Time was something we had plenty of; time to suffer and watch others suffer even more.

When the food came we were ready to eat anything. It was a bowl of soup which was more like dish water – thin and absolutely tasteless – and half a round of black bread. This was to be our ration for the first twenty-four hours. We were still hungry, but we had only just scraped the surface of prison life. The first meal was a picnic compared with the reality to come. Immediately after that skimpy meal we were marched into the courtyard and given ringside seats or standing positions to watch the first massacre. There were about forty prisoners to be killed, men and women, and their captors used every atrocity imaginable.

One by one they slit the women up the middle to about the chest bone, disembowelled them and left them standing until they'd done the whole crowd of women. Then they shot them as they lay moaning and screaming on the ground. They made some of the men dip their arms into buckets of acid which was so strong that when they removed their arms the flesh hung down like huge gauntlets.

We were forced to watch all this, helpless to do anything about it. Even if you closed your eyes you could never close your ears or your memories to the awful horror of those screams and cries. We had to witness many more of these massacres before we were freed. Each time we were marched back to our cell to a life which grew more grim and we were perpetually hungry.

At the beginning we had to work. We were lined up outside our cell and chained together like a lot of convicts on a chain-gang. We were marched through jeering crowds to the railway station where we had to unload sacks of millet from the trucks and carry them to the waiting carts. Some men became so weak, they would collapse under the weight of the sacks. Too feeble to work we were of little use to our captors, so back in the unrelieved misery of our cells we went on to reduced rations. For the remainder of our imprisonment our daily diet consisted of a raw fish about the size of a herring and a handful of nuts. We were so hungry that we would have fought over the food had it not been for our commander. He made us stand back against the cell walls and would call out our names one by one. The food was thrown on to the floor and each man would rush out, grab a fish and some nuts and return to the wall to devour them ravenously.

Suffering is one thing, but watching others suffer, especially your comrades dwindling to skin and bone and scratching on the ground for scraps of food, is even worse.

We were allowed out into the courtyard for half-an-hour each day to go to the toilet and have a wash. The toilet was simply a hole in the ground with a couple of bricks to put your feet on.

Having no soap we used to use the grit around the tap to wash our hands and faces a little. In that one half-hour of release we had to drink enough water to keep us going for the next twenty-four hours. This made us all pot-bellied and we began to look as if we were pregnant.

One of the things which helped keep us sane was a piece of glass one of the lads found in the courtyard. We used this to cut our hair away from our eyes and make ourselves a little more comfortable. Our main preoccupation was to hide this glass from the guards who used to search the cell at least once a week. They even dug up the earth floor to make us even more wretched, but they never did find it.

We were covered with lice in our hair, on our bodies, even in our eyebrows. To make matters worse some of the other prisoners would throw packets of lice into the cell through the grid in the door. We even went round our shirts with our teeth in a vain attempt to kill the eggs in the seams of our clothing.

The first chap to die was a mechanic called Marsh and it was that piece of glass which ended his suffering. He committed suicide, cutting the arteries in his wrists during the night and lying down to die. In the morning the guards almost fought over his clothing. They stripped him and left him in a pool of blood for three or four days until the flies in the cell were unbearable. Four more of my friends died in that cell and each time the same thing happened. The body was left where it lay until it had almost decomposed.

After almost a year of confinement, word went around the prison that a minister of the Georgian state was to visit the prison to interview Astare Nasarate about the release of Georgian prisoners. Georgia, which was holding out against the Bolsheviks, was separated from us by a wide river which the Georgians were defending quite efficiently from their bank. Held up in their advance, the Bolsheviks had resorted to negotiating with the Georgians and we had high hopes that this visit would give us, at best, a chance of release or at least a way of letting the outside world know we still existed.

When the Georgian minister arrived, he soon found that we had a Georgian interpreter among our party, whose job would have been to interpret everything necessary when we arrived at the Caspian Sea. The minister immediately negotiated for this man's release and it was only by this lucky chance that we were able to pass out a message for the British ambassador. The missive was hidden in a locket which Commander Fraser had somehow managed to conceal from the guards for all those months. It contained a picture of his mother. The Georgian swallowed this and was eventually released.

Some time after he left the Georgian minister came to the prison again to meet our commander. It was that interview which finally enabled us to leave that terrible place. We were removed to a disused school where the Georgian minister gave the commander some Russian roubles with which we were able to buy some horse meat and black bread to supplement our diet. We also bought a bar of soap so we all had a bath, one at a time under the cold water tap in the courtyard. It didn't have much effect on our lice. We were still infested because we were wearing the same clothes we had been captured in and they were getting more than a bit ragged by then.

After some weeks we were marched to the station, unchained this time. We were put into trucks and away went the train for the first stage of our journey towards freedom. At the border between Azerbaijan and Georgia we had to walk across a bridge. We were met on the other side by a Colonel Stokes and taken to a real train with carriages. There was no delay. The train left as soon as we were on board and we were given a very light meal of a quarter of a slice of meat, a little bread and a bar of chocolate. At every station my chum and I tried to get some bread, but we were still under guard and watched very closely. If we had succeeded I expect it would have been curtains for the pair of us. We saw Colonel Stokes smoking a cigar and followed him until he threw the end away, then pounced on it, had a couple of draws each and passed out for the count.

When we arrived at Tiflis (now Tbilisi), the capital of Georgia, we were given a complete change of clothing, including underwear, but we were still lousy. Our old clothes were thrown in a heap and burned. As the train took us steadily nearer the comfort of our own people, there was another complete change of clothing and our diet was gradually increased until we were on to a full slice of bread and meat at each meal.

When we arrived at Batumi, a welcome sight greeted us – a British destroyer. She took us back through the Black Sea to the Bosphorus where we were taken aboard the flagship, HMS *Iron*

Duke. There we were bathed and our entire bodies were shaved, even our eyebrows. We were given fresh naval clothes before going up for a light dinner with the admiral who thanked us on behalf of the Navy and made a speech. It was then that he broke the news that we would not be going directly back to England. We were to be the Navy's guests for a Mediterranean cruise on board a sloop, HMS *Heliotrope*, which had been fitted out for us and where we would be fed carefully until we were strong enough to return to England.

On board the *Heliotrope* our hammocks had already been slung for us and it was not long before we snuggled down and enjoyed the best night's sleep we had had for many months. Special messing arrangements had been made to cater for our tender stomachs and we had a doctor on board. Down in the bathroom I saw myself for the first time in a full-length mirror. What a sight – no eyebrows, no hair and a belly that stuck out a mile beneath ribs you could hang your hat on.

We were soon on a full diet, we even had the choice of a glass of port or a bottle of Guinness with our lunch. We called at no ports, just isolated bays in different countries where we went ashore to play football, swim or take any exercise to make us a bit fitter. Soon the hair started to grow back again and we began to look a little more presentable. Our troubles were not over though. During the cruise two of our chaps were taken ill. The doctor could do nothing for them so we called in at Malta where they were taken to Bighi Hospital. We later heard that they both died. The irony of their deaths after such an ordeal was lost on none of us. There were only twelve survivors from the twenty-nine cheerful volunteers who had started out.

We arrived at Plymouth to find we had become celebrities in our absence. The reporters were kept away from the ship and we were sworn not to communicate with the press in any way or give speeches or lectures about our captivity. All the papers could say was that the men had returned from the 'Black Hole of Baku'.

On board the *Heliotrope* we had whipped round to buy a ceremonial sword for Commander Fraser which he graciously received during our dinner with the Minister for Foreign Affairs, Lord Curzon. He was very proud of that sword and used it on all ceremonial occasions during the Second World War when he was Commander-in-Chief of the Home Fleet. His mother, Lady

Fraser, had written to the families of all her son's men telling them not to give up hope, even though we had all been reported missing, believed killed. She had also put each family in touch with another which was not too far distant so that they could share their troubles. It helped draw our families into that deep sense of comradeship which had held the survivors of Baku together.

Lieutenant Roy Smith-Hill,

Royal Marine Light Infantry

I was born in Cumberland and joined the Royal Marines in 1915. I trained at Deal where the training seemed based on what the Navy wanted, rather than on what we might have to do on land. I felt the military side was ignored. We did naval gunnery, naval boatwork, even torpedoes and electrical work. I then went to Whale Island for further gunnery training. I had the feeling that we were only expected to go ashore to deal with skirmishes, not any major action. Always you heard, 'We'll send a detachment of Marines' – we never did any land training on land.

Royal Marines would make up as much as a quarter to a third of a ship's company. The Marines' mess deck was always next door to the quarterdeck. The Marines were traditionally placed between the naval officers and the men. All rifles were in the Marine mess (barracks).

In the big ships there was always a Marine band which would play at evening quarters and morning colours. At those times, the ensign was raised or lowered. At sunset, the ship's company would fall in.

After Whale Island I was posted to the newly raised 6th Battalion, Royal Marines Light Infantry, which consisted of 'A' Company provided by Eastney, 'B' Company from Chatham, 'C' Company from Portsmouth and 'D' Company from Plymouth, along with a company of the Royal Marine Artillery. The whole battalion was formed up at Bedenham, near Gosport, with Lieutenant-Colonel Kitcat in charge. The battalion had been raised for mainly ceremonial duties during the plebiscite being held in Schleswig-Holstein, which would decide whether it stayed part of Germany or was returned to Denmark. So we were there to man polling stations and the like, but to exert no political influence. We therefore began to do an awful lot of polishing brasses and ceremonial drill.

We embarked in early August 1919 on the troopship *Czar*. Just prior to our departure we were told of a change in plan. We were now going to North Russia to bolster the forces available to General Rawlinson to cover the evacuation. We certainly did not expect to fight. In many cases morale was low. The men had not been given the chance to volunteer for Russia; the Royal Marines Adjutant-General had simply vouched his word for us at the War Office. Colonel Kitcat hadn't helped, because he thought it wise not to pay the men the day before we left Bedenham so that we wouldn't leave any drunks behind. The men had joined up for patriotic reasons; now, with the First World War over, in which many of them had fought, they certainly didn't want to lose their lives fighting in Russia. All companies had a number of raw recruits, some very young, and prisoners-of-war who had recently been returned from Germany and had had no leave.

On board we were given a talk by a senior officer who told us that our front in North Russia was 600 miles long and was held by small outposts.

There were no roads, and communication was maintained by riders in the summer and sleighs in winter. There was a rumour that we were to make an attack on Onega, some one hundred miles from Archangel, where there had been heavy fighting. If this was the case we would not get away before winter. This filled us all with dread. The feeling was further enhanced when passing the bleak Lofoten Islands. There was a sudden commotion in our wake. Everyone on board had a theory about what it was. I thought, 'God never walks here and the Devil never blows his horn'. We all felt uneasy. As we came into Murmansk I could not believe we were in the northernmost part of Europe; but for the porpoises we could have been off Margate. When we got ashore we found American, French and even Serbian troops in the same area – it was a mix-up and the mud didn't help.

The next day our train left ten hours late for Kandalaksha and 'C' and 'D' Companies left for Kem to relieve 1,600 army troops. We had a week's rations with us and the men were in cattle trucks. As the sun began to set half a dozen rifle shots rang out. We looked out of the window but could see nothing, but some of the officers seized and loaded their revolvers, thinking the train was being attacked by Bolsheviks. I suggested that, as the front was 500 miles away, perhaps it was our men trying to stop the train. This turned out to be correct. One of the men, while shutting the door of his van, fell out on to the line. The train had gone on about a mile before it could be stopped. We told the driver to back the train and sent off the stretcher bearers and the doctor and waited for the train to shunt. The gradient was a bit steep, so the men had to push the train before we could get moving. It was weird walking back along the line, by the shore of a dismal lake in the half light to find what was left of the unfortunate man. We slid him on a stretcher through the window, moaning but unconscious. The doctor did his best but he died at midnight. The rest of the journey was spent with a dead body. Not a good start.

At Kandalaksha, we were billetted in Sussex Village, named after their first inhabitants, the Royal Sussex Regiment. We were to keep two platoons in the village, mine and Eastman's, whilst Bramall's and Beazley's platoons were to occupy huts along the coast. The object was to have outposts in the direction of the Finnish border, about sixty miles away to the west. Later in the week I left the village by train to go to Kem to draw money. While I was there, I met Colonel Kitcat, who seemed to be very active and enterprising. I arrived back at Kandalaksha with a haversack full of roubles and 190 woollen jackets for the officers and men. Within a couple of days we heard a rumour that General Rawlinson had declared his plan of action. With two other regular battalions, we were to force our way over 250 miles to Petrograd. Although we didn't really know what was ahead we were prepared to fight. We really believed that one good British battalion was worth more than ten Bolshevik battalions.

We arrived in Med-Gora on 28 August. The camp was in delightful surroundings overlooking Lake Onega on which, we heard, the Bolo's (i.e. Bolsheviks) had a destroyer. We tested the Lewis guns at the rear of the camp and on 30 August loaded supplies and set out for Kapaselga. About four of us sat on the edge of the truck with our feet dangling, singing popular songs. On arriving at Kapaselga we each unrolled our valise and slept.

The next morning I went to our battalion headquarters and saw Hanson who told me that in their attack on Koikori, the night of 29 August, the Portsmouth Company had failed to reach their objective. They had met with concentrated machine-gun fire from well prepared positions, defended by tough, very experienced Red Finns and had lost three killed and eighteen wounded, including Colonel Kitcat. They had retreated leaving much of their gear behind. The next morning we left for Svyatnavolok. About sixty men, chiefly mine and Eastman's, bivouacked on the Tivdiya side of Lake Lijmozero, the remainder were on the Kapaselga side. We left there and marched to another lake which we rowed across and then marched to Svyatnavolok.

On 2 September we practised wood fighting under Major Williams and the next day with my platoon we formed the advance guard. Our packs were left at Svyatnavolok and we only took one blanket, waterproof sheet and a haversack ration of bully beef and biscuits (with short intervals we were on this diet until 19 September – we craved sugar). We had been told the enemy might lie up either side of the track so our rate of advance was only one mile per hour because the bush had to be searched for about fifty yards on each side. Bramall's platoon patrolled for two versts (a verst is about two-thirds of a mile or 1200 yards) on the road to Koikori. The following day two aeroplanes bombed the Bolo (Bolshevik) position and twenty minutes later a Bolo soldier gave himself up. He had no boots, socks or rifle. He said that other Bolos wished to give themselves up. Captain Watts then took two sections up, but the enemy changed their minds and fired at them with machine-guns. On 7 September we were relieved of our outposts by Serbians. They were very smart and very professional soldiers. One of their men was killed by chance by an 'over'. They were outraged and staged an unauthorised attack on the enemy to teach them a lesson. We practised our attack and planned out how we were to take Koikori. We left at noon for the 12 Verst post. In Russia, the road is marked every verst with a post to indicate the distance to the next village or town. When we arrived we relieved 'C' Company and rested knowing that we formed the first wave of the attack the next day.

I was given a Very pistol and cartridges which were to be fired as signals to the howitzers to increase the rate of fire, or to increase the range. At about 6pm a Bolo patrol threw grenades and fired at us – a little taster of what was to come. In 'B' Company we heard that the men were anxious that the officers should not try to win any medals. They feared that they might do something rash when in action and that their men might become unnecessary casualties. But of course they accepted that the officers would take the same risks as the men.

At 8am the next day we left 12 Verst post and marched to 15½ Verst post where I found Beazley was sick and his platoon, which had been sent out on patrol, was engaged with enemy patrols. The 'overs' from the Bolsheviks hit the trees above our heads. On arrival at 15½ post, we turned to the left along a small path which led round the Koikori side of a small lake. At 11.45 Major Barnby came to my platoon and told me to increase speed. Our 4.5-inch howitzers were firing over our heads. At about 12 noon the Russian guide, a machine-gun officer, and myself climbed a small hill from the top of which we could see Koikori's church. We could not see the river but there was a small ridge in front of us at a distance of about 150 yards. We heard a couple of the enemy close to us, talking, so I went back and fetched up a section of my platoon to clear the hill. In the meantime the guide had disappeared. I called two machine-guns to cover my platoon and fetched a section of Beazley's platoon. I then returned to the top of the hill where I found the machine-guns ready for action. Nearby were Major Barnby and the Machine-Gun Corps officer. One of our guns then opened on the trenches near the church, while I tried to see any of the enemy through glasses. None were visible, but they replied with rifle fire hitting a M G Sergeant in the stomach. Major Barnby gave me orders to take my platoon through the undergrowth, round the base of the hill. While this was being done I told Bramall to bring up his platoon onto my right and to advance in the direction of some hayricks to the right of the church. I then went down through the bush and passed the word back for the Platoon Scouts. One appeared and, without waiting for the remainder, we advanced to the hedge on the left. There we broke a hole through at the bottom and I saw through my glasses the sangars (breastworks) to my front. I had a machine-gun sent up and opened fire. I then sent my platoon through to line the hedge on the enemy side. At the same time two scouts cleared the sangars with bombs. The platoon then advanced in extended line two yards apart to the ridge and occupied it. The Bolo were now fighting back strongly and we were being fired on by a machine-gun from the right and snipers from the front and left.

The men on the crest then began to shout to the hill for our men there to cease fire as they were hitting my platoon. I had lost quite a few wounded, but they were still firing from the hill so I drew my revolver and went up and shouted, 'Marines, stop fighting'.

No one answered, but I was suddenly shot at and realised the enemy had gained possession of the hill behind us or that they had been there already prepared. I ran back to find that Major Barnby was wounded, and not pleased to hear my news. Captain Watts was also there. Realising we were in a difficult position, Barnby ordered the company to retire. I passed the order to Bramall on the right and shouted and blew my whistle to the men on my left. Taking the men with me, I retired to the left of the hill back to the woods. I had had nine casualties, five of whom were killed, most of them in the last half hour of the attack.

Before this battle had started we had been led to this position by a Russian guide, but now he was nowhere to be seen, though it was later reported he had been seen in the village. Many of my men had been shot in the back even though we were facing the enemy. My servant, Private Davey, was killed in this way. He had been with me for four years. We had simply been betrayed by the guide.

As I left the field I noted that the time was 2.30. We had been in action for two and a half hours.

I did my best to reorganise the company and manned outposts on the Koi–Svy road at about 15½ post. I went off to get orders and, on my return, found the company collected on the road, looking very down. On asking why they had left their positions they informed me that they had been ordered by Major Strover, of the Machine-Gun Corps, to 'Get the hell out of it' as they were not needed and that he would find someone 'who was some use to man the positions'.

I was told that one man had been seized and kicked down the road for no specific offence. When I heard this I was extremely angry and went to Major Strover to give him my account of what had happened and to ask him to convey his orders for my men through me. He told me that those who did not want to fight would be marched back with Major Laing to 12 Verst post.

At 12 Verst post the next morning Major Laing addressed 'B' and 'C' Companies and asked for volunteers for the outpost line. About sixteen men and NCOs volunteered from 'B' Company and about three from 'C' Company. The rest refused. These numbers were insufficient to man the posts. Major Laing then ordered me to accompany him to the report centre, which I did with Lieutenant Bramall. On my return to my company, I was told that about 56 men had left for Svyatnavolok. I reported this to Major Laing who ordered a cyclist to be sent after them to tell them they would be fired on if they attempted to enter Svyatnavolok. Thankfully this didn't happen. I was then sent alone to Svyatnavolok to take charge of the men who had marched back.

When I arrived I found them quite glad to see me and friendly. As there were no NCOs, I ordered them to fall in at 8am the next day. When they mustered, I told them that they would be court-martialled and could be shot. They did not believe this, and said that several parties of Marines who had been sent to *Glory III* had burnt their rifles and that nothing had happened to them.

The following day at 8am I found the men correctly fallen in, dressed, clean and standing to attention. I took down their names and issued rations.

Later, a stretcher party arrived carrying the body of Captain Burton, covered with a blanket. He was buried out at Svyatnavolok and the only mourners were a few old Russian women and myself. He had been adjutant of the battalion and had been shot in a sniping duel with one of the enemy. He was very brave and cheerful. But sniping duels were not his job.

On 11 September the remainder of 'B' Company arrived at Svyatnavolok and the 53 men rejoined their sub-units. As the senior subaltern of 'B' Company I was in command.

A few days after our arrival in Murmansk, all the battalion officers were summoned to Force Headquarters and were addressed by, I think, General Rawlinson. He told us what he thought of us, saying that there were no bad men, only bad officers and that the Commanding Officer had the main responsibility. Ninety-three men were court-martialled. Colonel Kitcat, who had recovered from his wound, told us that as Commanding Officer he accepted the main responsibility. A few days later the battalion was drawn up in a hollow square, with the men who had been court-martialled. The Commanding Officer read out the charge against them – and the punishment. Thirteen had been sentenced to death. I watched the faces of the men and saw that they merely looked bashful, not shocked. The 53 men of my Company were among those sentenced.

Captain Watts was also tried by Field General Court-Martial. He asked me to be his Prisoner's Friend (to defend him). He was charged with cowardice and for 'using words calculated to create alarm and despondency in that he did say "The whole bloody company is lost" "or words to that effect"'. Surgeon Commander Wilkinson spoke on Watts' behalf and told of his wounds at Gallipoli, of a severe fall in 1915, and that he had recently suffered an accident on his cycle and had fallen, cracking the back of his head. But it was all in vain, he was found not guilty of cowardice, but guilty of the second charge and cashiered. With some difficulty we found him a suit of plain clothes and he was sent home in a collier.

We had an uneventful passage to Glasgow where we boarded a special train and eventually arrived at Chatham station. An orderly met us with a message from the adjutant asking us to wait until the Divisional Band arrived to play us back to barracks. I felt that we would never be forgiven if we allowed ourselves to be played back in triumph, so I ordered the company to fall in quickly and reached barracks while the band was still getting ready to leave. I then reported to the Commandant, Colonel Graham. No news of our ignominious disaster had reached him. As my story unfolded, he was overcome. His tears made dark, pink spots on his pad of blotting paper.

The battalion was quickly disbanded and its members drafted away to various ships and establishments in ones and twos. It was feared they might start another mutiny if left together.

When the Field General Court-Martial was held in Murmansk, one of the accused was in the hospital ship. When he recovered he was tried by District Court-Martial in Chatham on the same charges as the others. He was found not guilty. This complicated matters still further and threw doubt on the validity of the Field General Court-Martial. On 22 December the Conservative MP, Lieutenant Kenworthy, asked in Parliament if Walter Long, the

First Lord of the Admiralty, was in a position to announce the decisions of the Admiralty in respect of the Marines held in prison. Long first praised the qualities of the Royal Marines throughout the war and announced that those sentenced to death would have their sentence reduced in twelve cases to one year and one for two years. Twenty men had their five-year sentence reduced to six months and fifty-one sentenced to two years would be released after six months. Two under the age of nineteen had their sentence reduced to six months, and six others under age were released.

Colonel Graham sent for me and officially informed me that I had incurred their Lordships' severe displeasure – i.e. the Lords of the Admiralty. I asked to be court-martialled but this was refused. The Brigade Major later told me that it was not a bad thing for a young officer to receive their Lordships' severe displeasure because it would get his name known. When I left the Marines many years later, it was as a Brigadier.

We had been ill-prepared for our attack on Koikori. Few officers and certainly none of the junior officers had any experience fighting in these circumstances. Our time had been at sea. We had thought that we were to act as a relieving force, while the evacuation of other battalions took place. In the subsequent court-martial it was obvious that the NCOs and men had lost faith in their officers. On the disbandment of the 6th Battalion, no further battalion took up the number six.

Lieutenant-Colonel Arthur de Winton Kitcat

Royal Marine Light Infantry

Lieutenant-Colonel Arthur de Winton Kitcat was the Commanding Officer of the newly formed 6th Battalion Royal Marine Light Infantry. This is his letter, published for the first time, to Brigadier-General Charles Trotman, the Colonel Commandant

of Royal Marines, Portsmouth. He wrote this letter while on an
ambulance train on 3 November 1919.

Ambulance Train
3.XI.19

My dear General

Things moved rapidly after I posted my last letter to you.

Then all prospects seemed very bright and rosy and now here I am a very chastened and humiliated officer on my way back to Murmansk with a bullet wound in my left foot.

I posted my last letter at Kem. Within a day or two I got orders to follow 'C' Company with my Battalion headquarters and 'B' Company to Kapaselga. We arrived on Thursday 21st. At Medvyeja Gora the Brigade headquarters we stopped for an hour or two. The remains of the Royal Marine Artillery Company were there. General Rawlinson was also there but left that afternoon.

Brigadier General Price was engaged in a conference so I did not see him. It was 8pm before we reached Kapaselga. I was to take over the command of the sector (No.2).

The next morning I went round two defences with him. They were very extended but he had got wire up along the whole front except at the north side of the village. It took us over two hours to walk around. When we got back I found a message from Brigade headquarters to say that I was to be ready to move our Company away the following day for some special duty and that a General Staff Officer would come to my headquarters that afternoon. The GSO was a Lieutenant-Colonel of Guards who had come out on Rawlinson's staff – a very capable, nice fellow. He explained that the duty was to be an attack against a neighbouring village and preliminary to that we were to move to a certain village named Tyvidia in our occupation where a further conference would be held on Sunday.

Please forgive pencil but my pen has run dry and I cannot get any ink at present.

Accordingly, to continue my story, the next morning we commenced the move. This entailed a march of some four or five miles to a lake side. Here an argosy of boats was gathered to take us over. It was a pretty sight. The boats were very rough, something like whalers. They were mostly pulled by women, young and old. The men all thoroughly enjoyed it and so did we officers.

It was 'C' Company (Portsmouth) I was taking. I saw Laing tumble into a boat manned by two quite presentable lasses. He himself took the fore and aft oar and looked a suitable Viking.

Each boat accommodated four to six men according to the amount of baggage in addition to the crew. There were some thirty odd boats to convey the two platoons. The other two platoons and two field guns were to follow the next day. It was a long pull across the lake – some eight miles. I suppose we arrived at the other side somewhere about 1.30 and then we halted for dinner. No transport had arrived to meet us. The village we were bound for was a mile or two away.

Williamson, Burton and I went on ahead after our lunch. It was late that night before all the baggage got transported with a good deal of ammunition. A young Captain of 11/Middlesex was in command at the village Tyvidia. He is a capable, energetic and young fellow but had been rather harassed recently by the Bolo. Under him was another very capable fellow named Small – not a regular officer but just the man to deal with the Bolo. He was in command of a Company of partisans and some splendid work he has done with them.

Our arrival bucked them up considerably. The men were provided with splendid quarters here. It was such a very pretty village with a fine trout stream running through it.

Next morning the General Staff Officer arrived by sea plane. The result of the conference was that our objective was changed to another village called Koikori.

This entailed a further move of the force to another village for starting point by name Svyatanavolok.

Officer in Charge, a Major Williamson, was present at the conference. It was decided that I should go to the village with him that afternoon and Williamson came too.

This entailed a march of about five miles through forest by one of the awful tracks. It was a very pleasant walk more or less. These woods are well stocked with game, Capercailzie etc. This brought us to the side of another lake where there were boats to meet us. Laing and one of his platoons came with us. The other platoon conveyed one of the guns by another route entailing a longer water journey. It was six miles straight across this lake.

The village stood about a mile from the landing places on a rise and the view from it was beautiful. This country all about is lovely and what a place to spend a holiday in peace time, with fishing and shooting to one's heart's content! Williamson and I were billeted in the priest's house – his drawing-room. It was very clean and nice and the people were very nice too.

In spite of its cleanliness I made the acquaintance of the first Russian bug there! Fortunately I discovered him before he had discovered me! He was a very fine specimen. Ugh!

It took some time to collect the Company and baggage at this village and it was not until Thursday morning early that the last party got over. The attack was to take place on Wednesday morning.

The column paraded in time to move off from the village at midnight.

We got off all right and nothing occurred on the march until we reached a point eight miles on where we had arranged to halt for an hour. I was feeling rather sleepy and we were just about to halt when suddenly a burst of rifle fire broke out in front. Everyone instantly dived, myself among them, for cover in an open wood. Presently somewhat wild firing was opened up through the column but that was soon stopped. I then moved up to front and the account there was that the firing was opened from some 200–300 yards further on and that four men had been seen making off and had got away. No one was hit in the front, but one Serb at the rear of the column was mortally hit and died that day. This shot could not have come from the party in front as the Serbs were in dead ground from it. I supposed that an isolated Bolo had fired it from a spot further forward on our flank. Then appeared 'B' Company, a shot or two fired from both flanks but the echoes in the wood made it difficult to be sure. We moved forward again and presently found the position the Bolo had fired from.

It was just an outpost group with lying cover provided. The Bolo left various odds and ends behind him, some wallets with paper, food and blankets.

We remained here about half an hour and then pushed on. There was a road junction and I think we stopped in order to get a party of partisans posted on the road which joined ours.

Koikori was twenty versts from the village we started from.

We saw or heard nothing more of the Bolo until we got about one verst from Koikori.

At about two versts from that village is a ridge. From this ridge the road runs along a projection from the ridge and then makes a turn to the right and runs down hill to the village. Shortly before reaching this ridge I had gone on ahead to reconnoitre. Laing was with me and Burton. When we reached the bend in the road I mentioned I saw below and near the church, which was very prominent and well clear of the village, some Bolo trenches. I pointed them out to Laing who was taking note of these when, biff, up came a burst of machine-gun fire. So evidently the Bolo were expecting us. I had seen a few men leisurely getting into one of the trenches.

The trenches were some 500 feet away from us and some 50 feet below. On our right was some cultivated ground for about 200yds to the wood. We very soon began to get some attention from the wood. Also some firing from further away on our left.

Then I tried to think what I ought to do and found I couldn't think at all.

I felt it was foolish to remain in this road and yet couldn't bring myself to give the order to withdraw from it. There was some extraordinary reluctance to do so.

There was the ridge some 200–300ft behind which provided an excellent point of assembly. Then a subaltern who commanded the M.I made suggestions. His advice was either to go into the wood or push down the ridge on our left where the ground was more or less open. I felt miserably undecided. If I had only had strength of mind to order Laing to form up his Company to rear of the ridge this could have given me time for quiet thought. The Bolo was expecting us so there was no particular hurry. From this position I could have put in a strong attack either on its left or through the wood on the right. Further I might have given the men time for rest and food before moving. It makes me sick to think of what did happen.

I weakly agreed to the platoons being moved out to our left and they pushed in an attack on the side of the church. The young officer helped very ably in this. The advance got on unopposed for a short time and then came under a heavy burst of machine-gun and rifle fire. The men made a spirited reply but the advance was held up. An officer got badly hit then through the left lung. I was afraid he was killed but I hope he will recover all right now. I went forward with this attack and things were pretty warm.

We made very little progress after this and then the Bolo fire ceased almost entirely. There were a few snipers making themselves unpleasant, on both flanks and they appeared to be working back. At about 11.15 I went back a little to the men for another push and it was while I was doing this I got a shot through my left foot. Burton was with me and applied first aid very skilfully. He sent word to Williamson, although I was out of action – I felt that this attack on our left was futile so sent word to Burton to withdraw. I met Williamson later on and told him. He proceeded with the withdrawal and returned right away back to Svyatanavolok.

Well that is the pitiful story. I will draw a rough map to show things clearer.

I have been given such an opportunity as has seldom fallen to the luck of anyone.

Our programme was to take Koikori and burn it. I ought to have succeeded in this without difficulty. I can now see that my best course would have been to have pushed through the wood. I should probably then have effected every object without a casualty. As it was we had 4 killed and 15 wounded.

I did not think that I could have made such a hopeless mess of things. I suppose I was suffering from 'wind up' but I did not realise it.

One thing stands out perfectly clear is that I am not fit to command troops either in the field or out of it.

I feel I ought to be court-martialled and at least cashiered but if I am to be spared that humiliation I must at least retire from the service. I have served so badly. Of course this failure acted badly on the morale of the men. Brigadier-General Price told me that the Company had got out of hand and that he was going over by sea plane to enquire into the matter. The Chatham Company was arriving that day or had already moved and I hope they will have restored the Portsmouth Company to a better outlook on things. They were all in splendid spirits before that day and seemed cheerful enough even after it.

We have now arrived at Murmansk and I understand that a hospital ship is due to leave for England on 17th. I expect I shall be coming home in her.

I will come round to the RMO in case you should care to see me.

I hope soon to hear good news of the doings of the 6th RM. I believe that Chatham, Portsmouth and Plymouth Companies are all assembled at Svyatanavolok.

Yours sincerely

(signed) A de W Kitcat.

Note: Colonel Kitcat, as part of the administrative action following the mutiny, was placed on the Half-Pay List.

Captain Thomas Jameson

Royal Marine Light Infantry

In 1918 I was serving on *HMS Kent*, a County Class armoured cruiser. She and her sister ship, *HMS Suffolk*, were 9,800 tons and were distinguished by their three tremendous funnels and bare appearance. In June 1918 we sailed from Plymouth destined to relieve *Suffolk* which was lying at Vladivostok, but by the time *Kent* reached Hong Kong she needed extensive repairs to her engines. We did not reach Vladivostok until 3 January 1919.

During this time Russia was in the grip of civil war, her forces divided between the Bolsheviks, or Reds, and the Mensheviks or Whites, and *HMS Suffolk*, along with other ships of the Allies, was keeping watch on the gradual move eastwards of Bolshevik influence.

In 1918 the Allies had hoped to persuade the Bolsheviks to permit Allied troops to land in Russia. When these efforts proved unfruitful, secret negotiations were started with the Whites. In April the Japanese had landed troops at Vladivostok to extend their power and influence in the Far East. Additional British, French and American troops landed in Murmansk whilst American, British, Japanese, French and Italian troops entered Vladivostok.

During the war Czech soldiers, who formed an unwilling part of the Austrian-Hungarian Army, allowed themselves to fall into Russian hands and these now provided the nucleus of a Czech Legion which was organised to fight on the Allied side. This numbered about 40,000 men and the Soviet government agreed to allow them to transfer to the Allied western front via Vladivostok, but this was opposed by Trotsky who ordered local Bolshevik authorities to disarm them. The attempt failed and the Czechs turned against the Soviet government, routing the Bolsheviks in the cities and the areas along the Trans-Siberian Railway.

During this period the Legion was strengthened by sizeable numbers of Czechs and Slovaks who had been exiled in Russia before the war and then recruited for service into Russian formations until freed by the Russian capitulation. By July 1918 the Czechs numbered over 70,000 and they not only took part in the fighting west of the Ural mountains but occupied and controlled the railway as far east as Irkutsk.

Anti-Bolshevik groups on the eastern side of the Urals formed a government at Omsk with Admiral Kolchak as its head. Allied recognition was given to Kolchak and, at the beginning of 1919, White forces were being supplied with quantities of war material varying from arms and ammunition to British service uniforms.

Kolchak's Omsk government ruled from Lake Baikal almost to the Volga, about half of Russia. In the south Denikin's White Army was preparing another offensive whilst, in the Ukraine, a joint Franco-Ukrainian formation was planning operations against the Reds in that area. In the north-west General Yudenich, with British naval support, was preparing to advance on Petrograd. On the eastern front Kolchak directed most of his forces towards the north-west in the effort to link with the White troops around Archangel.

In the autumn of 1918, in response to an appeal by the White Russians, who were extremely short of artillery, a small detachment of Royal Marines, with one 6-inch gun and four 12-pounders, were landed from *Suffolk* and mounted on platform trucks for service on the railway between Omsk and Ufa. They proceeded to the Ussuri Front where the 6-inch gun assisted the Czechs in driving the Bolsheviks westward. This supporting role came to a halt at the end of November when, owing to the extreme cold, the recoil cylinder of the gun froze up and further fighting became impossible. Russian guns using oil in their recoil cylinders froze up on the same day.

This Allied detachment withdrew to Omsk, and because they were suffering from extreme cold and poor food, the Admiralty ordered their return to Vladivostok at the end of March 1919. Meanwhile it was decided to allow the officers of the Royal Marine detachment to remain as a Naval Mission. Their role was to assist Admiral Kolchak in forming a Russian Naval flotilla to operate on the River Kama as soon as the ice cleared and navigation became possible.

This was the situation when we reached Vladivostok in January 1919. On our approach we had experienced severe gales and the ever-increasing cold caused icicles to hang from yards, rigging and the sea boats. Entering the Gulf of Peter the Great in the wake of an icebreaker and in a snow storm, we berthed below the town between a Japanese battleship, the *Mikasa*, and an American cruiser. Onlookers described our arrival as most picturesque and worthy of a place in an exhibition of Christmas cards!

This extreme cold was a new experience to most of us and its effect on everyday routine was soon to be seen. The guard and band paraded on the quarterdeck to salute the American cruiser, *Brooklyn*. The arms drill was faultless but the only sound we could hear from the band was the drums – all wind instruments froze up after the first few notes. This appealed to the Americans' sense of humour and we learned our lesson.

In February Captain Wolfe-Murray, the head of the Naval Mission assisting Admiral Kolchak, visited HMS *Kent*. He proposed that the guns from HMS *Suffolk*, which had been in service on the railway, should be transferred to vessels on the Kama River and become an integral part of the Russian Naval flotilla to be formed at Perm. The Admiralty would approve this scheme if sufficient volunteers from the Royal Marines serving on HMS *Kent* were forthcoming. Each member of the RM detachment was asked if he would volunteer for this expedition to Siberia. In outlining the expedition due prominence was given to the following points:-

Kent was due to be relieved soon by HMS *Carlisle*. We would be involved in Civil War. The vast country we would enter was still in the grip of the Siberian winter (35° below zero) with famine, disease and the language difficulty being only a few of the problems which we knew we would encounter. Our base would be Vladivostok and the theatre of operations was likely to be in European Russia, west of the Ural Mountains, over 4,000 miles away from Vladivostok.

Out of a total of 64 NCOs and Privates, 63 volunteered. The odd man out was in cells and had no vote. Whatever prompted so many to volunteer for further active service under these conditions, it showed that the spirit of adventure was not lacking. But we little thought that we would travel some 10,000 miles before seeing Vladivostok again!

The strength of this small force was based upon manning the 6-inch gun and the four 12-pounders and consisted of one Captain Royal Marine Light Infantry (RMLI), one Lieutenant (Mate) RN, one Gunner (WO) RN, seven NCOs RMLI, twenty-two Privates RMLI, one PO Armourer RN, one Sick Berth Attendant RN, and one Surgeon RNVR.

The 6-inch gun required a crew of ten whereas each 12-pounder gun was manned by six men including the Captain of the gun's crew. To complete the 6-inch guns crew, and owing to the distance from magazine to gun, three Russians were trained and included in the crew.

The main preparations for the expedition included the provision of suitable winter clothing from the Canadian Forces who had opened an Ordnance Depot at Vladivostok. All members of the detachment were supplied with a complete kit including shoe-pack boots, breeches, lumber jacket, a thick sheepskin lined waterproof coat and musquash fur cap with ear flaps. This excellent equipment gave a significant boost to morale as well as comfort in facing the arctic conditions prevailing in Siberia at this time.

We decided to carry two months iron rations and, by an all-round subscription, a quantity of luxury food from the ship's canteen. It was necessary to estimate future needs beyond immediate comforts and to provide against infection and sickness which we knew were only too prevalent in that country. Hygiene and sanitation were very limited under the arctic conditions, and we carried twice the weight of our food stuffs in disinfectant. In the days to come we soon discovered that this precaution had been wise.

The next problem was to find an interpreter and in this we were most fortunate to obtain Lieutenant Ewing.

Born of an English father and Italian mother, he was educated in Paris and London where he qualified as a barrister and, when war broke out, he was working in Russia. He endeavoured to join the British Forces but failed to pass medically on account of bad eyesight. He decided to serve with the Russians and, through the influence of the Tsarina, he was appointed as a Cadet to the Guards Division of the Russian Navy and soon obtained a Commission. He spoke several languages fluently. Approval was obtained from the Admiralty accepting him as an Interpreter with the rank, pay and allowances of a Lieutenant, Royal Navy. He proved himself invaluable in every way throughout the expedition and we were most fortunate to have him with us. After the expedition returned to Vladivostok I managed to have him appointed to General Knox's staff but I later learned that he had been captured by the Bolsheviks at Nijnuidinsk in February 1920 and I fear they would not have hesitated to take his life.

Our detachment travelled in the express train leaving Vladivostok at 10pm on 6 April 1919. We were given sleepers and with meals served in a restaurant car we were reasonably comfortable.

The single track meant that trains had to travel by sections in both directions and consequently stops at the end of each section were usually of unknown duration. It was inadvisable to move far from the train as little or no warning signalled its departure.

Travelling to Omsk in the express (4,500 miles) was full of interest and we saw evidence of Bolshevik activity almost daily. Twice the railway had been cut by raiding Red bands wrecking trains and shortly after passing Harbin (in Manchuria) we saw a train which had been de-railed and lay at the bottom of the valley. After this our train was preceded by an engine and truck carrying spare rails and travelling about a mile ahead of us.

The main railway station consisted of a station house and some twenty parallel tracks, two of which provided for trains moving east and west. The remaining tracks were completely filled with wagons of every variety, mostly tarplushkas (cattle wagons in England) and each one was filled to capacity. Troops lived in some of them but the majority were occupied by whole families and it was quite obvious that they had existed there throughout the winter. It is difficult to describe the utter filth and squalor that existed in those stationary wagons.

The tracks were about twelve feet apart. The occupants of each wagon existed without a water supply or any means of sanitation other than a hole cut in the floor and for cooking and warmth a small stove in the middle of the wagon. These incredible conditions made one realise how crude these wretched people had become and wonder what would happen when the spring came and thaw set in.

We were glad to leave Omsk on 26 April and to continue our journey to Perm, something over 1,000 miles to the west. The line ran through Ekaterinburg where some of us had an opportunity to visit the opera which provided a very welcome interlude. On the way back to the station we passed the house where the Imperial family had been so barbarously murdered on 16 July 1918. It was surrounded by a very thick double palisade of high stakes completely blocking it off from the road which ran above it.

Crossing the Ural mountains we came into European Russia, arriving at Perm, a large town on the Kama River, on 28 April. This was the end of our journey as far as the railway was concerned. Perm had been recaptured from the Reds by the Czechs only a few months previously, but not before the peasantry had experienced the ruthless brutality of the Bolshevik regime. The bodies of the many who suffered death were disposed of through holes in the ice, as we were to realise when the thaw set in. It was during our first night at Perm that a sudden thunderous roar awoke us and we were somewhat alarmed until we learned that it was the ice, about 3 feet thick, breaking up. The weather became noticeably warmer and the ice broke up and moved away in about forty-eight hours.

I soon made contact with the headquarters of the Kama River flotilla where I met Admiral Smirnoff and some of his staff officers. They were busy converting river tugs and barges into fighting vessels. I was told that we would be given a Kama tug which normally had towed barges and rafts between Perm and the Caspian port of Astrakhan, and a barge on which we were to mount our 6-inch gun. Both vessels were to be brought to a position close to the railway to facilitate the transfer of the guns from the wagons on which they had been mounted.

The Kama River flotilla was to consist of three fighting Divisions, the 1st and 3rd Divisions to be prepared at Perm and the 2nd Division at Ufa on a tributary of the Kama River three hundred miles to the south. Each Division was to be composed of six fighting ships carrying 3-inch or 4.7-inch guns and four machine-guns. One ship mounted with AA guns was allocated to each Division as well as a barge on which were mounted one or two 6-inch guns, minelayers and auxiliary tugs. In addition each Division had its own Base Ship, a repair ship, barges to carry fuel, kite balloons, ammunition and other stores.

The preparation of these vessels was a formidable task owing to lack of material and a great amount of improvisation had to be resorted to, especially in converting field pieces into naval guns. It was at this stage that I met Commander Vadim Makarov, son of the Admiral who was C-in-C of the Russian fleet in the Russo-Japanese war. He spoke excellent English and had served with distinction as commander of a destroyer co-operating with the British Fleet.

By 1 May the ice had practically all disappeared. The thawing of the side streams caused the river level to rise appreciably and added to our difficulties when we came to mounting the 6-inch gun on the immense barge. The unit allotted to us was a fast oil- or wood-burning tug and both vessels were detailed to the 3rd Division commanded by Captain Fiersdosiff.

We named the Gunboat *Kent* and the barge *Suffolk* after the parent ships carrying the SNO's flag at Vladivostok. The former measured 170 feet long and 40 feet wide which included the paddles on each side which were eight feet wide. The barge, towed by a tug, was so large that the 6-inch gun appeared as a mere spot in the photograph. The two vessels were within easy reach of the Motovilska factory where railway engines were built and repaired and which was now used to make the naval gun mountings for the gunboats.

So far the ships had only had their decks strengthened by means of props, and a great deal of work had to be done before we could become fit for operations. To add to our problems we had not been informed by the British Naval Mission that the pedestals of the 12-pounder guns had been removed to enable these guns to have overhead cover on the railway trucks. These pedestals had been disposed of somewhere in Siberia and the gunlayers were to fire the guns from the kneeling position.

So, in addition to building platforms across the *Kent* fore and aft, it was necessary to make pedestals to support the gun cradles and fix to the platforms. After considerable discussion, Makarov and the senior Engineer Officer, Commander Berg, decided that wooden pedestals could be made at the factory. This was done and consisted of five discs, each 5 " thick and about 2 feet in diameter, providing a 25" pedestal for each of the four guns. The work was accomplished in a remarkably short time, but the method of construction created a serious problem when they came to be positioned between gun cradle and platform. The Russians, in building the pedestals, placed one disc on top of the other, fastening it down with a number of strong screws which were positioned indiscriminately. The base of each cradle had 13 holes in its flange through which bolts would secure it to the pedestal; but in this instance it would be necessary to provide bolts over 4 feet long which would pass through the wooden pedestals, through the three balks of wood laid across the deck for a platform, and then through the deck and a metal plate against which the securing screws were to fit. Our Russian carpenters started to bore the 13 holes in each pedestal but their awls soon struck a metal screw and were broken. A further conference with Makarov and the engineers, and again an improvisation, solved the problem. Blacksmith's furnaces were produced, the bolts made red hot and then hammered down through the wooden pedestals, burning and driving their way past the screws encountered until all four pedestals, the platforms and the deck were able to accept the 13 bolts per gun.

This process resulted in each hole being somewhat wider than the diameter of the bolt, and I could not accept this slack fitting as likely to a hold a gun down firmly when the shock of firing was set up. The Russians agreed and once again the problem was solved. Barrels of resin were supplied from local resources since it was a product extracted from the forests and much used for industrial purposes. By heating this resin and pouring it into the holes as each bolt was driven down and allowed to cool, it was considered that any play between bolt and the enlarged hole would be taken up by the solidified resin.

Even now I demurred and suggested that each gun should be tested by firing on different bearings and elevations and depressions before proceeding to the battle zone. Without hesitation I was given permission to carry out these tests against the hills on the other side of the river, assured that the local inhabitants in that area were of no consequence! We carried out the tests and the improvisations proved remarkably satisfactory as only one bolt appeared to require further strengthening.

While this task of mounting the 12-pounders was taking place, the transferring of the 6-inch gun from the platform wagon on to the barge was being carried out and not without a number of problems not least of which was the lack of a crane powerful enough to lift the seven-ton barrel and the mounting of similar weight. The river was rising over a foot a day, due to the thawing of the tributaries, and only a system of wedging and skidding could be adopted. This manual work was largely carried out by women since all men of military age had been conscripted for Kolchak's Siberski Army. It was, however, accomplished remarkably quickly.

While this work of arming the two ships was in progress many other jobs were in hand, including the making and erecting of two masts in *Kent*. Two tree trunks were floated down to the ship, and Russian carpenters using principally an adze soon created the masts. They not only produced them as efficiently as our Dockyards might have done, but mounted each between two uprights from the deck, fixing the mast with two pins so that by removing the lower pin the mast could be lowered in case we had to move under low or broken bridges.

To convert a tug into a gunboat entails considerable constructional work. Living quarters were required for over 60 crew, since the previous complement was less than half this number, as well as storerooms, magazines and many other things, such as armour plating fixed around gun platforms and wheelhouse. We found that the Russians could supply us with a Vickers Medium Machine-Gun but without any mounting. This provided yet another problem to be solved by improvisation. To do this we modified a rail wagon buffer so that the flange or base could be secured to the deck with the stalk upright and provided with all the mechanical fittings which are found on the upper part of a machine-gun tripod. This improvised mounting was surprisingly efficient and even permitted the gun to be elevated to a greater angle than on a tripod.

The demand for skilled labour was great since so many vessels were striving to complete conversion to fighting ships at the same time and this meant that the detachment had to carry out a large share of the work. It may have been the novelty of constructing their own ship, or an energetic outlet after a long period of inactivity, but everybody put his back into it, and in a short time the *Kent* was ready to proceed downstream and assume her place as a unit of the Kama River Flotilla. Four ships of the 1st Division had commenced their conversion to gunboats earlier and had left Perm so that *Kent* received orders to join the 1st Division temporarily.

On 7 May 1919 we started work at 6am completing the final mounting of the guns, fixing the armour plating to gun platforms and wheelhouse. Then, we proceeded alongside and cleared for taking in oil fuel. The connection did not fit and it was 10.30am before oil was passing into tanks. Next we carried out gun trials, which proved successful.

At 2pm the Naval Mission departed. After taking in 150 rounds per gun at the magazine it was arranged that our gunshields should be taken by another vessel – *Startni* – for fitting later and we moved to the factory to draw stores. Owing to an error this was delayed, but eventually we were ready and, taking *Startni* in tow, we proceeded down the Kama river after a very long and tiring day. We were now on our way to the operational role for which we had come so far, and this evoked a sense of stimulation and excitement in us all.

Everything in Russia seemed so large to us. The river, now swollen by the thaw of tributaries, varied in width from half a mile to two miles, the bridges were immense structures and the barges so vast that even their tillers measured 30 to 40 feet in length.

Enormous stacks of wood cut in three-foot lengths were to be found at intervals for the use of tugs. Shoals on the river bed were a constant hazard even though we only drew 4'6", but fortunately our skipper knew the Kama well.

We passed the large town of Sarapul on 9 May, approximately 300 miles from Perm, and the next day we stopped at Elabouga, coming alongside the Base Ship *Nitalia* (1st Division) after passing Admiral Smirnoff's Flagship, which we saluted with a guard. I then visited the Admiral, who gave me an outline of the operations and dispositions of the Armies which we were supporting.

Admiral Smirnoff had served a considerable period with the British navy and had been awarded the CMG. He spoke perfect English. Before the Revolution he had been Chief of Staff to Admiral Kolchak who then commanded the Black Sea Fleet and when the latter became Supreme Ruler and Commander-in-Chief on the Siberian Front he appointed Admiral Smirnoff as Minister of Marine in the Omsk government.

Our operational roles were twofold. To give support and protection to the armies fighting on land adjacent to the river, covering any units which need to cross from one bank to the other and the engagement and destruction of Red ships.

The *Suffolk* had mounted the 6-inch gun before we left Perm, but during a firing test it was found that the gun failed to run out properly, due to faulty springs. Efforts to strengthen the springs by inserting washers gave improved performance, but the movement was very slow. Spare springs were sought from the parent ship at Vladivostok. Meanwhile *Suffolk* proceeded downstream and arrived at Elabouga on 14 May to be greeted with an attack by two Bolshevik seaplanes. Two of the three bombs dropped straddled *Suffolk* but no damage was sustained. Gunfire from the flotilla was directed against the second seaplane which came down, alighted above the base and surrendered. By this time the first seaplane returned and, after also being subjected to our gunfire, descended and likewise surrendered. Neither plane was damaged and although the reasons given by both pilots differed considerably, it was proved that engine trouble caused the first plane to surrender, while the occupants of the second, seeing their companions alight, mistook our flotilla for their own. The pilots were naval officers and, as such, were regarded as the most ardent Bolsheviks which, without doubt, meant instant execution.

The same day the Bolshevik flotilla made its first appearance west of the confluence of the Kama and Viatka Rivers and opened fire on the guard ship *Gregiasshi* (3rd Division), which returned the fire with her 3-inch guns. However the Bolsheviks easily outranged her and, in a short time, a shell penetrated the *Gregiasshi*'s boiler-room and she was put out of action. Six ships of our flotilla proceeded downstream from Kotlovka and engaged the enemy flotilla, but no satisfactory results were obtained because the high ground commanding the junction of the Viatka and Kama Rivers was strongly fortified by enemy artillery, and also because of the superior range of the enemy's guns, in many cases more than double ours.

The Reds were able to maintain their position. *Kent* followed the Flagship of the 3rd Division and closed towards the enemy but, without range finders and relying on observation, we found we could not cross the target. The enemy's shells on the other hand not only dropped between our ships but reached the Base Ships and the village of Kotlovka. Though the river appeared to provide room for deployment this expanse was caused by the floods and it was necessary to follow the channel of the river when normal. Orders were given to the flotilla to withdraw. *Suffolk* now appeared and opened fire with her 6-inch gun on an enemy battery concealed by a church in the village of Salkolka, putting it out of action, after which she engaged the Red ships causing them to retire downstream.

The Siberian army fighting to the south of the Kama River was now retiring eastwards and great difficulty was experienced in keeping up communications owing to the flooded state of the river, especially over the southern bank. After two attempts the Bolsheviks crossed the Viatka River and compelled the Siberian Army on the northern bank to retire, and consequently the flotilla was ordered to withdraw to Elabouga. The river was now rapidly subsiding and great caution had to be exercised when manoeuvring, especially after dark.

Orders were received for *Kent* to proceed to the Bielaya River, which flowed into the Kama on the south side and some five miles upstream. On 23 May the flotilla moved back to the Kama, and, after completing refuelling we received instructions that the flotilla would return to Elabouga after dark and, as the Bolsheviks were in possession of the south bank, we might expect trouble on the journey down if detected.

Taking all precautions to conceal our movements we proceeded at full speed to Elabouga, arriving there without incident. We later learnt that the despatch of the flotilla to the Bielaya River was intended rather to deceive the enemy than to take part in any operations in that sector, and our return to Elabouga was quite unknown to the Bolsheviks.

Our Intelligence Department informed us that the Red flotilla was to come upstream about noon to give support to their army units advancing on the north side of the Kama river with the object of capturing Elabouga. At 1pm our Guard Ship reported their approach and at 1.30pm the flotilla weighed anchor, and the 3rd Division, followed by the 1st Division and *Suffolk* (seven ships and a barge), proceeded at full speed, *Kent* being third ship of line. The enemy had chosen a good position with a dark background (their ships were painted dark green) at a range of eight versts from Elabouga (approximately five miles), and immediately opened fire on our base. Though under heavy fire our flotilla lost no time in getting within range. Fire was opened by *Kent* at 8,100 yards at the leading enemy ship. We used lyddite★ as the Russian ships only possessed common shell, and we could identify our fall of shot by the yellow colour of the explosion. At first we were short but soon our approach brought us within maximum range, and, laying on the flashes of the enemy guns, effective fire caused the leading ship *Terek* to beach herself in a burning condition. The enemy had eleven ships in action and after their leading ship was lost the remainder sought to turn and proceed downstream. *Kent's* fire was directed at their second ship first by one of her after guns, which could bear by firing over the intervening land on the inside of the river bend, and then by the two foremost guns. Repeated hits by lyddite were scored on her at a range of 4,700 yards. *Roosal*, their Flagship, was also compelled to make for the bank, reaching it in a sinking condition and burning fiercely. Her crew jumped on shore wearing white life-belts and provided an ideal target for our machine-guns.

The rapidity and volume of fire seemed to demoralise the Bolsheviks and, had our ships possessed a superior speed we should have had a better opportunity of routing them still further. Our second ship of the line proceeded alongside *Roosal* and endeavoured to put out the fires and salve her, whilst the 3rd Division Flagship, followed by *Kent*, continued the chase. Rounding the next curve the enemy flotilla disappeared except for one smaller vessel which offered us an easy target and was sunk on the right bank, her crew deserting her.

Captain Fiersdosiff in *Gordi*, and *Kent*, continued downstream, but when the former proceeded around the next bend she came under heavy fire from the enemy and, being badly hit, a shell knocking both foremost guns out of action and damaging her bridge, she turned back upstream signalling *Kent* to form a rearguard. *Kent* turned astern of *Gordi* and with the use of her oil fuel, created an effective smoke screen and engaged the enemy by bursting shrapnel beyond the high ground while both ships retired upstream. The enemy made no attempt to follow. *Suffolk* opened fire from a position of five versts below Elabouga and with her superior range she gave effective support to the flotilla until our ships passed out of sight. During this action *Kent* fired 288 shells

★ An explosive consisting chiefly of fused picric acid, named after Lydd where the first tests were conducted.

and *Suffolk* 42. Neither ship was hit directly but both received minor damage from splinters.

Both *Kent* and *Suffolk* took part in the operations against enemy ground forces, chiefly on the north bank as well as engaging the Bolshevik flotilla when their ships came within range. These engagements were usually sporadic owing to the lack of reliable information, for not only was it difficult to distinguish between friend and foe, but it was evident that the White forces had no cohesive control.

It was hardly surprising that these conscripted and illiterate Siberian peasants, lacking both training and leaders, had little enthusiasm for the cause for which they were fighting. Their rations and clothing were inadequate to the point of destitution, whereas the Bolsheviks through their propaganda promised payment in silver, good conditions and privileges for success in action and this induced many of the White forces, sometimes whole units, to desert to their enemies.

On 29 May Admiral Smirnoff hoisted his flag in *Kent*, the first and only instance of a Russian admiral flying his flag at the top-mast of a British man-of-war! We proceeded downstream to where a minefield was being laid under the protection of the 1st Division.

Reports were now received that enemy ground forces on the south bank had succeeded in reaching the junction of the Bielaya River and the Kama and were endeavouring to capture or destroy some barges at this point. One of these barges was carrying a large amount of oil fuel and its towing tug had made off after letting go the barge anchor. The only available ship of the 3rd Division, *Grosni*, proceeded upstream and reached this barge at the mouth of the Bielaya River about 7pm. The Red troops on the bank opened up a fierce fire with rifles and machine-guns but *Grosni* managed, by going astern, to pass a wire light around the anchor cable and, moving forward, slowly the wire raised the anchor and the barge was towed away. Some casualties were suffered by *Grosni* including her gunnery officer who was killed. It was now decided that all ships should retire to a position north of the Bielaya River and, with *Kent* leading, we reached the mouth of this river shortly after dark. Four large barges were on fire and this enabled the enemy to molest the retirement of the flotilla. From a fifth barge and some buildings on shore they opened up a lively fire. *Kent* covered the passing of the flotilla with her 12-pounder guns and machine-guns. Enemy fire was too high to be effective and only the funnel and masts were hit.

At this time *Suffolk* was engaging enemy targets from positions near the mouth of the Bielaya River, and reports from Army headquarters confirmed that at least one battery had been destroyed. By her bombardment of the village of Dirabigski the Bolsheviks were driven from a strong position commanding a reach of the river through which the flotilla was about to pass.

The 6-inch gun in *Suffolk* was still giving a great deal of trouble and it was necessary after every round to run the gun out again. It was decided to make and fit another box cap to increase the compression on the springs, and *Suffolk* was instructed to proceed to Sarapul, where the work would be done by the repair ship. Sarapul, fifty miles upstream from the mouth of the Bielaya River, was a large town, nine-tenths of it situated on the right bank of the river and spanned below the town by a substantial bridge carried on four piers. Base ships, consisting of several large three-deckered passenger vessels, provided the headquarters, repair ship, and hospital as well as barges for carrying fuel and transporting troops from one bank to the other.

Rations and fuel were supplied to ships as required and as opportunities occurred during operations. The rations consisted mainly of black bread, a loaf usually some eighteen inches across, meat in casks, often bear's meat, which had been packed into the cask with ice and salt before the end of the winter, and potatoes. There was little variation and not infrequently the bread was sour, even moist and green at the centre of the loaf whereas the meat had not always kept edible owing to faulty casks.

My batman visited a small village hoping to find eggs available and managed to exchange a piece of soap, a commodity which had not been seen for many months, for a small bag of white flour. Returning on board he expressed a hope of making us some white bread, but then realised he lacked any yeast. He was not, however, defeated for, at our next meal, a white loaf of bread was put on the table. When asked how he managed to produce such a wonderful loaf he explained that he had used the fermented greenish centre of our ration bread as a substitute for yeast or baking powder. Never did white bread taste better than this loaf!

In a light-hearted moment I decided to have a Commodore's

pennant made by a Russian sailmaker and, assuming the role of the Senior Naval Officer commanding more than one ship, I flew the pennant at the yardarm when we next went into action. The pennant and the order, including specification, I have kept as a memento of a personal and quite unofficial jest!

I then received orders for *Kent* to rejoin the Flotilla at Nikola Berezooka, some twenty-five miles downstream.

Shortly after passing under the Sarapul Bridge, we observed what appeared to be a battery of field artillery digging into position about two miles below the town, and apparently the guns were laid towards Sarapul. It was hard to believe that enemy guns were so close to the town where both White Army headquarters and the Naval command had so recently assumed a Base. On arrival I immediately reported our observations to Admiral Smirnoff and he told me that a report had just been received by wireless (his ship was the only one fitted with radio) to say that Sarapul was being attacked by Bolshevik forces. A conference of Commanding Officers was called, and *Grosni* and *Kent*, the two fastest ships, were ordered to proceed at once and hold the Bridge until the remainder of the Flotilla reached Sarapul.

This situation was a typical example of the utter lack of reliable information and the resultant critical positions in which we found ourselves. *Grosni* and *Kent* reached the Bridge and were relieved to find that the only one span available to the passage of vessels was still open. The other spans had already been blocked or actually broken.

The sun was coming up, an uneasy silence prevailed and though we observed some troops moving, it was deemed prudent to maintain observation only until such time as the rest of the flotilla arrived.

At 5.35am the flotilla, carrying barges and tugs, appeared around the bend below the bridge, the 1st Division engaging enemy artillery on the right bank. At 5.50pm *Grosni* and *Kent* were told to lead the flotilla and all ships to proceed at full speed. Targets were difficult to locate and enemy guns put down barrage fire on point after point upstream into which we ran unavoidably at maximum speed. We opened fire independently at any moving troops or occupied buildings.

Our 12-pounder guns, using lyddite, swung on to targets and at point-blank range maintained a rapid rate of fire especially at targets on the waterfront. I pointed out a field gun firing at us through the back door of a house close to the edge of the water, and a shell blew house and all sky high. Captain Fiersdosiff later told me, 'You used your guns like revolvers and it was a heartening sight'.

The flotilla took approximately one hour to pass the town, and one would have expected heavy casualties running the gauntlet on a comparatively long waterfront, but only one of the gunboats, the *Startni*, immediately astern of *Kent*, was sunk. We turned to pick up survivors but the next ship rendered this assistance. *Kent* was near-missed several times.

This lively operation gave us a sense of some satisfaction since it showed that, though training and efficiency were sadly lacking in the White troops, the Bolshevik forces were not particularly skilful and had let pass a brilliant opportunity of destroying the flotilla. We were fortunate that the one span of the bridge had been completely ignored by the enemy, who were already established within a short gun range. The arrival and entry of the Bolsheviks reflected little praise to the intelligence and fighting units of the Whites and their Army Headquarters set up in Sarapul. The attack was completely unexpected and resulted in a 'sauve qui peut' of the defenders, including the ships then forming the naval base on the river.

The senior NCO of the *Suffolk* experienced this at first hand when he went ashore with his dog for a walk. All the river craft had either gone or were getting under way including *Suffolk* which had left a tug to bring him off and, although she had fired four rifle shots as a signal for his recall, Taylor could not hear them on account of the din in the town. The tug then lay off, but the captain spotted Colour Sergeant Taylor and sent a boat in for him.

No sooner had the boat touched land than a rush was made for it and she was almost swamped by the panic-stricken soldiers. The situation was serious, and Taylor had to threaten this mob by drawing his revolver. To make matters worse, after he had got into the boat, he found that his dog was still on shore so he ordered the boat to put back and get him, and then there was a real row and he threatened to shoot the whole lot of them.

They caught the dog and were away just in time for, as they shoved off, the Reds were fairly close, their cavalry leading four deep. At that moment one of our ships with a 3-inch gun opened fire, which halted their advance and, in the confusion Colour Sergeant Taylor made it back to the ship.

The Base was now established at Galova and the flotilla was employed between Galiani and Galova in giving artillery support to the Army. *Suffolk*, whose gun was now giving less trouble, was kept extremely busy. Galiani changed hands several times but was finally lost to the Reds on 7 June. Between 7 and 10 June *Kent* and *Suffolk* took part in engaging the enemy's infantry and field batteries. These operations were fraught with constant disappointment as our army units seldom took advantage of the effective supporting fire, and it was obvious that their morale was very poor. On 8 June *Suffolk*'s gun caused the Bolsheviks to withdraw into a wood, and, as they emerged on the other side, several of our gunboats opened fire with lyddite and shrapnel, causing a considerable number of casualties.

On 12 June we received an encouraging message of congratulations from Commodore Edwards (*HMS Kent*) who, with General Knox, had received a cable from Admiral Smirnoff commending the efforts of our detachment.

On the same day the *Suffolk*, together with two Russian 6-inch guns mounted on barges, successfully engaged and put out of action three enemy batteries as well as blowing up a large ammunition dump.

When Admiral Kolchak informed the High Commissioner of his recent action in awarding decorations he directed that they should be handed back. This was a disappointment as they would have been a treasured souvenir of this expedition, and especially so when we learnt that Russian awards to British servicemen on the north fronts had been accepted.

British Army units, which had been training with Russians to form an Anglo-Russian Brigade, were withdrawn and returned to England, but no such instructions were received from the Admiralty, so we stayed in action.

The Bolsheviks were obviously concerned about our presence, and in one of their radio reports they stated 'Our Naval manoeuvres on the River Kama are being seriously hampered by the British destroyers'. This flattery at least gave us something to laugh about! Other references were made over the radio as well as in the press and on one occasion a message in English from Moscow was addressed to 'Jack Kent' urging us to discontinue our activities and offering immunity to retribution whilst giving us a safe return to our country.

About this time I was visited by Officers of the Secret Service on the Admiral's staff. At their request I arranged for them to interrogate my Engineer Officer and one of his men, and, at the same time to examine their belongings as they had reason to suspect them of being agents of the Bolsheviks.

In their investigations documents were found in the Mechanic's kit which proved beyond doubt that an early attempt was to be made to destroy the *Kent*. I later heard that the Mechanic had been shot.

Civil warfare always has an insidious effect upon those involved and, with a small force operating in a foreign country far from their base, the lack of security can quickly undermine morale.

The obvious instability of the White forces soon gave rise to rumours of impending disasters, even perhaps a repetition of our experience below Sarapul, and it was important that action should be taken to dispel the doubts and uncertainties. To this end I took steps to obtain more reliable information and also to prevent unauthorised persons from meeting the Russian and British crews. These proved successful and any loss of confidence in our security was soon restored.

The river was now down to normal depth and, as their draught was too great, the larger base ships had gone back to Perm. This also applied to the Bolsheviks and, with little threat from these ships, we were mainly employed supporting the Army and covering the constant transferring of troops and refugees across the river. All villages west of us were evacuating rapidly and a constant stream of droshkies carried the families and their belongings together with cattle and other animals. This is always a sad spectacle and perhaps even more pathetic in a Civil War. The Siberian Army retired further almost daily and the Red forces were rapidly becoming stronger and more confident. Lack of discipline and training was becoming more evident, in fact, the majority of casualties were self-inflicted while desertions were frequent and, at times, wholesale.

Defensive lines were vacated before the enemy made any attack, and the Bolsheviks were quickly gaining access to the wheat country in the Urals which was one of their main objects at this time. The harvest was one of the best for many years and was just ripe when it fell into the hands of the Reds. The weather was becoming very hot, and the mosquitoes, though not of the malaria carrying species, were most troublesome. The food also at this time was of a very inferior quality, but in spite of all this, the health of the detachment was good throughout the expedition.

The situation was obviously deteriorating and I took the opportunity of discussing the situation with Admiral Smirnoff. He agreed that the support we would give to the troops was now of little use and that they really needed more land artillery. I then suggested that we might obtain field mountings for our 12-pounder guns and transfer our services to the operations on land. He agreed and I immediately informed Captain Wolfe-Murray who, in his reply, said that he had wired Vladivostok for the field mountings to be sent to Perm at once. During the following days *Kent* carried out a succession of duties covering the crossing of troops and material to the south bank and acting as guard-ship.

On 18 June I visited a village. The inhabitants were very kindly but they were existing on little more than a small bread ration and tea made from mulberries. They exchanged milk and eggs, such as they had left, for some soft soap and a small bar of washing soap which they had not seen for many months. I recall that I gave an old man a pipe and a tin of tobacco at which he was overjoyed and insisted on giving us a bucket of milk and half a dozen new onions.

We continued to move back upstream passing Okhansk escorting a number of large barges and occasionally stopping to embark civilian refugees who were only too glad to move before falling into Bolshevik hands.

On 20 June we were now only 45 versts from Perm, the weather very hot and no provisions left – the Wardroom had a little black bread but it was green outside and very sour.

The same evening we proceeded in company with 3rd Division to Perm at fifteen versts per hour. At 5am the next day we fuelled ship and embarked ammunition preparatory to proceeding down again if necessary and this gave me the opportunity of visiting the Naval Mission and officers of the British Railway Mission. The situation was very obscure and it was quite impossible to ascertain what was happening at the front which meant that *Suffolk* might be left behind a retreating army and virtually cut off.

At this moment the British Naval Mission decided to move back to Omsk.

Before leaving, Captain Wolfe-Murray delegated to me the

responsibility of withdrawing *Kent* and *Suffolk* should Perm fall to the Reds. I at once visited the Base ship *Mariana* and met the Naval and Military Commanders who left me in no doubt how the situation was deteriorating rapidly. My first concern was for the *Suffolk* and I pointed out how vulnerable she would become if the front suddenly collapsed.

The Russians implored me not to recall her since to do so would further undermine the already demoralised troops on the Perm front.

On 20 June I sought an interview with the Admiral to reach a decision about the withdrawal of *Kent* and *Suffolk*. We agreed that the former should proceed to a point above the Motavileka factory where a jetty ran out which could be used to transfer our guns, ammunition, etc., to our original naval armoured train. She would commence stripping down the armament at once.

The Reds were now approaching Kungur, a large town some seventy miles south of Perm on the main railway line which might fall into their hands within hours. This meant that we would now have to rely on a small single line running east and later south joining the main line at Ekaterinburg, a distance of three hundred miles.

Next day, having received reports of further withdrawals by the White forces, I gave orders that *Suffolk* was to return to Perm forthwith. This decision proved to be fortunate for, on her arrival, I learnt that she had exhausted her ammunition twenty-four hours previously and had not been able to report this situation. She had fired 256 rounds in two days after *Kent* had moved north.

In Perm refugees were moving eastwards by all available means. Over 8,000 carts carrying families and their belongings were passing through the town daily and all trains, now using the northern line, were packed to capacity. As soon as *Suffolk* arrived, the work of dismantling her 6-inch gun began and, as no Russians were available, I was about to send the *Kent*'s crew to assist when all the spare ammunition, some hundreds of rounds, both 6-inch and 12-pounder, arrived in a sinking barge and we had to deal with this without delay. *Suffolk*'s crew, who had had little sleep for forty-eight hours, had to strip down their gun and prepare to get it off the barge, after which it had to be moved across the Motavileka factory to the main line for replacing on its original platform truck.

Since April the river had greatly subsided and, as a result, it was impossible to get the light railway of the factory to run close enough to the barge and it was necessary to build a staging out to the side of the barge so that the small gauge trucks could be moved to meet it at deck level.

The only available crane was not capable of lifting more than five tons whereas the 6-inch gun alone weighed seven tons without the mounting, but we found we could lift and swing one end of the gun at a time and eventually we managed to get the gun on to the two trucks.

With the help of a large contingent of women the gun had to be towed through the works for some considerable distance before reaching an arch crane spanning the railway. During this journey the leading truck fell between the rails and after finding that the available jacks were quite inadequate, we resorted to raising the truck and gun by use of wedges and chocks until the line could be repaired and the journey continued.

Time was exceedingly precious but the 6-inch gun was successfully fixed on to its original truck. While this work was in progress I managed to obtain an engine with which we moved the 6-inch gun to the remainder of our wagons near the *Kent*. This difficult task of disembarking the guns, ammunition and material weighing some 14,000 poods (1 pood = 36 lbs) and then loading them on to the train was carried out almost entirely by the crews of the two vessels.

We were able to obtain two wagons (3rd class with wooden bunks in three tiers) and our small train reached Perm station about 7pm on the same day as *Suffolk* had arrived back from the front.

Kent and *Suffolk* were then sunk by permission of Admiral Smirnoff.

Our problem now was to get our wagons attached to an out-going train and, though this was achieved, no engine was forthcoming.

The British Railway Mission under General Jack was providing the only effective control at Perm station and indeed our escape from this chaotic situation would have been extremely difficult without their energy and assistance. On General Jack's advice we took an armed party to the repair sheds (the Motavileka factory was the Swindon of East Russia) where we persuaded the Russians in charge to allot an engine and crew to our train, and with our armed guard on the footplate it reached and was attached to the train.

The next morning, 29 June, we pulled out of Perm with every wagon filled to overflowing. The town, congested with refugees and wounded, was rapidly showing a loss of control and panic was especially evident at the railway station.

Some three hours after our departure the Reds shelled the town and we heard that they occupied it from the North on the same day.

Travelling was desperately slow and far from comfortable with 37 of us living three deep in two wooden wagons. Early next day the train came to a halt and we discovered that our engine had completely broken down with no possibility of repair. We were 300 miles from Ekaterinburg and would have to cross the Ural mountains before reaching Omsk nearly 1,000 miles away.

The situation called for prompt action, and we decided to obtain sufficient horses to carry us and our so far untouched rations. We would have either to follow the railway east or trek north-west to Archangel where we might join our forces in that area. We were busily occupied in discussing these arrangements when, to our astonishment and not a little relief, we caught sight of an engine coming from the east. This engine, we learnt, had been sent at the instigation of Admiral Smirnoff who had heard of our escape from Perm, but as no further information had reached him he sent this engine to find us.

We reached Omsk without any further incident. There we learnt that the Admiralty had decided to withdraw the Force altogether and orders were received to return to Vladivostok as soon as accommodation on a train became available.

It occurred to me that it would be an advantage if we could avoid taking our guns and ammunition back to Vladivostok. After approaching the Russian Council and ascertaining that they would be glad to take over the guns at an agreed valuation I asked and obtained Admiralty approval for this transaction. It was a relief to be rid of this material especially as I was aware that the cordite might well be in a dangerous condition, after being subjected to temperatures varying from 40° below zero to a high summer heat, but I did not mention this to the Russians.

Whilst waiting for train accommodation I received an invitation from Admiral Smirnoff to dine with him and some of his staff on 28 July at the Aquarium, a restaurant in Omsk. It was an enjoyable meal, served in the garden. Looking back on this farewell party I recall my feelings of regret since it marked the end of my association with the Admiral and his officers. Throughout the operations on the Kama River their friendliness and good comradeship always made us feel that our presence and efforts were appreciated.

Almost as soon as we reached Omsk one of our detachment had to be admitted to hospital and it came as a shock when we learnt that he was suffering from smallpox. Surgeon Lieutenant Joyce had been sent back to Vladivostok whilst we were at Perm and though a relief was on his way to join us, he had not yet arrived. When we received our orders for leaving Omsk this presented a serious problem but on enquiry at the hospital the doctors declared the patient to be no longer dangerously ill and they were not opposed to letting him leave if we wished to take him with us. We gladly accepted the risk, and before he joined the train, we managed to construct a partition across one of our wagons, thus providing a crude form of isolation.

It added a little to the congestion but perhaps our efforts contributed to the fact that no further cases occurred.

Before our departure we were informed that Bolshevik activities were particularly directed against the railways and throughout the journey, some 2,500 miles, we could expect some form of attack, usually by wrecking. We were also told confidentially that a number of wagons of our train contained a large quantity of bullion which was being transferred to the National Bank at Vladivostok. This information, if it became known to the Bolsheviks, would add considerably to their interest in our train. Already one wreck had taken place not many miles ahead of our train resulting in over 250 casualties.

Czech detachments along the railway were most helpful in giving us information and, acting on their advice, we avoided travelling after dark in those districts which were known to be frequented by marauding bands.

The station at Taishet was completely burnt out as a result of a recent fight between a large band of Reds who had seized this section of the line and a Czech armoured train. A little further east we were delayed for several days by the wrecking of a train travelling westwards with, again, a high casualty roll. After passing Irkutsk incidents of train wrecking were more frequent and we had to take further precautions which included the provision of a pilot engine with a truck carrying spare rails for replacement preceding our train. In addition armed look-outs lay on the roofs of some of the wagons when travelling and pickets were posted when the train was stationary.

Our stocks of disinfectant proved invaluable at this time. Typhus was sweeping through Russia and vaccines against this and other diseases were not available. The mortality rate was estimated to be about 96 per cent. Colonel Clarke, Chief Medical Officer on General Knox's staff, contracted typhus but thanks to the skill of a Canadian nurse and a strong physique he was one of the few who survived.

Hospital trains had been organised and were moving typhus victims away from the worst stricken areas. These trains could be identified when they stopped near our train by the discharging of corpses to the side of the railway and we had to maintain a constant watch out for them.

As soon as we became aware of such a train halting near us I at once ordered our men into their wagons and to close all doors and ventilators to prevent mosquitoes reaching them from the vicinity of the typhus train. I would then take a few armed men and visit the stationmaster and demand that the distance between the trains should be increased to at least half a mile. This invariably resulted in some excuse being given which might stimulate a bribe before an engine could be found available. The demand was then repeated and supported by an order to my men to load their rifles. This only occurred on a few occasions but we were not far from our destination and I was determined that no effort should be spared to avoid infection even if it was necessary to resort to a threat of arms. At Harbin cholera was raging, in fact it was estimated that some three hundred people were dying daily, many in the streets. Except for a small party which I took into the town to obtain rations, no man in the detachment was permitted to leave the immediate vicinity of our train.

A few days later we moved on to Vladivostok which we reached on 18 August, 52 days after leaving Perm. It was a relief to feel that we had at last reached our destination and I can recall the surprise and thrill to find the band of the Middlesex Regiment at the station ready to lead us to *HMS Carlisle*. As we approached the ship the lower deck was cleared and we were given an extremely generous welcome by Commodore Carrington in the presence of the ship's company.

Thus ended our expedition. Never before had such a party gone so far (4,350 miles) from its parent ship and we had suffered considerable privations and lost a lot of weight during the long journey, but this was nothing that rest, relaxation and nourishment could not quickly restore.

We reached Portsmouth in November and my detachment marched into Forton Barracks, on *HMS St. Vincent*, where I said good-bye to them all and watched them march away to their Company Blocks. So ended this story of one small detachment of Royal Marines who had conducted themselves with credit in a most adventuresome journey which, without being momentous, must certainly be regarded as unique even in the annals of their travelled Corps.

Lieutenant Frank Layard

I served as watchkeeper and divisional officer on the *Benbow*, then second flagship of the Mediterranean Fleet. Our Commander was B.H. (Bertie) Ramsay who rose to fame in the last war, especially over Dunkirk and through organising 'D' Day. He was a strict disciplinarian who saw to it that his ship's orders, which covered pretty nearly every eventuality, were carried out to the letter which made for a well run, happy and efficient ship.

Life in the Navy was much as it had been in pre-First World War days. Foreign commissions lasted from two to three years during which time sailors were separated from their homes and wives. Married officers were slightly better off as, on the Mediterranean station at least, they could get their wives out to Malta, but at their own expense. On the further flung stations, however, few could afford the price of the sea passage. Thus long periods of separation faced all married personnel, officers and men alike.

Pay, although it was improved at the end of the war, was still pretty meagre. A lieutenant's pay had gone up from 10s.0d. a day to 17s.0d., a Petty Officer's from 3s. to 7s., and an AB's from 1s.8d.

to 4s.0d. So by the time a man had remitted home the maximum amount allowed he had not got much left to spend on himself. But ships were very self-supporting and most of a sailor's requirements could be obtained on board fairly cheaply.

In every ship, except the very smallest, there would be barbers, boot repairers (or snobs as they were called), tailors and dhobey firms. Official permission to carry out these services was eagerly sought as a means of supplementing a man's income. Soap and tobacco and slops could be bought cheaply from the Paymaster, the cost being stopped from a man's pay.

The Paymaster kept a supply of slops on board. Boots, socks, under-clothing, jerseys; in fact everything that made up a sailor's compulsory kit. A man would buy six yards of serge and a yard of jean, some tape and such badges as he was entitled to, and take it along to one of the ship's tailors to be made up into a suit.

In the *Benbow* one of the best tailors was Petty Officer Hook, a heavily built little man with a voice like a foghorn. His main duty as main derrick PO entitled him to a small caboose or locker on the boat deck just big enough for himself and a small table, and there he would sit in the dog watches with his sewing machine, his big scissors and yards of serge cloth, busily turning out suits for his clients.

In those times, we officers wore monkey jacket suits throughout the day. From colours to sunset the officer of the watch (OOW) wore a frock coat and sword belt and carried a telescope. Our rig on Sundays was frock coats with, at divisions, swords and white kid gloves. In Malta, when attending the Opera, we had to wear mess dress which was also the rig for dances on board. The sailor's daily working rig was 'No. 5's', a white duck suit worn with a silk and lanyard but without a blue collar. This could be washed when dirty and was therefore more suitable for daily work than a blue serge suit. Overall suits were only worn by the torpedo party and a few others if employed on dirty jobs but they had to keep out of sight and were never allowed on the upper deck. Caps had to be worn at all times and dockyard and other working parties would leave the ship in the rig of the day taking their overall suits with them.

After tea, when the rig of the day was no longer compulsory, the sailors shifted into night clothing, an old serge suit worn without collar or lanyard. When not worn these suits were kept rolled up and stowed in a sailor's tightly packed locker and an occasional airing became very desirable.

For this purpose four wire clotheslines were rove through blocks under the foretop and shackled to eye bolts by the jack staff. On the appointed Saturday hands were piped to divisions with night clothing and after inspection they took their suits up on to the forecastle and attached them with spun yarn stops on to the clotheslines under the supervision of divisional officers and POs. When stopping on, each piece had to be stretched out so that it overlapped the next one on the line. When all was ready the clotheslines were triced up taut and the clothing blew out in the wind. If any gaps, or 'holidays', appeared between the bits of clothing we would be in instant trouble with the commander.

As facilities for drying clothes were very limited they too were triced up on the forecastle lines at certain times. Only authorised lines could be used and on no account should clothing be hung up in the superstructure or on the guard rails or anywhere be visible from outboard. The appearance of many foreign ships in this respect used to cause much amusement and critical comment.

The men lived in the broadside messes on various mess decks. These messes consisted of a long wooden table hinged to the ship's side and hung at the inboard end from the deck above by a swinging bracket called a craw-foot. On each side were long wooden benches which in rough weather could be secured with deck bolts. At the head of the table, secured to the ship's side was a locker which held the mess traps, cutlery, plates and basins (which took the place of cups). On the inboard end of the mess table stood the mess utensils such as kettle, fanny and meat dish, all beautifully cleaned and burnished and on the deck at the head of the table stood the wooden mess bread barge. In the centre of the mess deck were nests of galvanised steel lockers, one for each man, in which he kept all his uniform clothes.

There was also storage on the ship's side for ditty boxes; these were small wooden boxes, about 12in × 9in and about 5in deep, with a lid, a lock and an inside tray. The ditty box was a very precious article in a man's kit. In a very public and crowded life it was one of his few truly private possessions, somewhere where he could keep photographs, letters and his small valued personal treasures.

These broadside messes (which really differed little from those in the *Victory*) were home for about fifteen men for two and a half to three years. It was a crowded, uncomfortable and hard life, but also a happy life with good shore leave, lots of sport, great esprit de corps and, in those days of big fleets, a fierce spirit of competition and rivalry between ships.

Before general messing was introduced, the system in the navy was known as canteen messing. Every man received a victualling allowance of 9d. a day, and a daily ration of meat, potatoes and bread, and a weekly allowance of tea, sugar and tinned milk. Each mess drew their daily and weekly rations which could then be supplemented to the value of their victualling allowance by taking up extra rations from the Paymaster and buying such extras as eggs, sausages, and sardines from the canteen.

Midday dinner was the main meal of the day. Very few messes could afford anything more than bread and margarine and tea for breakfast. On Sundays and when the mess could afford it, the main course at dinner was followed by 'afters'. This might be tinned fruit, a figgy duff, rice pudding or something else depending on the skill and imagination of the mess cook.

Before the days of general messing, on foreign stations officers used to engage a local messman who would enter into a contract with the mess committee to feed the mess to a required standard. A man with local knowledge of prices, of shops and markets could cater better and more cheaply than if it was left to some Chief or Petty Officer steward.

In addition to the Officers' stewards, one of whom was the wine steward, there were some six or seven Marine mess attendants under a mess corporal who waited at table and served drinks before meals. A certain number of the older three-badge Marines acted as officers servants, one to perhaps two or three officers, looking after his cabin and clothes, cleaning his shoes, bringing his shaving water, etc.

Our day's routine started at 0510 when the hands were called and ended at 2100 with Commander's rounds. Punctually at nine o'clock the little procession moved forward with the bugler in front, followed by the Corporal of the gangway with a lantern, then the Master-at-Arms, and then the Commander. As they approached each mess deck the bugler sounded the still, the Master-at-Arms ordered 'Attention for the Rounds', and the men stood up to attention. As soon as the rounds had passed hammocks could be unstowed and slung overhead. At 'Pipe down' at ten o'clock everyone had to be in their hammocks and mess deck lights were switched out leaving only police lights burning.

Every morning except Saturdays at nine o'clock Divisions was sounded off. We divisional officers would inspect our men after they had been mustered and reported all present by the senior divisional midshipman. Only those on a very limited excused list could be absent from divisions. When we had reported their divisions present to the commander, the Close would be sounded and all divisions would march aft on to the quarterdeck where the band had already assembled. The chaplain, the captain and possibly the admiral would come up from below, prayers would be read and a hymn sung. We would then march our divisions off the quarterdeck to give them about ten minutes physical training (PT). Both watches for exercise would then be sounded off and the men would fall in amidships and be detailed for the morning's work by the commander with the Mate of the Upper Deck and the Chief Bosun's Mate in attendance.

In appearance the *Benbow* was, at least in our opinion, the smartest ship on the station. The ship's side which was under constant care of the side party was always immaculate and without a blemish. The quarterdeck too was quite a show piece. Unlike most other ships the *Benbow*'s wooden decks were made of oak, and not teak, and under a weekly application of holy stone and sand the quarterdeck assumed a whiteness which a teak deck could never quite match. This large expanse of white deck together with shining enamel paint on 'Y' ret, guns and after super-structure, coachwhipped canvases and whitened awning stanchions and beautifully scrubbed 'Open work' wooden hatch and bollard covers, a taut well spread awning with the hemp tails of the chain earrings neatly cheesed down, the glistening brass tompions of the turret guns and the spotless starboard ladder with its green Sunday manropes, all presented a really impressive picture.

I was on watch one Sunday in Malta, Church had just been un-rigged, the deck cloths removed and the deck wiped down when I saw the Chief of Staff's barge approaching the starboard gangway. I hurriedly sent the midshipman of the watch to inform the captain and commander but before they could get on deck I was receiving the great man, Commodore W.W. Fisher (the Great Agrippa), Chief of Staff to Admiral Sir John de Robeck, at the top of the gangway. He apologised for making this unexpected visit and said he had come to look at our quarterdeck about which he had heard so much. I believe he was greatly impressed and offered the commander his congratulations.

During the winter, at the end of the exercise period when the whole fleet was at Malta, all ships gave dances on board to which the youth and beauty of the island eagerly sought invitations. There was great rivalry between ships, each one trying to outdo the others in the decoration of the quarterdeck, the sitting-out and supper arrangements, and the quality of the music served up by the Marine band.

In March 1922 the *Benbow* gave a dance which was quite a sensation. The quarterdeck was made to resemble the quarterdeck of an old ship of the line. A poop was built at the after end of the deck with ladders leading up each side, a dummy stern chase gun mounted aft, doors leading into the cabin underneath and a wheel and binnacle below. 'Y' turret guns were encased and disguised as boats and a framework of canvas and wood surrounded and concealed the turret with painted doors and slatted windows labelled 'Master Gunner's Store' and 'Bosun's Store'. Canvas bulwarks were built up around the deck and the centre stanchion of the awning ridge rope was made to represent a mast with belaying pins round its base. With the quarterdeck staff dressed in old fashioned uniforms and black tarpaulin hats and with not one bit of a modern battleship's quarterdeck to be seen the transformation was complete.

It had taken the best part of a week for the carpenters, painters and shipwrights to construct and set up this truly remarkable disguise during which time the ship had been out of routine and virtually out of action. While greatly admiring the result and congratulating all those concerned the C-in-C decided that this oneupmanship had gone far enough, and he ordered that in future ship's dances were to be run on a more modest and less expensive scale.

There was constant rivalry in the Fleet both in work and sport, each ship striving to be just that much better than the rest. One of the ideas thought up by our commander for getting a little additional attention was the special extra little flourish which he introduced for entering and leaving harbour. Instead of just one bugler he would fall in six buglers on 'B' turret for sounding off the salutes and on the quarterdeck he had a combined brass and bugle band. All this additional noise and showmanship made our arrival and departure from Malta quite impressive.

It was not all brightwork, bugles and 'bang me arse' however. There were intensive exercise periods at Malta and at Constantinople culminating in the C-in-C's competitive shoot for which a much prized cup was awarded. We never won this cup in the *Benbow* but I think our excuse was that instead of the usual Elswick-Vickers mountings, our 13.5-inch turrets were Coventry Ordnance mountings. Compared with the enormously sophisticated weapons in use today, it was almost a bow-and-arrow navy.

As second flagship we spent much time at Constantinople. Our admiral, Sir Richard Webb, was a member of the Inter-Allied Armistice Commission responsible for seeing that the Turks carried out terms of the Treaty of Sevres. There was a military occupation force of British, French and Italian troops and ships of all the Allied navies. At colours in the morning, by the time the national anthems of all these countries had been played, it was about a quarter of an hour before the 'carry on' could be sounded.

Amongst this Allied fleet with admirals, generals and high commissioners constantly coming and going the OOW really had to be on his toes. The guard and band, buglers and saluting gun's crew had to be in immediate readiness not only for the VIP who came on board, of whose visit one generally had some notice, but also for those who unexpectedly passed by in their barges either with or without their flags flying. The British flagship must, of course, be the smartest ship in the harbour – the quarterdeck spotless, awnings taut, lower booms and ladders squared-off, and boats and boat's crews immaculate. All this required constant attention and a sharp look out if the OOW was to avoid the sharp edge of the 'bloke's' tongue.

All inter-ship communication in harbour, and when in visual touch at sea, was by flags, lamp or semaphore, and so a good signal staff was of vital importance. In harbour by day general signals from the flagship were made by semaphore and after dark by masthead flashing light. It was wonderful how quickly a good yeoman or leading signalman could identify a whole string of flags at a great distance. He knew his signal books so well that he could instantly interpret the meaning of a signal immediately informing the captain.

In a flotilla after leaving the harbour a signal would be seen going up in the leader and the leading signalman with his eye to his telescope would sing out, 'Apples Isaac One, compass O Nine O, George one two – Hoist' and would turn to the captain and report, 'From the Leader, sir, take up flotilla cruising order number one, course 090, speed 12 knots'. A short signal of this sort presented little difficulty but sometimes a flagship would be seen smothered in flags with masthead as well as yardarm hoists and at a distance it really needed a trained and expert eye to identify the flags and interpret their meaning.

The annual meeting of the main fleets during the Atlantic Fleet's spring cruise was an occasion of some importance. In February 1922 after some tactical exercises the combined fleets consisted of three battle squadrons, three cruiser squadrons, a battle-cruiser squadron, eight destroyer flotillas and an attendant aircraft-carrier anchored in Pollensa Bay in Majorca. This was probably the greatest assembly of naval strength since the dispersal of the wartime Grand Fleet and it seemed nearly to fill this great bay. A truly impressive sight.

Today the shore is lined with hotels and villas and great apartment buildings and yacht marinas but in 1922 the only visible habitation was the little fishing village of Puerto Pollensa lying at the head of the bay, behind which rose a distant range of mountains.

During our stay of about ten days the admirals and captains and their staffs met and the exercises were analysed and discussed. There were sailing races for officers, junior officers and warrant officers, and much ship visiting and dining-out. Both fleet flagships gave evening 'At Homes' where one met many old friends and consumed a considerable amount of whisky.

I landed one afternoon with a shooting party and scrambled about in a large marshy area where there were a few duck and snipe. This was being attacked from all sides by countless other sportsman from the fleet and I think we spent more time avoiding being shot than shooting.

Before we went home to pay-off in March 1923 we became involved in the Chanak incident when we so nearly found ourselves at war with Turkey and, together with other ships of the fleet, we took up a bombarding position where we were ready to support the army with gunfire in the event of a Turkish attack. I remember riding around the defence line with some army officers and wondering what chance they would have of holding out if the whole strength of Kemal Ataturk's army was launched to the attack.

For an unmarried officer like myself, mess life was fun. We were hard worked, but we had plenty of time for shore leave and sport of every kind and during a long commission we made deep and lasting friendships.

Lieutenant-Commander Harry Hodgson

In 1920, having passed my torpedo course, I was sent in November to join the submarine depot ship *Titania* in the Far East. Our converted cargo-ship called in first at Japan. The Japanese had been on our side during the First World War, so we received a right royal welcome, stayed all over the islands and no money passed hands. We then sailed to our new base, Wei Hai Wei, in China. The local people were very friendly, there was good shooting and lovely picnic beaches where rather attractive ladies would disport themselves. After this rather hedonistic period, we returned to Hong Kong for the winter.

During my time in the Mediterranean in the first war, I had run concert parties in the *Forward*. So almost as soon as the crew of the *Titania* heard of them they asked me if I would join their concert party group, 'The Fairies'. They were all lower deck and very keen. We had a wonderful time doing shows in Hong Kong and other ports. When we heard K15 had sunk with the loss of all hands in June 1921, we set about raising funds for the dependants.

After Christmas of that year, we went off to 'show the flag' in the South Seas. One of the great beliefs in those days was that 'Trade followed the Flag'. We went to a number of ports where we were always made welcome. While we were at Penang, the Admiralty decided, because *K15* had experienced problems with hot weather, that we should undergo some hot weather trials in the

Malacca Straits. Although it was only January, the sea temperature was 80°. We were asked to remain submerged for as long as possible. We did this for several days and the results were dreadful because the crews were collapsing with heat stroke. Our report back to the Admiralty gave them some concern and a number of changes occurred before future trials were undertaken.

After that experience we went to North Borneo where we rested and did some pig shooting before going off on a goodwill visit to some American ships in the area: we were very impressed that they had certainly learnt lessons from their short time in the war and had adapted their ships accordingly.

We then went up the China Coast to call at all the British concessions. These concessions looked after all the British people employed in trade in China. It was a very pleasant time and gave us an opportunity to explore China. Certainly the most interesting place I went to was the Forbidden City, which had only just been opened, and with a guide, I was shown all the remarkable palaces.

Somehow I knew that one day I would become engaged so I bought yards and yards of silk. When I left China I had over 700 yards of it.

Lieutenant Brian de Courcy-Ireland

I went to Gonville and Caius College, Cambridge. They distributed us among the various colleges but Caius took thirty, all of whom had been sent to sea early. I shared a room with two friends who had been with me on the *Bellerophon*: the companionship continued. Instead of batwomen we had Marines who cleaned the rooms and lit the fires and so on. We had a Captain in charge of the whole lot of us and he had quite a staff of engineers and instructors. Our Naval training continued: navigation, engineering lectures that sort of thing. We were also allowed to select two subjects of our own choosing, I took Geographical Discovery and

English Literature. My lecturer in English Literature was Professor Macaulay Babington. He was very amusing, and taught us a great deal about English Literature and the Classics. We had a mixed class, both naval officers and girls from Girton and Newnham. The Professor did not like women and was determined to get rid of them. He used to read to us unexpurgated extracts from the Classics and would begin by saying, I think this will appeal to naval humour. When he got going all the young female undergraduates' faces got pinker and pinker and within a fortnight the whole lot of them had fled.

Cambridge was a tremendous escape. You see, we had seen an awful lot. So we had to adapt, adapt very quickly. At the end of the six months I left Cambridge rich in memories and learning and started on my naval courses at Whale Island to become a lieutenant.

Six months later, I joined *HMS Venomous* as an Acting Lieutenant. However, I found destroyers in peacetime rather boring after the war and in early December 1921 I applied to join the Australian Navy. I went out by Aberdeen White Star liner. A long and exciting five-and-a-half week journey that took us round the Cape.

On board I was meeting a completely different sort of person, without uniform or rank, and two men I met were to remain lifelong friends. At Melbourne I was suddenly told to disembark and report to the naval officer. He welcomed me and told me to report to Flinders' Naval Depot (FND). When I eventually arrived there I found the place was only half built and my accommodation was a tent. I reported to the captain the next morning. He was RN, and very welcoming. 'When did you do your long course?' I looked at him. 'Long course, sir, what do you mean?' 'The gunnery course.' I said 'I'm not gunnery, they told me I was coming out here to go to destroyers.' 'Well,' he said, 'I don't know anything about that. All I know is you've been appointed Gunnery Instructor to this Depot.' After I got over the initial shock, I asked him what type of guns the Depot had. 'Guns?' he replied. 'We don't have any.' So there I was, gunnery instructor to a gunless depot.

From my first day I watched FND reconstruct the Australian Navy. At that time every state had a militia and all of them wore different uniforms. Some of them very peculiar indeed. They seemed a hundred years behind the times. Nor did they have much discipline, but that was the way they were.

My job really, in the end, came down to training new recruits alongside John Cobby, who was also a RN fellow.

The first thing I found out was that the desertion rate in the first year was over 80% – after two years we got it down to 17%! This was very much down to three ex-gunnery instructors, all English, in particular Maurice Baldwin Backwood who was navy through and through with a great-grandfather who had been a vice-admiral and served under Nelson. He wasn't a big man, but my God he was tough. One day an Aussie challenged him behind the Mess blocks. A couple of minutes later the Commander reappeared, stopped a sailor and said 'Will you go along to the doctor, there is a rating at the back of the block who requires medical attention'. When they found the chap he was still flat out. The Australians understood that he meant business. Discipline became so much better with him in charge. Unfortunately he had been called up on a temporary appointment and left to be replaced by an utterly useless commander. On one occasion I had to take a defaulter up in front of him who had attempted to attack the Master-at-Arms with an axe. The Master-at-Arms was quite capable of dealing with that sort of thing, but the defaulter argued that he was only going to cut firewood with the axe. This commander hadn't a clue, hummed and hawed for a couple of minutes and then he had a 'bright idea'. He smiled and said 'I think the best thing you two fellows can do is go and bury the hatchet.' I walked out of one door and the Master-at-Arms walked out of the other. We looked at each other and shook our heads. The commander disappeared the next day.

All the men were volunteers but they had £5 per week minimum wage, which in those days was a lot of money. However, the only people who ever joined the Navy were either wanted by the police or just needed to hide somewhere. The Depot was an ideal place because it covered 7,000 acres, most of which was bush. So if someone didn't like it there, he could simply walk out. The first thing we had to do, therefore, was make a boundary. For this we got hold of an Irishman, who had eighteen oxen and an enormous plough. He ploughed three furrows round the perimeter to show the boundary. It took him three months. That was the sort of situation we were in. No standing orders, just a lovely time. We had fishing on the creek, shooting and riding; I had a koala bear as a pet and kept bees, so it wasn't exactly a naval life. I really missed it when I left after just over two years.

I was twenty-four when I got back to England and was appointed to *HMS Frobisher*, a cruiser, 10,000 tons with very unusual 7.5-inch guns. Not a happy ship. She was a flagship of the cruiser squadron out in the Mediterranean. We commissioned in Devonport and had twenty-four officers. The first day the captain fell us all in. He said, 'I don't believe in leading, I drive. You will do anything that I order. Now, the Officer's and Ship's Company will sit down.' So we all sat down on the deck. He then said, 'Stand up'. So we all stood up.

I was one of four watchkeepers on board and had to turn out at 5.15am with the hands and scrub decks, not exactly normal, but you couldn't just stand and watch the sailors do it. If you had the middle watch you were allowed to sleep in till 6.15. This captain used to turn up sometimes and prowl round to see if we were up. He was a bachelor, never went on shore and always slept on board. The sailors christened him Pontius Pilate. Thank goodness we had with us Commander Woodhouse, who finally became a distinguished admiral. He was an ex-rugger captain of England, a grand chap who held the ship together, and was admired by everybody.

During our time in the Med we visited Spain, where I went to my first bullfight. It was awful because a rather drunk Spaniard, who thought the matador wasn't doing his stuff, jumped into the ring and of course the bull gored and killed him. He became a hero, all the audience stood up and cheered him as he was carried off. That was the first and last time I've been to a bullfight.

We also visited Italy and the French Riviera, where I had to take part in a march in honour of something or other. We went to Majorca twice, Sicily and Sardinia, and we went to Albania because there was jolly good duck shooting. We had to leave in a great hurry because the Albanians had arrested some people who had tried to blow up the President. They were going to execute them and thought it would be nice to have the Royal Navy there to show us what might happen if we stayed much longer. We then went to Greece, and in particular Corfu. This really was old England because they play cricket there. It was a matting wicket and the umpire wore a frock coat and bowler hat and their cricketers wore bare feet, almost unbelievable. They were good and took on the Mediterranean Fleet every year. In an English Church I met three very old ladies who had been governesses to the British army children during the latter years of the occupation. They now ran the Church. It was fascinating. They had arrived as young nannies and governesses sixty years earlier.

Our next call was the Black Sea and Bulgaria. We had King Boris and a very Bulgarian band to lunch on board. He then invited us to play tennis at his villa on the coast of the Black Sea. Actually we didn't really play tennis because the grass was a foot and a half high and the net had about two threads on it. I think we were supposed to play a six-a-side with the ladies-in-waiting as the opposition! So we gave that up. I was then instructed to go for a walk in the woods with one of the ladies-in-waiting, who could talk a little English. As we were walking through a glade a man came towards us and she said to me, 'Oh, it's my Pa'. As he past her she curtsied absolutely to the ground. When he'd gone past I said, 'Look, you're a bit frightened of your father, aren't you, your Pa?' 'Oh,' she said, 'I used the wrong word, he's the Czar.' That was King Boris.

We had to leave there in a hurry because somebody, in the usual Balkan way, had bombed the cathedral. The culprits had been caught and they were either going to hang or be shot. We were asked if we would like to see that as well! We made a hurried signal and left. We didn't quite know where to go so we went to Constanzia in Romania. The night we arrived there was a big fire in the dockyard and the locals seemed quite hopeless in their attempts to put it out, so we lent them our fire party. That didn't go down at all well because the owner of the warehouse was burning it down to get the insurance. I got four days leave and went to Bucharest with some of the other chaps and then up to the Carpathians, where we saw a big oil well on fire. You could see it fifty miles away, like an enormous Bunsen burner. It took them six weeks to put it out and with considerable loss of life too.

We then returned to the ship. The Queen came down with her bag of medals for the chaps who had put out the fire. She was Queen Mary who was the grand-daughter of Queen Victoria. She also brought with her a daughter called Ellena who was sixteen and a son called Nicholas who had been made an honorary sub-lieutenant in our Royal Navy. We gave them lunch and then showed them round the ship. We were just about finishing when the Queen said, 'Where's Ellena?' We looked round and there was no daughter in sight. The Queen kept muttering about how naughty sailors can be. We eventually found her in the gunroom having a whale of a time with the midshipmen! So again we then left there and went back to Malta, taking her son, Nicholas, with us. He was only there six weeks before he developed one of those complaints you get if you sleep with undesirable ladies, so we had to ship him back.

That was the sort of life in those days. However, towards the end of the year something happened which had a great influence on my career. There was a court-martial on board of two young seamen who had been caught ashore. They were both homosexual, so there had to be a court-martial. The first lieutenant and myself were told off, as prisoner's friends, to defend them. The captain was prosecuting. He was appalling. He shouted at them and called them liars. I remonstrated, but the Court told me not to make a fuss. But I did. I showed them the regulations and I made them write down in the minutes what the captain had said. At the end of the court-martial they reduced the charge, gave them six months and discharged them from the Navy for gross indecency. The result and the sentence went to the admiral and then the C-in-C who both made their comments before it went to the Admiralty. The Admiralty came back at once. The captain had given them severe displeasure. The verdict was therefore cancelled. All records were to be expunged and the two men were returned to the ship immediately. That placed the first lieutenant and myself in a very awkward position with the captain. The two lads asked to see me after the sentence and thanked me for my defence. One of them said, 'We think we got off very lightly considering we'd really done it. Hope you don't mind, sir, but we're going to go on doing it.' I obviously couldn't report this to the captain so I went to the Commander and he sorted it out with his seniors. However, I still felt very uncomfortable. The watchkeepers and myself decided that we'd had enough of this, so we all applied to do an observer's course in the Fleet Air Arm. The lot of us were relieved, and we left the ship.

Three of us left and joined the Fleet Air Arm because we wanted to get out and because the Admiralty were very keen on Fleet Air Arm entries at that time. So I did an observer's course at Lee-on-Solent, where I met my wife-to-be on 22 July 1926, I am reliably informed. The course was from March to November. We were flying an aircraft called the *Walrus*, an amphibious type. To get it from its hangar into the water to take off, we had to cross a main road with traffic lights!

Then I went to HMS *Furious* in November 1926. Initially we were only trained to land on water. We were flying the Blackburn Bisons not long after the first steel deck landings in 1927. We were still a bit hesitant at that time – I lost a few friends who tipped over the side, and I once did a forced landing in Scotland. I was with her until 2 January 1928. It was mainly navigation, such as leaving a carrier on exercises and finding her again, but we did a certain amount of practice bombing. We used to fly for about two and a half hours. From the Blackburn Bisons I went to a Blackburn Blackburn. Her top speed was about 65 knots and she stalled at 60 knots.

Then I was appointed to Leuchars in Scotland, forming a squadron which was going out to China. That didn't last very long, because the group captain there switched me since he wanted me to stay and become a ground instructor. I taught navigation until summer 1929. After a very short session in the *Argus*, I was appointed to HMS *Hermes* in China in December 1929. I went there with my wife and baby. Arriving in Hong Kong I found that I spent nearly all my time at Kai-Tak, an airfield which had just been made on the mainland opposite Hong Kong. I flew there mainly, only boarding the ship occasionally. Then I was given the difficult job of some air reconnaissance over China. We had to do it at 13,000 feet without oxygen and we didn't carry parachutes in those days. I had to wield a very heavy camera, which weighed about forty pounds. I suffered a sort of heart attack and was invalided home. Fortunately it happened on the ground. I think it was due to the weight of the camera and very, very bumpy flying without oxygen at such a high altitude. You really had to hang on for dear life.

The surgeon captain was absolutely convinced that I was going to die and he was terrified because he had a rather heavy casualty list. Having reported to the Admiralty that he was sending me home by the first available boat, he promptly had a heart attack himself. Naval life was full of those sorts of wry ironies, but there were no major incidents in China. We led a very interesting life, though I never left Hong Kong. The ship was re-commissioned in the middle of our time out there so I had to go back to England. They said that either I or one of my friends would have to go back there on the new commission, but they wouldn't say which. We took a gamble on it and left my wife out in Hong Kong and I was the chap who went back.

When I got back to England, the Naval Hospital at Chatham said they couldn't find anything the matter with me and if I just took it easy for a month I'd be okay. They passed me fit as a seaman and I was appointed to RAF Gosport in August 1931. They said 'You're just the chap we want. We've got a big photographic job for you.' I asked if they minded if I had a check up first, which they agreed to. The doctors said, 'You're never going in the air like that, you're going straight back to Naval Hospital.' So I was sent straight back to Haslar. Haslar said, 'This man's been passed fit to be a seaman. If he's fit to be a seaman, he's fit to be an airman.' So they sent me straight back to the RAF. The RAF sent me straight back to Haslar and it seemed as though this was going to go on forever. So I sat down and wrote to ask the Admiralty if I could have a shore job for a short time, while I was getting composed again. They gave me a senior officers' tactical course which I completed. By this time I said, 'To hell with the doctors' and went and joined HMS *Furious*, where I stayed until 1933.

I was unlucky. I damaged my knee badly in rough weather, so I was sent to Haslar again where the doctors made a complete and utter mess of it. At the end of three months they informed me that there was nothing more they could do for me, but if I wanted a second opinion, I could go and see a specialist in London. I got an appointment with Trethowan, a great man. He was absolutely furious. It took him ten minutes to find out what was wrong. He said, 'A bit came off your kneecap and has got in the joint. I shall have to operate, I can't guarantee that I can save your career, but I shall do my best.' He took me to the great St Agnes' private hospital. He operated and I recovered all right and when I was fit enough I went back to Haslar for treatment. They were very surprised to see me especially when I went to sea again. We went from the Blackburn Blackburns to the Fairy III-D and after that the *Fairy III-F*. We then did some early trials with the Swordfish and the Shark, but we chose the Swordfish.

On the *Furious*, apparently the naval doctors had told the Admiralty that I would never really be fit again because of my leg so when the position of senior observer became vacant, they appointed somebody junior to me. They knew they'd made a boob but they weren't prepared to alter their decision because they had already made the appointment, so I would just have to stand to one side. My captain was seething, and the admiral of the aircraft carriers, Sir Alexander Ramsay, was even more angry. It seems that I had come under his eye at some time, so he went to the Admiralty and said, 'I am not going to allow this to take place. De Courcy-Ireland is going to come to my flagship and I shall decide whether or not he's fit.' So I was appointed to his flagship *Courageous* and he kept a very benevolent eye on me which was rather embarrassing. At the end of about three months he made me the senior observer.

My pilot was an RAF Squadron Leader called Gerald Boyce, a Canadian who had volunteered for the job and a great character. We were trying out our deck landing at night. Beginning with floodlights and then cutting them out one by one until we could hardly see the deck. Came a time when we reckoned we'd had enough, I was standing up behind Gerald to help con him on. So we packed it in and reported to Admiral Ramsay. 'Well,' he said, 'what did you think of that?' 'Well,' drawled Gerald, 'I'll tell you, Admiral. There was a man once walked across Niagara Falls on a tight rope, but they built a bridge for the others.'

On another occasion we were practising live bombing with 500lb bombs on a sandbank off Leuchars. First we had to get the seals off the sand. Then on the first run in, when I pulled the toggle to release the bomb, it jammed. Nothing that I could do would release it.

'I'll give her a waggle,' said Gerald and started throwing the aircraft about. 'For God's sake stop that,' I shouted. 'We are bang over St Andrews golf course.' Anyway no bomb had fallen or gone off that I could see.

We returned to base. As we came in to land he said, 'Look, supposing that bomb is just loose: when we land it might fall off or go off. So the moment she slows enough I'll go over the port side and you go over starboard.'

That's what we did and did we run! The aircraft careered on and came to a halt. 'What's up?' they asked when we reached the control tower. 'You been taken short or something?' We explained. The senior armourer examined the bomb rack. He returned looking angry. 'Whoever loaded this bomb,' he said, 'Never took out the safety plug. But nevertheless there is no bomb there.' For some years we lived in hope that it didn't land on the Royal and Ancient.

I put in for a staff course and went down to Plymouth to take over temporarily on a cruiser. After three weeks I received a telegraph telling me I was to report forthwith to Admiral Ramsay as I'd been appointed his staff officer. It was a Sunday. I had to pack up, see the C-in-C, and get up to Portsmouth. Admiral Ramsay met me and said 'I'm sorry about this, my senior staff officer's had a nervous breakdown and you've got to take his place. I think you've got a wife here, haven't you?' I replied that I had and that she'd just had a baby. He asked whether it was a 'toggle' or a 'grumet' which in Navy parlance means a boy or a girl. So he said 'Well, go and kiss her and I'll have a boat in for you tomorrow morning at half past eight and we sail'. So I did just that.

The following day he said, 'You're my temporary staff officer, senior officer of operations, and you're also my guest.' I had to live with him for the duration of the commission which he didn't reckon would last more than a month or so. It was the Abyssinian crisis in 1936. We sailed at 20 knots escorted by a flotilla of destroyers from Spithead to Alexandria in Egypt without stopping. We went through the Straits of Gibraltar at night, passing an Italian ship who were astonished and sent frantic signals about us. We arrived at Alexandria and stayed there for a year. I lived with the admiral for four months and eventually I said, 'Look, I can't go on like this, sir, I really must pay my mess bill or something.' He said, 'What's the messing in the wardroom?' I replied that I thought it was about two shillings a day, so he said, 'Well, you can give me two bob a day.' So we went on like that until he was relieved. He wanted to take me back with him but the Admiralty said that I was to be the continuity man. So I had to take on the new admiral, Admiral Lawrence. I stayed with him after I came back to England. We used to do quite a lot of exercising. I flew over all sorts of places when the admiral felt like it. It was still the *Swordfish*.

We were never given any refresher courses or extra training but I didn't have any problems coming back from flying duties and then rejoining the ship at a higher rank than before. The chap below me was a fellow called Caspar John who later became First Sea Lord. My wife came out to Alexandria for some time; she used to follow me anywhere. When I got back, I found I was appointed to the Admiralty as director of training and staff duties under a chap called Sholto Douglas who after the war became head of the BOAC. I spent two years at Bush House. I wrote a couple of manuals for the Royal Air Force and had a very good time there until January 1939.

Lieutenant Stephen Richardson

Fleet Air Arm

In the course of the First World War the Navy and the Army created their own air services, the Royal Naval Air Service and the Royal Flying Corps respectively, each developing its own expertise in spotting, bombing, and attack. But to simplify the production of new aircraft and engines, the government in 1918 united the two Services under the combined control of the Royal Air Force with excellent results.

As the range of both aircraft and radio increased, it was found that cooperation with the Fleet required an expertise that was difficult for most RAF pilots to achieve, many of whom were serving only on short service commissions. The government therefore approved the training of naval officers as pilots and the development of aircraft carriers, while the technical care and maintenance continued to be fulfilled by the RAF. In practice this worked well for many years until the Navy could train its own riggers and fitters. The Admiralty therefore arranged that the Air Ministry should train 54 pilots to begin with. This was in 1924, and I myself, as a young naval Lieutenant, was one of those who responded.

The training of the pilots began at RAF Netheravon, on Salisbury Plain, and the type of aircraft used was the Avro 504K. This was a two-seater bi-plane with open cockpits. It had a rotary engine, in which the five cylinders and crankcase to which the propeller was attached all rotated round a fixed crank. It worked on the two-stroke principle: each cylinder had a spring-loaded air inlet valve which was not adjustable so that, for the engine to run, petrol was piped into the crankcase to mix with the air.

The air inlet valve was spring-loaded and automatic. This meant that when the pilot opened the petrol supply, it poured into the crankcase and there got mixed with the air until the mixture was right for combustion in the cylinders to take place. For these reasons there was only one flying speed, which was about 50 knots. When gliding in to land with the 'throttle' closed, however, care had to be taken to maintain a gliding speed sufficient to keep the propeller turning in case, on landing, one needed to take off at once, and in any event taxying was not possible without using the engine.

These aircraft had two open cockpits, the front one for the instructor and the rear one for the pupil, and in each was a full set of controls, namely ignition switch, petrol tap, and control column (commonly called the stick, or joy stick). The stick's fore and aft movement controlled the setting of the elevator (the hinged flap of the tail plane), i.e. to climb, dive, glide, or fly level. The stick's sideways movement controlled the angle of roll. Steering was by a pivoted bar worked by the feet.

The engine, as also that of certain motorcycles, was lubricated by castor oil, and this gave the exhaust gases a smell which always remained associated in our minds with the joys of aviation. Because the speed of the engine was a fixed one (it either went or it didn't go at all) except when picking up speed or slowing down to stop, its use for taxiing was controlled by interruption of the ignition by pressing a button on the stick, thus obtaining a short burst from the engine during the brief periods when the button was released.

The design of this aircraft evidently dated from before the introduction of the tail trimming gear needed to adjust flying balance according to variations in the loading. Consequently when we flew solo, with the front (instructor's) cockpit empty, the aircraft was 'tail-heavy', so that when taking one's hands off the stick, the nose of the aircraft immediately went up sharply, and unless level flight was regained speed would be lost and a stall would result.

A 'stall' is the result of interruptions of the proper airflow over the wings, so causing the essential lift this gave to be suddenly removed, and normal control is then lost until proper flying speed is regained. The shape of the wing is so designed that part of the air it meets is deflected slightly upward by the leading edge of the wing and then passes over the top of the wing just clear of its surface, thus causing a suction which is capable of equalling two-thirds of the weight of the aircraft while the air passing under the wing presses up to the extent of one third of the total lift that the wing provides.

If, however, the nose of the aircraft is raised too high above the direction of travel without any increase of engine power to maintain the forward speed, a point will be reached at which the flow of air over the top of the wing will suddenly break up and the lift will as suddenly vanish, and, because this nearly always happens to one wing before the other one, down will go the wing affected and the nose of the aircraft with it, which is known as stalling. The pilot's instinctive response will be to counteract the fall of the nose by pulling the stick back, but if he does so it will prevent the aircraft from gaining the speed needed to restore correct flow over the wing surfaces, so that the condition of stalling is maintained, height is lost, and the aircraft locked in a spinning nose dive until it hits the ground. Hence the only cure for stalling is to recover the forward speed necessary, and this in turn requires the stick to be pushed forward until the proper flying speed has been regained.

The Avro 504K was, apart from its very draughty cockpit, a pleasant and easy aeroplane to fly. With the instructor in the front cockpit and the pupil in the rear cockpit it was reasonably well balanced when airborne, but there was no tail plane trimming gear to correct fore and aft disbalance. The great day came when the instructor allowed one to fly by oneself but then, with the front cockpit empty, and there being no tail trimming gear, the aircraft was slightly tail heavy, necessitating slight but continual forward pressure on the stick, but one soon got used to this. Being fitted with dual control meant that there was a complete set of controls in each cockpit, i.e. flying controls as before mentioned, an ignition switch, and petrol control (i.e. throttle control in modern aircraft). For the engine to work both ignition switches had to be 'on'.

There was a broad canvas belt to hold one in one's seat during unusual manoeuvres, but this was so loose that if one wanted to fly upside down one had to hang on to the bottom of the seat with one hand to stop one from slipping through the belt. And as all this was before the days of parachutes it added spice to the experience.

After a while of enjoying solo flying, the question arose in my mind as to what would happen if, whilst flying, something went wrong in the empty cockpit. Would it be practicable to do something about that? Would it be possible to change cockpits safely while in the air? The only answer was to try it out. Being a Christian who believes in God as being fully responsible for what he has created, and requiring responsibility in his followers, I got his permission to try out this idea of changing cockpits in the air. So I took the machine up to 3,000 feet which I reckoned would be high enough to allow correction to any misjudgements on the way down. I then, reckoning it unwise to keep the engine pulling normally, put her into a steady glide, undid the belt, and stood up to climb over to the front cockpit. But, the front cockpit being empty, the aircraft was tail heavy and up went the nose at once, spelling quick loss of speed, a probable stall and spinning nose dive, the jerk of the latter perhaps slinging me out of the machine. So by putting the nose further down first, I was able to get into the front cockpit before the nose had come up again. All was well thus far and I returned to the airfield. But, viewing the ground from the front cockpit, I was not sure if my judgement of height for a good landing was adequate, so decided to take the machine up high again and get back into my usual rear cockpit.

This time when I let go of the controls the machine was nose heavy and I went into a dive at once, so that at my second try I pulled the nose up above the gliding angle as high as I dared (for I reckoned that if the machine stalled and went into a spin the centrifugal force might sling me out), and got over into the rear cockpit before anything untoward happened. Thus, with the belt on again, I returned to the airfield and landed grateful for the assurance thus gained.

The next day I happened to be flying solo in a similar machine, and was at 3,000 feet on a nice clear day when suddenly the engine stopped. I tested everything that I could reach, e.g. petrol level, engine control, ignition switch etc. and found nothing wrong. To have force-landed on Salisbury Plain would not have been all that dangerous, though certainly inconvenient, so I decided to investigate the controls in the front cockpit using the previous day's technique for getting there. And there I discovered that the ignition switch was 'OFF', whereas it should have been 'ON' together with the switch in the rear cockpit to have permitted such flying as had been achieved. So I moved it to 'ON', and at once the engine responded. I returned to the rear cockpit and flew back to base.

But I never had God's permission to change cockpits in the air just for fun.

Lieutenant Shannan Stevenson

During 1925–1927 I was a young naval officer serving on the China station in a Yangtze River gunboat, HMS *Bee*, one of what were known as the Insect Class. They were little ships of about 625 displacement tonnage, about 240 feet long and with a draught of 4½ feet.

At this time there were about a dozen Royal Naval gunboats operating on the Yangtze. Our duties were to patrol the river, which was navigable by steamships over the 1,350 miles between its mouth and the port of Chungking, and to safeguard as far as possible the lives and property of the many British subjects who lived and worked in the Yangtze ports.

Going upriver from the mouth, which is just around the corner from Shanghai, the Yangtze runs through a thousand miles of flat land and the river bed is mostly mud and sand. But at the port of Ichang (1,000 miles up) there is a sudden and dramatic change. From there for the next 250 miles to Chungking the river narrows and runs between high limestone cliffs and the river bed consists mostly of rocks. It abounds in dangerous rapids, whirlpools and cross–currents.

Coming downriver from Chungking was a hazardous operation, made worse by the fierce strength of the current rushing through the narrow channel and the fact that the ship must go faster than the current. Otherwise she would not respond to her rudder.

The thousand miles from Ichang downwards to the mouth were not so hazardous. Although the river was wide the navigable channel was very narrow in places and the sands banks were for ever shifting. We had charts, but they were rarely up to date. We used to run ashore quite often, but the ship was designed for this – she had a flat bottom and her propellers worked in tunnels so that they were protected from contact with the ground.

When we stuck on the mud we usually found that full speed

astern on both engines would have the desired effect, and we would slide gracefully back into the channel and try again. Fortunately the Admiralty were fully aware of these difficulties, and I think I'm right in saying that the Yangtze was the only waterway in the world where a naval officer could run his ship ashore and not be court-martialled.

Another hazard the navigator had to put up with was the Chinese raft. Huge quantities of timber were transported down the Yangtze and the Chinese merchant found it cheaper and simpler not to charter a ship for this purpose. Instead he would lash the timber together to form an enormous raft – up to half an acre in size – and for a small sum he would engage a few men to pilot the raft downriver to its destination, perhaps a journey of several hundred miles.

The crew of the raft were always accompanied by their wives and families. They built little wooden houses on the raft and brought their pigs and dogs and chickens with them. The raft had the appearance of a floating farming village!

These rafts had no means of propulsion; they merely drifted with the current. The crew managed, by means of long oars, to keep the raft in the channel, but of course they were very sluggish to manoeuvre and so were a danger to all ships. On one occasion, when we were at anchor off the port of Changsha, one of these rafts collided with us and got completely stuck across our bows. We started to drag our anchors and things were not looking very bright. Our own sailors and the crew of the raft then set about cutting the raft in half, and in due course half a raft drifted past us on each side.

Another touch of local colour we had to negotiate was the farmer taking his ducks to market. If you've got a river handy you might as well make use of it and hundreds of ducks, with clipped wings so that they could not fly, would paddle their way downriver in convoy. The farmer would follow in his sampan and keep his flock together with a long bamboo. But of course they occupied the main channel to take full advantage of the current, and it was a tricky operation trying to overtake them without damaging or dispersing the ducks.

During part of my time in HMS *Bee* I had the great pleasure of having as a shipmate Prince George, the fourth son of King George V, who later became the Duke of Kent. In our Yangtze days he was a serving officer in the Royal Navy and was regarded by himself and all of us as just that. He was known by us all as P.G.

On one occasion he and I and the ship's doctor were invited to visit some English friends who were at a holiday mountain resort at Kuling near the port of Kiukiang. The normal way of getting there was to go by Sedan chair borne by four Chinese coolies. The young and energetic did the climb on their own feet.

Prince George and I decided to climb and the doctor, who was rather portly, elected to go by chair. We set off first and, when we neared the top, a Chinese photographer, who had evidently heard of Prince George's approach, rushed towards us in great excitement. He said to Prince George, 'You belong English King's son – yes?' Prince George then replied 'English King's son very fat man – come up in chair by and by'. And we proceeded to our destination.

Some time later the doctor arrived and told us that on the last stages of his journey a Chinese photographer had followed him taking innumerable photographs. He couldn't understand it. I must add that, before we returned to our ship, Prince George called at the photographer's shop and let him take all the photographs he wished.

In the main we led a fairly peaceful life, joining in the social activities of the British community of the ports at which we called, including the excellent snipe shooting available on the banks of the Yangtze.

During the second half of 1926 we encountered more serious problems. The country was in a state of civil war, and British ships were liable to be boarded by Chinese bandits demanding free passage. Far more seriously, on 2 September 1926 we heard from HMS *Cockchafer* at Wanhsien, a riverside port halfway between Ichang and Chungking, that a local bandit war lord, Yang Sen, had seized two British ships belonging to the China Navigation company, the SS *Wantung* and SS *Wanhsien*, and were holding six British officers hostage. The *Wantung* and *Wanhsien* were each manned with four hundred of the Yang Sen's soldiers and the banks of the river were lined with thousands of troops. Negotiations had broken down and the officers were in serious danger.

This action took place on 6 September. HMS *Kiawo*, a requisitioned merchant vessel led by Commander Darley of the *Despatch*, grappled on to and boarded the *Wanhsien*, supported by HMS *Widgeon* and HMS *Cockchafer*. In the confusion the master and officers of the *Wanhsien* escaped onto the *Kiawo* and two of the three officers of the *Wantung* managed to jump overboard and were rescued by the supporting gunboats. Few of the troops on the *Wantung* and *Wanhsien* survived and thousands of soldiers on the foreshore were killed. But we lost Commander Darley, two lieutenants and four ratings in the action.

Anti–British riots were not uncommon in those days. They would start without warning, and for no very obvious reason, except that we knew the Chinese students were usually at the bottom of it with their slogans 'China for Chinese' and 'Out with the foreign devils'.

The British settlement at Hankow was next to the Chinese city, so we were always the first to bear the brunt of any anti-foreign feeling on the part of the Chinese. When trouble started a recognised alarm signal was given on a steam siren and any naval officers and men who happened to be ashore would return to their ships as quickly as possible. The Hankow British volunteers – the civilian male population – would assemble at their headquarters immediately, put uniform on, get their rifles off the racks and wait for orders. The British gunboats would then send landing parties ashore to guard the boundaries of the British settlement, and they would be supported by the Volunteer Corps.

The worst riot I experienced was in early January 1927. On 3 January we received the news that a huge mob was heading for the British concession, so a landing party was sent ashore and the Hankow Volunteers were mobilised. There were just thirty of our men to protect the Concession's waterfront and they had express instructions not to open fire on the crowd. Meanwhile British women and children were gathered together on the far side of the Concession, ready for evacuation.

As the mob approached they bombarded our men with bricks, chunks of stone and broken pieces of metal, but they were kept at bay with baton and bayonet charges. Many of our men were injured, one of them stuck with his own bayonet when he slipped and dropped his rifle. Thomas Ellis, who was in charge, stopped a brick with his face and had to go to be patched up in hospital.

After dark things quietened a bit. I went ashore to relieve Ellis and spent a tense night at Volunteer Quarters. We had no idea what the next day would bring. In the morning I received orders to return on board as the Chinese military authorities had promised to protect the Concession on the condition that all landing parties withdrew. This promise was worth nothing at all because by 4pm the Concession was packed with howling mobs. That day was the birthday of my wife-to-be, Daphne, and we had planned to go to her tea-dance party at the Race Club and then to dinner with friends!

The next day the crowds gathered again and at 2.30pm we decided to evacuate all women and children. I went in a tug with an armed party to collect refugees and took them to British merchant ships at anchor in the stream. All one lady had with her was a small attaché case containing a sandwich and a toothbrush. I heard an alarming rumour that Daphne was trapped by the crowds and couldn't be evacuated, and spent an agonising few hours until hearing that she was, in fact, safely aboard a merchant ship.

Meanwhile, the remaining British civilians were in fear of their lives as we were expecting the crowds to invade the Concession's buildings under cover of darkness. Suddenly, rain began to fall and within fifteen minutes the crowd had dispersed. But for the rain I can't imagine what would have happened.

Leading Seaman Stan Smith

On board HMS *Broke* during 1926 a notice went up for volunteers to go into the Brazilian jungle in search of one Colonel Fawcett, an explorer who had gone missing. His fate was the subject of a lot of speculation back home. Some thought that he'd been captured by a tribe of Amazon Indians, others that he was a prisoner in the depths of the jungle, or that he'd been kidnapped and made king of some native tribe. Nobody knew, so the Navy decided to send in a party to try and locate him and unravel the mystery.

I was one of the twelve volunteers accepted and placed under the command of Lieutenant Bradley, a very nice chap. We set sail for the Xingu River and went up it as far as we could by ship, reaching Bara, a town which was the centre of the rubber trade. It was a thriving industrial town with trams, cabarets and dance halls.

We were kitted out with khaki shorts and a jacket. All our personal necessities were to be carried on packs on our backs. We were issued with rifles and ammunition and each of us also carried a large sharp Bowie knife at our belt. Porters were recruited to accompany us to carry the stores and the trade goods which we were to distribute in friendly villages in exchange for a safe passage or information about Colonel Fawcett.

We plunged deep into the jungle, paddling on up the river in canoe shaped boats as far as we could. We travelled by water for three days until we reached some falls which we could not negotiate. There was nothing for it but to hit the trail on foot, so we hauled the boats up into the bush, camouflaged them with branches and undergrowth and, with the porters well loaded, headed off into the jungle. Led by a guide who was supposed to deal with the natives for us, we slogged on and on. At times we had to hack our way through the jungle, it was so dense.

Thankfully, when we came to a village, the natives were friendly. Our lieutenant had a good long talk with the chief and gave him and some of his followers some of the trading goods we had brought with us; strings of cheap beads (probably from Woolworths), little mirrors and other bright objects and knives. We carried on for days. Sometimes we would only make about a mile a day through the interlacing vines in the humid, suffocating heat. At each village we asked for news of Colonel Fawcett, but even where the villagers were friendly, there was none.

As we penetrated further into the jungle a gradual change came over the natives we met. Our reception was less and less friendly until we began to find ghost villages, totally deserted yet with signs of recent habitation. We had the unnerving experience of knowing we were being watched by hundreds of unseen eyes all around. Even so, we would still leave small gifts at some point in the middle of the village, hoping they would find them after we had gone and realise that we were trying to be friendly. They didn't attack us in any way or show any signs of hostility.

We passed the remains of several old settlements, ancient towns which to this day are still being discovered. But we had no time to explore. One day we came to a clearing in sight of one of these villages and we made camp. During the evening we were attacked by pygmies using blow pipes. We had to open fire on them. I don't know if we hit any of them but the noise of the guns probably scared them away. Unfortunately, one of our chaps was hit in the shoulder by a dart. We gave him what first aid treatment we could and tried to suck the poison out of the wound, but he gradually became worse.

There was no alternative but to send him back to Bara with one of our party and two of the bearers. We made a rough stretcher from boughs and vines and sent them off to follow our trail back as quickly as they could. That was the last we saw of any of them. We heard nothing more of our wounded comrade; whether they were killed or simply got lost and starved to death we shall never know.

Immediately after the attack all our bearers deserted us. We awoke in the morning to find they had simply crept away during the night. We could not carry on much further transporting all our stores and food so we discarded some of the extra clothing and food, packed it all up carefully and hid it in the bush. Then, just carrying the minimum of food for survival and the clothes we stood in, we set out again, travelling light. We tramped on for two days but food was getting very short. Then we came to a swampy patch of jungle where we were pestered by swarms of mosquitoes. It was a sweating, stinking infested sump to the world which was also populated by leeches. These slimy, fat, repulsive suckers clung so hard to our legs that we had to yank them off.

We had a consultation. If Colonel Fawcett had come within a hundred miles of this God-forsaken place we might never have known anyway and we would have probably perished in attempting to find out. We had done our bit and nobody could expect more so we did an about turn and began the long hard slog, picking our way back through the jungle the way we had come. On reaching the clearing where we had left our stores, we had a jolly good meal of corned beef and biscuits, packed some more food in our haversacks and continued our homeward trail. The going was fairly easy and we made much better time going back than we had on the outward journey because the trail was still clear and we had marker trees to guide us.

Mercifully our boats were still intact but we had nobody to paddle them so we made ourselves some rough paddles from the jungle. We steered one boat and towed the other. Fortunately the tide was with us so we made fairly good progress, although our craft was not very manoeuvrable and we were a lot weaker. At one of the friendliest villages, however, we had more than enough volunteer paddlers, in fact we had to select a crew from among them.

So we arrived back at Bara. We had tried but failed and come back with a totally different crew. There was time for a run ashore, some onion beer and a few smokes before we returned to our ship. Without delay I found myself back aboard HMS *Broke* at Malta.

Lieutenant-Commander Harry Hodgson

After *Titania*, the submarine depot ship, I joined HMS *Renown* as a Lieutenant-Commander. On 6 January 1927 she set sail for Australia to open the Government buildings on the site of the new Federal capital at Canberra. Aboard for this royal tour, were the Duke and Duchess of York, and *Renown* was under the command of Admiral Norton Sulivan.

Having crossed the Atlantic we called at Jamaica where we illuminated the ship with light bulbs to make the design of the Rose of York. The Duchess, who the previous year had given birth to her daughter Elizabeth, was given a grand welcome. We then sailed through the Panama Canal, the biggest ship then to have passed through.

When the ship was being refitted for the tour, I arranged to have my cabin open on to the quarterdeck which was about a hundred yards long. During the tour dances were held on this deck, and I often danced with the Duchess. Between the dances she would come to my cabin and we would chat together; she in fact taught me to Charleston. We danced to a gramophone which I had had installed during the refit. I was told off because I had requisitioned an American cine-camera and one or two people thought that rather unpatriotic! However, the film I made of the tour proved very popular with the royal family.

The Duke had rather a bad stutter, but he controlled it very well. As he came to a word which would cause him to stutter, he would click his fingers and he got through. I watched him give a number of speeches on the tour, all of which he got through very well. He was helped too, I think, by a New Zealander who practised Mesmerism.

After visiting the Marquesa Islands in February we passed over the Equator where the 'Crossing of the Line' ceremony was duly observed. The Duke and the Duchess entered into the spirit and were initiated. The Duchess was spared the customary shaving and ducking. But not the Duke of York. The ceremony was witnessed by practically the whole ship's company, some of whom were perched in precarious positions along the 15-inch guns. King Neptune and Queen Aphrodite (well portrayed by a sailor) were attended by the Herald, a bodyguard of trumpeters, doctors, judges, barbers, clerks and bears, all suitably rigged out. The Duke was presented with a large copper plate of the Order of the Old Sea Dog. The Duchess was invested with the Order of the Mermaid. After that, a considerable amount of 'ragging' went on and few survived not being ducked.

During the voyage we rigged up netting on one side of the *Renown* so that members of the royal family and their entourage could play deck tennis which, I must say, the Duchess played very well. We called in at Fiji where the natives entertained us to a fine display of dancing. That was our last port of call until New Zealand where we stayed eight days. The Duke and Duchess were given a very warm welcome at Auckland. We had a tour of this beautiful country and saw the hot springs and attended the opening of a new power station. The Maoris entertained us with a tremendously exciting tribal dance display. The Duke and Duchess went big-game fishing in the Bay of Islands where the Duke caught a superb 120lb mako shark. The Duchess, in another boat, struck lucky with a large basket of khaiwhai and schnappers. She was equally successful when she went fishing in the rivers.

When we visited the South Island the Duchess developed bronchitis and had to recuperate at Government House. She soon recovered and we set sail for Australia. At Sydney we had an unbelievable welcome. The Duke dressed in naval uniform and accompanied by Lord Cavan, met a number of veterans of the Australian Army. We entertained the local children who were particularly excited by the giant chute we had fixed up from one deck to another. Our visit to Melbourne was timed to coincide with Anzac Day, 25 April. The crowds were vast, bigger than I had ever seen. The Australian servicemen, either in uniform or suits, marched in a seeming endless line, ten abreast. The Duke took the salute and *Renown*'s Marine band set the pace. It was a proud moment for me as I was asked to lead the parade. The city was ablaze with colour and noise. It was a wonderful day. At Canberra in May, the Prime Minister of Australia handed the gold key to the Duke who opened the new government buildings. We then moved on to our last port of call in Australia, Fremantle, where we were often entertained by local families.

We left on 23 May and went through the Suez Canal before arriving back at Portsmouth on 27 June. The members of the royal family bade us farewell and the ship's company stood to and gave them three rousing cheers. The trip back had not been without incident because we had a fire in the engine-room which, before we were able to extinguish it, had caused the deck to become extremely hot. Had it got worse, we would have been in trouble because the nearest ship was 1,000 miles away. A month later, we were back with the Home Fleet doing harbour drills and exercises. This was not quite so glamorous. However on 11 August the following year, the sailors of HMS *Renown* towed my new wife and me through the village of Holybourne, she resplendent in silk!

Able Seaman 'Ginger' Le Breton

I joined HMS *Dorsetshire* as an able seaman in 1930 and had a wonderful cruise with her around the West Indies, where I played a lot of cricket. Back in England, while we were enjoying ourselves, the country was going through a bad time with nearly three million people out of work.

During September 1931, when we were back at Invergordon with the Atlantic Fleet, there was a buzz about our pay, which along with the other armed services, was to be cut. We thought it would be about 10% all round, but instead we heard that a shilling a day was to be deducted from everyone. Well, most able seamen were on 4 shillings a day so for us it was a reduction of 25%, but for a petty officer, who was on 8s 6d. a day it was only about 10%. This began to cause a great deal of bad feeling. Many of the men were married and had hire purchase commitments at home with fixed weekly repayments. This scheme was going to be implemented within about three weeks, which did not give enough time for those with families to sort things out.

As a torpedo man I spoke first to Lieutenant-Commander Cameron, my divisional torpedo officer, and explained that the men knew how to do percentages and that this reduction was unfair to us. He was very understanding, but there was little he could do.

On 15 September the Atlantic Fleet was due to go to sea on exercise. That was the morning we all decided not to turn to. Meetings had been held in naval canteens in Invergordon and in all the other ships of the fleet and it had been agreed that only able seamen and stokers, and those of equivalent rank, would take part. On the *Dorsetshire* we turned to for breakfast and then gathered on the fo'c's'le. That just seemed to happen. We saw other ships of the fleet close by and cheered. We were supporting each other; they had not turned to either.

We were then told that our commander wanted to speak to us so we went down to the upper messdeck. Commander A. C. 'Alfie' Collinson was a tough, heavy sort, a bull of a man. When he came forward we could see he was angry with us, but he was a belligerent man in any case. He railed at us and when he realised he wasn't getting his way he shouted, 'If you won't fall in, go down below to the lower messdeck.' Of course we just laughed at him and he stomped away.

A little later we were told that our captain wanted to speak with the ship's company on the fo'c's'le. Our captain, Arthur John Power, was a lovely chap and very popular. The first thing he did when he joined the ship was to call us all together. He told us that if we saw him walking around the upper deck with his cap under his arm, then we were not to stop our work or salute him, we were to carry on with whatever we were doing. We appreciated that: we liked him.

When he came forward to speak to us he did so with his cap under his arm. He was staking his reputation on this move. He told us that if we turned to, he would see us through. Then he quietly said, 'I am going aft. I have work to do. I hope you will do the same.' To a man, we followed him aft to our muster stations. It was a remarkably moving moment and one that I will remember for ever.

From the Atlantic Fleet seven captains were relieved of their command. Captain Power was the only captain from the Invergordon Mutiny to obtain further promotion. The next day the Admiralty ordered all ships to return to home ports. The mutiny was only a short affair, but it did a lot of damage to the reputation of the Navy and to our country. We had two ratings discharged from our ship on the grounds that they were engaged in subversive activities and others were drafted to various barracks. We were fortunate that we had a captain who understood his men.

Petty Officer Stan Smith

I was ordered to qualify for petty officer and gunnery instructor. This time I qualified and took classes right through to seaman gunner. I was transferred to HMS *Cumberland*, bound for China, where I had my first taste of the mystic East, Geisha girls and all.

From Nagasaki we went back to China where I had a spell of shore patrol, working with the English police and studying their different routines. During this time I saw a terrible number of public executions. The prisoners were often only petty thieves, forced to steal because of desperate poverty. They would be paraded through the streets accompanied by the executioners with their long axe-like knives. When they reached the public square their wrists were tied to their ankles. In this kneeling position their heads involuntarily rolled forward and the executioner would stroll down the line, efficiently lopping them off. This head would often be handed over to the shopkeeper who had accused the condemned man. He would hang it in a basket outside his shop in the same way a farmer might hang dead crows over his fields as a deterrent.

The numerous executions seemed to indicate that the deterrent was not particularly effective.

After our spell in Shanghai we started our voyage up the great Yangtse River and sailed almost a thousand miles to the city of Hankow. Our task was to minimise the ever-present risk of looting in that area. We sent patrols in all the passenger boats plying between Hankow and the villages upriver and put guards on all the merchantmen that came up.

One day we received a distress call from a ship somewhere between Hankow and Nanking. We upped anchor and steamed downriver as fast as we could but we were too late. The ship had run aground and her crew had been massacred. Every movable thing had been taken out of the ship, all in a matter of twelve to fifteen hours. Even the steam pipes, copper pipes and engine fittings had been unbolted and stolen. From a nine thousand ton merchant vessel she was reduced to a useless old hulk. It would have taken a British dockyard months to pull apart the inside of a ship that size, but the Chinese looters had done it in hours.

We then got word that some kind of big celebration was taking place on shore, so out of curiosity some friends and I got leave and attended. We should have guessed what all the fuss was about – another public execution. We went up to Torture Field where about twenty were executed that day. They might have considered themselves lucky compared with the torment other prisoners were subjected to. Some were simply in ordinary stocks, like the traditional English ones, and people were throwing all manner of offal and rubbish at them. Others were chained to a stake, each with a wooden collar around his neck so he couldn't feed himself. These poor wretches depended on the scraps people threw at them for survival. Still others were strapped down over bamboo shoots which gradually grew right through their bodies. Yet more were buried up to their necks in ant hills and were gradually devoured. For us it was a sickening sight and we didn't linger, unlike the locals who treated it as a form of entertainment.

I was lent to HMS *Glowworm*, one of the famous flat-bottomed Yangtse River gunboats of the Navy at that time. We saw China as she really was as we patrolled the upper reaches of the river. We saw women whose feet had been bound from birth and as a consequence were so small and deformed that they could hardly walk. Often we saw women come down to the water's edge, give birth and then go back to their work in the paddy fields. Life was hard as well as cheap and it all seemed to centre on that great river.

We reached some rapids which the old *Glowworm* had no chance of getting through unaided. So hundreds of Chinese were recruited on either side of the river with huge ropes snaking back to our fo'c'sle. With the engines going full ahead and the Chinese pulling, we got through the rapids and reached the calmer water above.

At night we would show only the barest glimmer of light on the upper deck for *Glowworm* both by name and by appearance would attract thousands of insects; rice flies and great flying crabs, or 'doodlebugs' as we called them. If these hit you, the impact would break the skin and give you a nasty cut. We swept them up in heaps under the small lamps we carried on the upper deck.

We went ashore for the exercises although there was no great fun in it. There was very little to do and no beer to drink, apart from our daily ration of one bottle, and even that was onion beer and not worth drinking. I think it was the boredom which incited me on my next escapade. For no apparent reason my mates and I bought a baby donkey with the intention of taking the animal on board and keeping it as a mascot. So we smuggled it on board and took it down to the store room. This involved getting him through a circular hatch and into the room where all the ship's stores were kept. We built a stall with cotton waste bales to conceal the donkey from sight. Somehow he was not discovered, even when the commanding officer went down to check the stores during captain's rounds.

Going back through the rapids, we must have done about 25 knots with the roaring bubbling water carrying us through the Yangste and back to Hankow where I had to rejoin my ship. I later heard that the donkey was discovered. By this time he had grown so large they couldn't get him through the hatch. They had to take a complete plate out of the side of the ship to get him out and the chaps involved all got stiff punishments.

On 9 June 1931, as we lay in HMS *Cumberland* in the harbour at Wei Hai Wei, special sea duty men were piped to their stations, the ship weighed anchor and got under way at 0800, heading out of harbour towards the China Sea. We thought it was just another torpedo or gunnery exercise.

Once outside the harbour we went to general quarters, guns

Crew of 'Q' Ship, HMS *Hyderabad* in service uniform.

The same crew disguised as merchant seamen plus cat held by Captain.

The deck of HMS *Vindictive* on the morning of 23 April 1918 prior to her attack on Zeebrugge.

The blockships, *Intrepid, Iphigenia* and *Thetis* sunk at Zeebrugge.

Seaman on board HMS *Barham* await the surrender of German Fleet on 21 November 1918.

HMS *Queen Elizabeth*, on board which the surrender was signed, triumphantly flying the flag of Sir David Beatty and preceding HMS *King George V, Ajax, Centurion* and *Erin*.

Royal Marines
and sailors of
HMS
Southampton at
Murmansk
1919.

The detachment
of Royal
Marines from
HMS *Kent* and
Suffolk
alongside their
six-inch gun in
Siberia.

HMS *Renown* manoeuvring at speed.

Duke and Duchess of York aboard HMS *Renown* en route to Australia in 1926. They are playing Mrs Gilmore and Lt. Cdr. Harry Hodgson.

Royal Marines embarking for China in 1927.

HMS *Bee* on the Yangtsze River in 1927.

Fairy Flycatchers on the deck of the HMS *Eagle* during manoeuvres off Rio de Janeiro in 1931.

Men of HMS *Exeter* in jubilant mood on the return to Devonport after their success at the battle of the River Plate in December 1939.

HMS *Royal Oak* sunk at anchorage by U.47 at Scapa Flow with loss of 786 men. Fathers, brothers, mothers and sisters anxiously scan the list of survivors. One young girl has found the answer.

and circuits were tested and all the normal procedures of a warship preparing herself for a state of readiness were carried out. As we passed fairly close to SS *Yuta* she signalled that she was thought to have struck a submerged vessel, probably a submarine, and that oil had appeared on the surface, along with some debris from the wreckage.

We proceeded to the position given by the merchant ship but could see nothing. The captain piped for volunteer boat crews. I took the second cutter. We were lowered and a grapnel was placed in the boat. We were told to grapple along a line parallel to the ship.

There was a current of about 8 knots running which made it hard work to pull the boat. So we worked with the current, trailing the grapnel astern, all morning until our grapnel suddenly caught up on something. We tried to shift it, pulling on the grapnel, but it wouldn't budge an inch, so I signalled back to the ship. Marker buoys were sent out and they had to be placed well above where I was to allow for the tides.

By this time, several ships had arrived on the scene and were standing by. One of them was an American vessel which carried deep sea divers who were going to try to locate what was underneath us. Their task was not made any easier by the strong current. We were just idly pulling the boat to keep stationary against the current and maintain our position near the marker flags where the submarine was thought to be. Around mid-afternoon there was suddenly a tremendous upheaval in the water and up bobbed seven human beings. Half my crew were over in a flash, swimming out to bring the survivors back to the boat.

When we got them into the boat we found that their faces and necks were so black and swollen that it was impossible to get the Davis escape gear from them without cutting it away. So I did precisely that with a sharp knife. We got them on board and managed to pump some air into them before taking them back to our ship. Soon after we got back to our station, four more submariners suddenly bobbed up to the surface. They were all in a bad state, but we managed to get them on board, cut off their gear and revive them. One was a Chinese cook and he was in the worst shape of all. We gave him artificial respiration, but he died.

The motor boat came alongside and took us in tow to the

Cumberland. We didn't know if there were any more survivors to come, but there were plenty of boats and ships around to take care of them. We later learned how the survivors owed their lives to the experience, presence of mind and bravery of their chief coxswain, Chief Petty Officer Willis.

Apparently, the submarine had been hit just abaft the conning tower and the whole after part of the boat, complete with crew members inside, had been lost. The eleven survivors were in the fore part. Firstly CPO Willis led them in prayer and they sang a hymn. Then they rigged up jack-stays along the bulkhead so that they could stand on them with their mouths close against the roof of the submarine. They then got into their Davis escape apparatus which, in those days, only really consisted of a mask. Standing on the jack-stays around the hatch, CPO Willis gradually flooded the compartment by opening the valves until the pressure in the submarine was more than the pressure above the hatch. They were taking a big chance, because if the hatch had only just popped up a bit and then shut down again, they would have all been lost. Fortunately the hatch blew clean open and was forced back by the weight of the water which kept it wide open. Those that were on the ladder shot up through the hatch and the remainder escaped in one big air bubble.

The submarine was HMS *Poseidon*. CPO Willis was made a terrific fuss of when he got back to England and the *Daily Mirror* took up a fund on his behalf and bought him a bungalow. He received a hero's welcome. Some weeks after the event we had to attend a court of inquiry in Hong Kong and I got hauled over the coals by a commander for cutting the Davis escape gear off, because it was vital evidence. Apparently, I was supposed to have pulled it clear or unbuttoned it. I spoke out of turn and pointed out that it had been a choice between saving the Davis escape gear or the lives of the men inside it. He didn't enjoy being spoken to in those terms and I was instructed to pipe down.

I learned afterwards that my grapnel had caught in the brass handrail around the conning tower. The flutes had jammed right underneath and couldn't be shifted. A diving ship went out there to examine the submarine and see whether she was worth trying to salvage. Somebody yanked the grapnel and brought up half the brass handrail with it.

We had to assume that the men we had seen come to the surface were the only survivors of the *Poseidon*. Down on the bottom the American divers had tapped all around the hull but received no answering sounds from inside.

We now did a cruise around the Yellow Sea, visiting various volcanic islands and also Formosa (now Taiwan). We just had time for a run ashore there before the ship received an urgent call to go back to the Yangtse. The river was in flood and what grim tasks awaited us. The river had burst its banks and there was water on both sides as far as the eye could see. Small communities had been engulfed, the water lapping around the roofs of the houses and homeless villagers were desperately trying to salvage some of their belongings, using rafts and gaining access to their dwellings by making holes in the roofs. There were bodies floating down the river in an endless stream: buffalo, cattle, pigs, people.

I have never seen such a scene in all my life. We went back to Hankow and started rescue operations, using every available ship's boat and taking them as far inland as possible. They sailed over telegraph poles, football fields, villages and all devastated relics of human occupation.

The rescue operation went on for some time. I vividly remember pulling a man out of the Yangtse only to see him jump straight back in again. Buddha had declared that he was to die in the Yangtse and who was I to stand in the way of fate? Another time a raft came floating downriver with a small boy entwined in the lashings. We got him on board and he told us, through an interpreter, that his mother and father had been washed away and he was the only surviving member of his family. We adopted him and christened him Chick. In Wei Hai Wei Chinese boys came on board voluntarily to look after each mess. They would prepare the meals, wash up, go ashore to buy the provisions, all in return for the leftovers or 'gash' of each meal. To supplement this meagre reward we would club together to give them a few dollars at the end of the trip.

As captain's cox'n, I had quite a lot to do with kitting out and training our new Chinese cabin boy, or no.3 hand. We dressed him appropriately for his new role in life and he learned to speak English quite quickly. He used to prepare the vegetables and generally make himself useful. He turned out to be a very good cabin boy and was eventually taken on officially by the Royal Navy. After we had paid off at the end of that eventful commission, the next lot of 'Cumberlands' inherited Chick and he remained with the ship as one of the captain's valets.

The 'sew-sew' girls, the cobblers and the tradesmen selling many and varied commodities brought the seething world of Hong Kong commerce right on board our ship. The 'sew-sew' girls were particularly helpful, turning our worn-out collars and maybe making an old suit look as good as new. We used to go ashore up on the Peak where there was a good restaurant and by ferry to Kowloon where we spent our time hunting for souvenirs and curios to take home to our families. But before that could happen the unpredictable Asian climate, prone to extremes, caused yet more devastation in the form of a typhoon.

Immediately on receiving the warning the ship was prepared as if for action. Awnings were taken down and all stanchions and everything movable securely lashed down. When the hurricanes hit us we had two anchors down and steam up to go slow ahead to keep the anchors holding. I have never seen wind and rain like it. It blew so that, if you forgot to hold on to something, you were swept along the deck. An auxiliary oil tanker, lying just off the dockyard wall, was lifted bodily out of the water and deposited some fifty to sixty yards inshore. Afterwards she had to be dismantled and reassembled in dry dock before she could be refloated.

The storm did enormous damage. Junks and sampans, which crowded the harbour, had disappeared as if by magic. They had heard the forecast and scurried away to shelter. The place was totally deserted. Tremendous damage was also done on shore and there was a great clearing-up operation to be done when the hurricane had gone.

By this time we Cumberlands had completed our two and a half years on the China Station so we began our journey home.

The *Cumberland* went into dock at Chatham. When we moored in the basin to pay off we had come to the end of a commission which I don't think anybody on board could ever forget. The Royal Navy between the wars was a benign policeman with a beat covering all the world's seas, but of all the areas in which it served none could have been more strange, more fascinating or more brutal than the China Station.

Engine-Room Artificer Trevor Lewis

Hong Kong was the main base for the Far Eastern Fleet. It providing dockyard facilities for all ships and submarines, sports clubs, accommodation, and the magnificent China Fleet Club which the government had built specifically for Royal Navy personnel. This offered accommodation at cheap rates for men on all-night leave, a large restaurant, an English tavern and all kinds of indoor recreation. There were other homes for servicemen, such as the Mission for Seamen, the Methodist Church Home and the YMCA, but the China Fleet Club, known throughout the China Station as 'The Blue', was our very own club.

When we in HMS *Danae* arrived in Hong Kong in the mid-1930s, the Garrison was very strong. They were stationed there along with the Royal Engineers, the Welch Fusiliers and the Seaforth Highlanders. Consequently inter-service rivalry on the cricket, football and rugby fields played a big part in our daily routine.

Certain customs in the Far Eastern Fleet were quite different from those in the Home Fleet, especially regarding the matter of catering. Each chief or petty officer's mess was allowed to employ a Chinese messman who would buy all the food ashore and be responsible for the cooking. He was paid weekly or monthly and each member of the mess would pay a mess bill and be relieved of all catering duties. For a few shillings a month we lived like the proverbial fighting cocks. Similarly we took advantage of the laundering facilities, for which the Chinese are renowned. When we were at sea we used to save up all our dirty washing for the return to base. The messman would recruit laundry maids – little Chinese girls with pigtails down their backs – who were all probably related to him. They would come on board every day at 5pm to collect the dhobeying and bring it back twenty-four hours later spotlessly clean and beautifully starched. They charged six cents apiece, irrespective of size, which was nothing as there were 100 cents to the Hong Kong dollar and sixteen dollars to the sterling pound. With their funny little ways and pidgin English they caused a lot of amusement, but they were always scrupulously honest and could be trusted to search through our kit for dirty laundry.

Since we had left Australia the ship's group, The Danae Singers, had been in temporary decline and I had been recruited by Mr Lee, our warrant schoolmaster and choirmaster, to help teach some of the seamen and stokers to write their letters home and to read more fluently. It was quite common in the 1930s to find seamen who had had very little education, but they still made very good and well-disciplined ratings.

After our 23,000-mile journey around the world the *Danae* went into dry dock for maintenance and, on completion of this, we joined up with the Fleet exercises in a mock attack on Hong Kong. We were in company with the heavy cruisers *Cumberland, Berwick* and *Suffolk*, our sister ship *Capetown*, ten destroyers and two flotillas of submarines. Altogether 20,000 men were mobilised ashore to repel the attacking forces in the biggest exercise ever staged by Britain in the Far East.

The Sino-Japanese War, which had broken out in 1931–32 over the invasion of Manchuria, had been rumbling on ever since, but in 1936 tension suddenly flared up again and hostilities were resumed in earnest. The Far Eastern Fleet suddenly found itself in a war situation.

In early April *Danae* was ordered to pick up the British Consul and take him to Shanghai from Foochow which lay some two hours steaming up the Min river. The Min, like many of China's rivers, is a fast flowing stream with a current of about five to six knots, against which the junks going upstream were propelled laboriously by eight or ten men. Those coming downstream glided swiftly by without any human effort apart from steering. Foochow is one of the five Treaty Ports, so called because of the treaty signed between the Chinese and western powers to open up certain ports for foreign trade.

We lay for four days with no sign of the consul and accordingly moved downstream to the gulf of Lian Kiang just north of the mouth of the Min river. Our objective was to visit the cemetery, and clean and tend the graves of the British servicemen who had died fighting during the Boxer Rebellion of 1900.

Mid-April found us off the estuary of the greatest river in China, the Yangtse Kiang, which meets the Whangpoo river at a confluence that empties into the East China Sea. The sea for miles around is a dirty brown colour owing to the large amount of silt brought down from the interior. Shanghai, which lies on the Whangpoo river some twelve miles from the mouth, became the most important city in China after being made a Treaty Port with the large International Settlement and the French Concession, alongside Greater Shanghai which was entirely Chinese.

Everything was peaceful during our eight-day visit. The Danae Singers came into prominence again by broadcasting and making two gramophone records, although what the Chinese thought about our singing was anyone's guess. The place was teeming with life but had a darker side, like all great cities. The ship's company were warned not to wander from the main thoroughfares and there was no all-night leave. In truth, most of us were glad to return to the safety of our ship by 2200 hours.

After showing the flag for the comfort of British nationals we left Shanghai, passing the US Asiatic Fleet in the estuary and exchanging the usual courtesies before making for Nanking where the Yangtse river is over one mile wide. Nanking had been the seat of the Chinese government since 1928. It is the largest walled city in China lying about three miles from the river bank. Several ships from the Chinese Navy greeted us upon our arrival with gun salutes and we were honoured with a visit by the Chinese admiral which was a first for any of our ship's company. HMS *Gnat*, one of the river gunboats, came down from Hankow for our visit. The gunboats served two-year commissions up the river without seeing the open sea, so it was a time of swopping old sailors' yarns and updating them with news from home.

After a five-day visit we began the 200-mile journey downstream to the sea. Reaching the estuary we turned north, heading up through the Yellow Sea for Chefoo on the northern coast of the province of Shantung, the only port in that area open all year round. The Yellow Sea is really part of a large gulf of the Pacific Ocean and is so called because it is discoloured by the yellow mud brought down from the interior by the Yellow River, also known as China's Sorrow. We were supposed to celebrate the Coronation of King George VI on 12 May 1937 along with the rest of the fleet but one of the ratings went down with smallpox and the entire ship was placed in strict quarantine. The sufferer was rushed into isolation ashore and everyone on board was inoculated immediately. There were plenty of sore arms for several days afterwards but fortunately no one else contracted the dreaded symptoms.

Still in quarantine *Danae* moved further along the coast to the Naval base at Wei Hai Wei in north China where we spent six weeks in between spells at sea. The base is situated on an offshore island where facilities were provided for the fleet such as a sports ground and a naval canteen which was by far the most imposing building in the place. By the beginning of June the rest of the Far Eastern Fleet had joined us to escape the trying heat of South China. Free of quarantine restrictions we were able to join in the football and cricket matches against other ships and prepare ourselves for that most gruelling of all sports, pulling a whaler at sea. The ERA's mess entered a crew of which I was a somewhat reluctant member. Thankfully it was the last time I would ever have to participate in this form of punishment and after a two-mile slog we managed to come a commendable third.

Early in July fresh hostilities broke out between China and Japan which meant an arranged trip to Peking and the Great Wall had to be cancelled. Instead we were ordered to Chingwangtao with half a flotilla of destroyers to stand by for further eventualities. Equally abruptly on 13 July *Danae* received orders to proceed to sea and rendezvous with the flagship HMS *Cumberland*. Here the Commander-in-Chief, Admiral Sir Charles Little, was brought across in a launch with the British ambassador to China, Sir Hughe Knatchbull-Hugesson. We received orders to take the ambassador to Nanking with all despatch.

Nearly three months had elapsed since our previous visit to Nanking during which time the Yangtse River had been in flood and vast stretches of land on either side were under water. The current in the main channel was very strong and the water was like dark brown soup. Bamboo rafts with whole families on board were carried down from the interior. One or two entire villages floated by on several rafts lashed together complete with bamboo houses and scores of men, women and children all heading for the open sea. We had to navigate with extreme care whilst still maintaining our speed of 20 knots owing to the urgency of our mission. Arriving at Nanking on 15 July, we found several ships from different nations had gathered there. After the customary salutes all round we fired a special one for the ambassador as he disembarked.

The weather was hot and very sticky, in contrast to the bracing air of north China, and the ship's company were not allowed leave ashore because of the war situation. Reports were coming in of heavy fighting around Peking and the advance of Japanese armies southwards.

For two weeks we lay at anchor in midstream wondering what the outcome of all this would be. We received orders to proceed downriver to Woosung at the mouth of the Yangtse to oil ship from the Royal Fleet Auxiliary *Pearleaf* before going on to Shanghai. Just as we were preparing to oil we received a signal warning of a particularly virulent typhoon sweeping in from the East China Sea with winds of 80–100 miles per hour. Frantic activity ensued as we cast off all the hoses, battened down all the hatches, and secured everything that was moveable between decks whilst simultaneously heading out to sea from the estuary. The greatest dread in every captain's mind is to be caught in harbour or any restricted anchorage by a typhoon in the China seas, so we were thankful to make it to open water when the typhoon struck. The eye of the storm passed over us and for three days we steamed into the full force of the wind with our 40,000 horse-power at half speed, but we were treading water, trying to forge ahead but remaining practically stationary.

There was a continuous roar from the wind punctuated by sudden enormous gusts strong enough to lift a ship bodily from the water. It was a terrifying experience but somehow we survived it. At least forty sea-going ships were lost or wrecked in that typhoon; and three weeks later, on 1 September, the 10,000-ton mass of the British India liner *Talamba* was flung like a matchstick one hundred yards up the beach by the combined onslaught of wind and waves. The Hong Kong Electric Company tried to gauge the velocity of the winds but the needle went off the gauge after 160 miles per hour.

Four days later than planned we were able to oil ship before proceeding up the Whangpoo River to Shanghai and berthing midstream opposite the Bund at Number One British Navy Buoy. We remained there for the next two and a half months as the British government's representative in the troubled situation. Most of the Western powers sent a warship to protect the large numbers of nationals living in the International Settlement (an amalgamation of various foreign 'Concessions') and the French Concession. The French cruiser *Lamotte Picquet* and sloop *Dumont d'Urville*, the US cruiser *Augusta*, two Italian destroyers, Norwegian, Dutch and Swedish sloops were all anchored off the Bund with other ships arriving from time to time. Our own destroyers *Duncan, Delight* and *Duchess* were engaged in bringing up troop reinforcements from the mouth of the river to man the perimeter of the settlement. They would berth alongside *Danae* and disembark men of the Ulster Rifles and the Welch Fusiliers who would then be ferried across to the Bund. The Commander-in-Chief, Admiral Sir Charles Little, flying his flag in HMS *Falmouth*, made frequent trips up and down the river, transferring his flag to *Danae* whenever he was required to be in Shanghai.

Tension mounted as the fighting drew nearer to the outskirts of Shanghai and on 12 August all servicemen on leave were suddenly recalled to their ships. The following day fighting broke out in earnest. The Japanese flagship HIJMS *Idzumo*, berthed just below Garden Bend, announced that she would fire on any ship proceeding up or down the Whangpoo River. Higher up the Chinese blocked the river with a line of sunken ships so we were effectively hemmed in with nowhere to go. The ship's company was placed on half rations immediately. Corned beef became the staple diet along with ship's biscuits which could have been made out of reinforced concrete.

For the next few weeks we experienced the realities of modern warfare, admittedly mainly as spectators, but it was still far too close for comfort. On 14 August Chinese planes attempting to attack the *Idzumo* dropped bombs on the intersection of Edward VII Avenue and Nanking Road – two of the busiest roads in Shanghai. It was like a holocaust. Some of the sights were really horrifying as the intersection was crowded at the time and many people were simply blown to bits. Over 1,000 people were killed, mainly Chinese, but several foreigners died, among them the distinguished American missionary, Dr F. J. Rawlinson.

Each day brought heavy bombing from both Chinese and Japanese aircraft in the Pootung and Hongkew areas and intense anti-aircraft fire from both sides of the river. We were slap bang in the middle of it all. The Bund was declared unsafe, all traffic was stopped and pedestrians vanished from the streets. Huge areas of Chapei and Pootung were on fire from the incessant bombing and our port quarter, McKenzie's Godown, and the cotton mill nearby blazed for two days. During a particularly hot exchange of fire from both sides of the river a shell exploded on the quarterdeck of *USS Augusta* killing a seaman and seriously injuring eighteen others. *Augusta* was secured to the same buoy as *Danae* so for us it was a narrow escape.

During the third week of fighting aerial torpedoes were dropped on one of the largest stores in the city, the Sincere-Wing Emporium – the Harrods of Shanghai. It was another scene of terrible carnage and again several hundred people lost their lives. Two platoons of seamen and stokers were landed from *Danae* together with our full complement of Royal Marines to assist the Loyal Regiment in guarding the International Settlement.

On 18 August the evacuation of all British nationals was ordered which required every available rating ashore. I found myself in charge of a platoon with a service revolver on my hip and six stokers armed with rifles. Our task was to escort evacuees from the collecting depot, see them safely into the waiting tenders for transfer to the *Danae* and eventually to Hong Kong. It made me recall the refugees at Valencia who were so grateful to the Royal Navy for rescuing them from the war zone. Some had only the clothes they stood in; others came loaded with treasured possessions; some brought along their family pets, only to find they had to leave them behind. Most of the men were bank officials, consular staff or shipping company employees who had lived in China all their working lives. Many of their wives were Chinese, some of whom did not speak much English but they smiled their thanks for our help and protection and in their quaint Chinese way each one bowed low before me thinking I was Number One Man. It was really quite touching.

One woman gave birth to a son on HMS *Duncan* during the passage downstream. An agreement was reached between the British and Japanese authorities to allow the passage of refugees to the river mouth. Within three days the evacuation of 3,000 British passport holders was completed, all safely ferried down to Woosung by the destroyers. In that time I lost count of the number of babies my team of six young stokers and I had carried and deposited safely on board. Perhaps it was good training for the future.

In the last week of August the ambassador to China, Sir Hughe

Knatchbull-Hugesson, was travelling by car from Nanking to confer with the Commander-in-Chief in Shanghai when the car was attacked by a Japanese plane. The ambassador suffered severe spinal injuries and the event brought forth a strong protest from the British government. Six weeks later the ambassador was brought on board looking very pale and drawn. He was carefully transferred to HMS *Falmouth* with his wife for passage to Hong Kong. He subsequently made a good recovery and later became British ambassador to Turkey throughout World War II.

There was still no let up in the fighting and from the ship we had a grandstand view of the aerial warfare by day. Fires raged for miles in the Hongkew and Pootung areas. Many of us had taken to sleeping on deck to escape the humid atmosphere between decks, and had to learn the exact moment to leave the camp bed once we heard the rattle of machine-gun fire overhead. On several occasions I must have beaten all existing world records in the twenty yard dash for cover.

During these weeks we had to make our own entertainment such as ship's concerts, in which each mess would take part, ukkers championships, crib matches and even competitions for writing and reciting poetry. None of these entries would have found a place in the *Golden Treasury*, indeed some needed to be heavily censored before recital. Nonetheless, my entry was very much a cry from the heart. I had been abroad for nearly three and a half years and was getting very homesick. Judging from the reception the ship's company gave it at the ship's concert, my sentiments echoed in the hearts of all. It won first prize and the chorus was sung, whistled and hummed throughout the ship for the remainder of the commission.

Cholera had broken out ashore so, once again, the entire ship's company was inoculated. There was the usual crop of sore arms for several days afterwards.

Early in September the fighting moved north of Shanghai, and at last we were able to breathe a little more easily. Shore leave was finally granted each day though for a limited period only. It was good to stretch the legs again after being cooped up in a stationary ship for so long.

Fighting of a different sort provided a light relief when a boxing match was arranged between the *Augusta* and the *Danae*. Although classed as a light cruiser, *Danae* was only one-third of the size and complement of the heavy American cruiser. The match was staged in a hall near the Shanghai Racecourse but the contest became so one-sided it was almost laughable. The Americans sauntered into the ring rigged up like professionals with boxing boots, silk shorts and dressing-gowns with their names emblazoned on the back, whilst our chaps turned out in regulation tropical shorts, singlets and good old 'pussers' plimsolls. It was a source of great amusement for all the spectators and of some embarrassment for our ship's company. The Yanks fought like professionals too and had easily won every bout on the programme until the last of the evening, billed as the star attraction – the Light Heavyweight Contest.

The British representative was our own ERA messman, a stoker first class, known to everybody on the ship simply as Geordie since he obviously hailed from Tyneside. Geordie was slow-witted, almost illiterate, and would never rise above his current rank, yet he was a very hard worker on board and an equally hard drinker on land. He usually managed at least one run ashore per month when he would always get into trouble, returning on board with a couple of black eyes, having lost his cap or his pay-book. He never caused any trouble on board and everybody liked him. When he came into the ring the spectators roared with laughter. He looked so comical in his long tropical shorts while his opponent danced around in professional style in his flashy red dressing-gown. Geordie was as strong as an ox and built like one. The American began punching him from all angles while the Yanks roared their man on. It looked to be another cakewalk with the British being completely whitewashed. In round three the same pattern was emerging when Geordie suddenly decided he'd had enough of this, shook his head like a wounded bull and unleashed an enormous swing. The American dropped as though he had been poleaxed, lying flat on his back and knocked out cold. The audience were literally stunned into silence until the British contingent erupted into ecstatic cheering. The Yanks were dumbfounded. Our pride had been salvaged and Geordie became the ship's hero for the remainder of the commission.

The ERA's mess achieved a certain notoriety in a quite different sphere when one of the younger ERAs, known to everyone as Knocker White, suddenly announced that he intended to marry a Chinese girl with whom he had fallen in love. She was a 'hostess' and dancing partner in one of the better class cabarets which abounded in Shanghai. They were genuine places of entertainment and not, as one would imagine, houses of ill-repute. The girl herself, we had to admit, was very beautiful.

Knocker was a real country bumpkin from Andover. He was brought up on a small farm and had about him a kind of rustic stolidity which he'd probably inherited from his parents. Nothing would shift him once his mind was made up. We all tried to dissuade him from taking this step, since the likelihood of a Chinese cabaret girl settling down on a small Hampshire farm was fairly remote. However, Knocker was adamant and nothing his mess-mates could say made any difference. Prior to the war no rating serving abroad was allowed to marry on the station without the commanding officer's permission. Usually the rating concerned would be drafted back to Britain by the first boat, but due to our circumstances this was impossible. The captain saw Knocker and advised strongly against the marriage but stopped short of actually forbidding it. The wedding went ahead even though with the restrictions on shore leave they were unable to set up a home. When we finally left Shanghai she tried to follow as best she could, since all the British women and children had already been evacuated. I believe it took her some twelve to eighteen months to reach England by which time World War II was drawing near. Unfortunately there was no happy or romantic ending to the story as poor old Knocker was killed in the first two years of the war. I have often wondered how she took to life in Andover.

One other very unpleasant, sickening memory of those three months tied up to the buoy lingered on in our minds long after we left Shanghai. During most of our time there another ship would be berthed alongside, sometimes one on each side. These were usually 'D' class destroyers and often the Commander-in-Chief's yacht HMS *Falmouth*. The Whangpoo river is noted for its fast current of 4–5 knots which brings down all the flotsam and jetsam imaginable from the interior. Much of the garbage would become trapped between the two ships, quickly accumulating into a solid mass which would have to be cleared by hand with boathooks. The 'D' class destroyers had a low free-board and the ERA's mess, which was on the starboard side of the ship, had four portholes which were only a few feet above the water-line, so the putrefying garbage was very quickly smelt in the mess. We became very familiar with one very distinctive foul smell; the stench of decomposing human flesh.

Invariably these proved to be the bodies of tiny little baby girls. In those days female babies were unwanted by the peasants and it was common practice, in the interior of China, to dispose of them by throwing them into the river. The task of freeing these poor little creatures and watching them swept along with the garbage of the river to the open sea affected all of us.

In the third week of October 1937, HMS *Dorsetshire*, a county class cruiser, arrived off Woosung to relieve HMS *Danae*. Shortly after, we slipped our moorings and proceeded downriver to the open sea and thence to Hong Kong. After storing ship and replenishing the larder, we left the Far Eastern Base and began the six-week return trip back home. Owing to the gathering war clouds in Europe, as well as the delay caused by the situation in China, our round-the-world return via the Panama Canal was cancelled. So it was Singapore, Colombo, Aden, Port Said, Malta, and finally Gibraltar on 5 December, before starting the last lap for home.

Surgeon-Lieutenant Dick Caldwell

I joined the Royal Navy as a qualified doctor in 1934 on a four year engagement. In 1936, I joined HMS *Norfolk*, the Flagship of the East Indian Squadron and had a marvellous time touring such places as Calcutta, Bombay, Mauritius and Zanzibar. We were based at Colombo and seemed to do little else other than attend parties, which never seemed to start before 2am, and play tennis.

In 1938, I went on a six week tour with the First Lord of the Admiralty, Duff Cooper, on the *Enchantress*. We sailed into the Mediterranean and visited Malta and Naples. There was little for a doctor to do but enjoy himself. What I do remember was a most violent storm in which everyone seemed very ill, myself included.

I thought in 1938 that I would leave the Navy. But a close friend of mine strongly advised me to stay. He said that he felt war was imminent and that if I left and was then called up later, I'd have to start at the beginning again. So I decided to stay and was posted to the *Royal Oak*. As I travelled up to Scapa Flow, I felt everywhere there was the shadow of war: a feeling of unease. Chamberlain's speech about 'Peace in Our Time' really had a hollow ring to it.

As war approached, I think the thought of going to war was exciting. In September when war was declared, the admiral called us together in the wardroom and gave us all champagne. He gave us the toast 'Damnation to Hitler'!

I thought, well, what do we do now. We went out on patrols only returning to Scapa, that huge desolate place, each time. On the night of 13 October, I had been playing poker and had been listening to gramophone records with two fellows I was never to see again. At half past twelve I picked my way carefully along the darkened quarterdeck to the hatchway leading to my cabin. I undressed and climbed on to my bunk.

We were in harbour – if such a term can be used to describe the wide, bleak waters of Scapa Flow – and after a not unadventurous spell at sea, no thoughts of the impending disaster could have been in anyone's mind, when at ten past one a muffled, ominous explosion shook the ship.

'Lord,' I said to myself, 'I don't like the sound of that much', and as I jumped down from my bunk I found my heart thumping a bit. I looked into the next cabin and saw my neighbour pulling on a pair of trousers, and out in the cabin flat five or six officers were already discussing how and where the explosion could have occurred. (One must remember the vast number of compartments and storing places in a ship like *Royal Oak*.) Eight minutes passed. It was cold, and one or two men drifted back to their cabins. Just as I decided to do the same, a tremendous shuddering explosion occurred and the ship took a list to starboard. I heard the tinkling of glass falling from ledges and pictures in what seemed to be the awe-stricken silence that followed; a silence that was suddenly shattered by a third explosion. All the lights went out, the list increased, and it was obvious to everyone that we were for it.

I got on to deck in my pyjamas, monkey jacket and one bedroom slipper – I dropped the other and remember deciding not to retrieve it. A fourth torpedo struck us and the mighty bulk of the battleship shuddered again and settled further into the water. These last three blows had occurred in the short space of three minutes, and it was now every man for himself in a sinking ship with the cold, black sea all around us. I suppose all of us have wondered how we would feel in a case like this; I know I have, and I was certainly shocked but, curiously, not frightened as we stood on the sloping deck in the darkness, wisps of smoke eddying round us. One heard shouts of reassurance, even of humour; and a sudden splash as men clambered over the guard rails and dived twenty or thirty feet into the water below. I had no plan. My mind was curiously blank with regard to my personal safety, although I can most vividly recall every thought and impression that passed through my brain; my new and rather expensive tennis racket, a book I had borrowed and promised to return, three pounds in the bottom of my drawer, a ship of this size must surely take a long time to sink (six minutes later it was out of sight), but above all these surprising thoughts: 'This can't be happening to me; you read about it in books, and see it on the flicks, but it doesn't happen, it can't be happening to me.'

The ship suddenly increased her list more and more rapidly. We were now on the ship's side and as she slid over, turning turtle, I lost my footing, fell, tried frantically to scramble up and dive clear and was thrown headlong into the sea. ('I'll be sucked down – that's what they say happens – what a fool I was not to jump sooner.') I seemed to go down and down and started fighting for breath. Then, as I came to the surface, the stern and propeller soared above me, then slipped slowly into the water and disappeared. A rush of water swept me head over heels, it seemed, and I went under again and came up in oil, thick black oil. I gulped it and retched at the filthy taste of it in my throat; oil, thick black oil smarting in my eyes. I swam and floundered about, hoping to find some form of support in the darkness. None of us had lifebelts. I heard cries round me, saw black heads bobbing, and I swam frenziedly again. I tried to wriggle out of my jacket, but found it heavy and slimy with oil. I repeatedly went under until quite suddenly I gave it up and thought, 'I'm going to drown'. Perfectly dispassionately 'I'm going to drown' and in a way which I cannot explain I wondered how to. And I thought of all the people I wanted to see again, and things I wanted to do – that was all I thought of – and then I saw a group of heads and then threshed my way towards them.

Somebody swam quite strongly past me and I caught his leg and tried to hold it. He kicked me clear. I saw an upturned boat ahead of me. How far was it? Or how near? Fifteen yards can seem insurmountable, and then I touched the freeboard, touched it and held on. 'I've made it, by God, I've made it; and to think a few minutes ago I might have been drowned'. I thought what a pity one can't thank inanimate things, I was so grateful to that support.

I tried to wipe the oil out of my eyes with my free hand, and then with my sleeve, and realised how stupid that was. My mind flashed back to a silent picture of Buster Keaton as a diver drying his hands on a towel at the bottom of the sea. I said 'Hullo' to the indistinguishable face beside me, and it said 'Oh, this bloody oil!'

There were about a dozen of us, I think, hanging on round a boat which kept steady as long as we did, but every now and then someone would try to improve his position or make himself more secure by clambering on to the upturned keel. Then slowly but inevitably our support would begin to roll over and back we would slip into the water, clawing frantically for a fingerhold on the smooth surface, and shouting at each other till the movement ceased and we were supported once more. This happened many times and every time meant a mouthful of oil and a thumping heart.

Time dragged on, with no sign of us being picked up. We strained our eyes in the darkness for some glimmer of light, but none came. We sang, 'Daisy, Daisy, give me your answer do'. *Daisy* was the name of the drifter attached to the *Royal Oak*.

At last we saw a mast head light which grew brighter and then the blacker darkness of a boat moving slowly towards us. We shouted again and again.

When she was within twenty yards of us we left our upturned boat and struck out in her direction. She had ropes hanging down, up which we tried to climb. I remember falling back into the sea twice. My hands were numb. I thought 'Mustn't lose now. Come on, mustn't lose now' – but have no recollection whatsoever of finally succeeding . . . I found myself sitting on a hot grating in the engine room, shivering uncontrollably from the cold which I had not previously noticed – most of us had this experience.

I stood up and vomited oil and salt water all over somebody sitting at my feet. I did this three times and apologised each time to him. He didn't appear to worry much, anyway.

We were taken to the *Pegasus* and given hot drinks and helped into hot baths, and splashed and scrubbed. They were very grand to us, and we began to talk and recognise people and shake hands and try not to notice friends that were missing. Over eight hundred were drowned that night.

Of the happenings during the following days before we disembarked and were sent south, I retain vivid memories which now seem so swift-moving and so violently contrasted that they really belong to a different story. The air raids, the shattering noise, a German pilot lazily parachuting down silhouetted against a bright blue sky, while his plane, broken up by gunfire, crashed in flames, on the hill-side; the sinister whistle of bombs from the raiders; the whole-hearted enthusiasm at an impromptu concert the night after we were torpedoed; the marvellous kindness shown to us by the Thurso folk; the sense of relief we felt in the train taking us south (a relief broken almost comically by a train-collision); the gradual acquisition of strange clothing, of odd meals and drinks, and so – at last – London; to find normality almost unreal after chaos.

Leave soon put that right!

Warrant Shipwright F.H.T. Panter

My first ship appointment as a newly promoted shipwright officer was to HMS *Ajax* on 11 January 1938. *Ajax* was a light cruiser of 7,000 tons carrying eight 6-inch guns in four twin turrets; 'A' and 'B' forward and 'X' and 'Y' turrets aft. She was also fitted with upper-deck torpedo tubes and a Sea Fox seaplane carried on a catapult amidships. Adjacent to this was a crane for lifting the aircraft from the water to the catapult.

I joined the ship at Chatham where she was being prepared for a two-year commission at the America and West Indies station based in Bermuda. Captain C.H.L. Woodhouse was in command with Commander D.H.E. Everett as executive officer. The first few weeks were spent getting her shipshape and settling down the crew.

From Bermuda our first long cruise was to the Caribbean Islands, then around South America, steaming down the east coast, through the Magellan Straits, up the west coast, through the Panama Canal and back to Bermuda, stopping on many courtesy calls on route. It was a pleasant cruise, marred only by the terrible earthquake that occurred in January 1939 whilst the ship was at Valparaiso. The epicentre was a town nearby called Talcuahana which was completely demolished. Our ship's company was sent there for four days to help provide relief with food, water, medical supplies, tents and blankets. I landed with some of my staff to make safe some of the buildings and help the homeless people until the Chilean Army arrived and took charge.

Once when the ship was anchored off a small Chilean town, we were presented with a huge live turtle on board with the compliments of the local dignitaries. We had no idea what to do with it so the commander decided that the ship's company should have real turtle soup with their evening meal, which was fine, until we tried to kill it. Butch, our marine butcher managed to turn the turtle upside down on the upper deck where it lay helpless, rocking on its armour-like shell. After several hours beating with a cleaver it was still alive, pulling in its head with every blow. Eventually it gave up the ghost and died. Then came the nauseous task of trying to cut, dig and scrape the flesh from the shell, which took all day and ended with a pile of bloody mess on the deck. The cooks tried to make some turtle soup, but by then nobody felt like eating it.

One Sunday afternoon when the ship was anchored in a small bay off Brazil, I decided to go shark fishing with a young pay sub-lieutenant. We tied a whole loaf of bread to a shark hook and using a piece of wooden box for a float, cast the line from the stern of the ship. We soon hooked a medium-sized shark and managed to drag it to the side of the ship. The line wasn't strong enough so we got a heavier rope, tied it in a noose around our line and dropped the rope over the shark's nose until we could tighten it under its fins. Then we tried, with other helpers, to haul the shark up on to the quarterdeck, but it seemed to catch on something on the ship's side. Meanwhile, below us in the stern of the ship, one of our engineers called Dickie Bird was taking a shower when he noticed the bathroom become very dark. Looking up he saw a shark's head looming through the porthole, apparently trying to smash its way in. Terrified, he ran screaming down the passageway to his cabin, stark naked and dripping wet. Poor Dickie never lived it down.

The *Ajax* docked in Bermuda early in 1939 for a small refit. She was expected to remain there for about six months during which time sports days, regattas and competitions were held as well as naval exercises, gunnery practice and speed trials with the other cruiser on the station, HMS *Exeter*. She was a slightly heavier ship of 10,000 tons, fitted with six 8-inch guns.

Murmurings of a sabre-rattling hot-head called Adolf Hilter, thousands of miles away in Germany, did not concern us much at that time, in fact I arranged for my wife, Gladys, to come out to Bermuda for a holiday. We spent a very pleasant six months together to the extent that we failed to realise the serious developments in Europe until the *Ajax* and the *Exeter* were ordered to sea a week or so before Britain declared war on Germany. Presumably the Admiralty didn't have too much faith in Neville Chamberlain's declaration of 'Peace in our time'. The holiday was over.

On the day war was declared the captain cleared lower deck, and all the officers and men not on duty mustered on the quarterdeck where Captain Woodhouse gave us the news. The chaplain said a few prayers, then we exercised action stations.

The *Ajax*'s task was to patrol the Atlantic Ocean. Only an hour or so later we had our first prize. We spotted a German merchant ship, the *SS Olinda*, steaming along bound for Germany. Captain Woodhouse ordered her to heave to and steamed the *Ajax* up close to her. We landed a boarding party and took off the master and crew who weren't even aware that we were at war. Captain Woodhouse was at a loss what to do with his trophy since he couldn't afford to leave a steaming party on her as we were thousands of miles from a British port. He had no option but to use the *Olinda* as a gunnery target and sink her. So *Ajax* claimed the first enemy ship in the war.

The following day the German merchant ship *SS Carl Fritzen* met with the same fate. The officers and men were taken off and the ship deposited on the bottom of the ocean. We then had two foreign crews on board, a mixture of Germans and Swedes. Later they were transferred to our store ship and taken to the Falkland Islands where they remained for the duration of the war. With two prizes to our credit, the captain earned the nickname 'One a day Wimpey', but it was a few weeks before we claimed the third, the *SS Ussukuma*, which joined the other two on the ocean bed.

At this point the war seemed quite pleasant to us, just cruising around the Atlantic looking for quarry while the *Exeter* was doing the same well to the south of us. Being the larger ship she carried the flag of Commodore H. Harwood, the flag officer of the American and West Indies Station. We were also helped by the New Zealand ship HMNZS *Achilles*, a sister ship to the *Ajax*, patrolling somewhere south of Capetown. A county class cruiser, *HMS Cumberland*, was also under the command of Commodore Harwood but she was having a much needed self-refit in the Falkland Islands.

The Treaty of Versailles, signed after the defeat of the Germans in World War I, had enforced certain restrictions on German warship construction. Consequently, new ships were not to exceed 10,000 tons nor could they mount guns larger than 11 inches in diameter. To keep within these limits the Germans used welded joints and seams as opposed to our lapped and riveted seams and new diesel engines against our oil-fired steam turbines. This combination gave them a speed of 26 knots and they could cruise for 20,000 miles without refuelling. Each battleship was fitted with six 11-inch and eight 5.9-inch guns and by using new alloy metals for non-essential parts they remained within the legal weight restrictions.

Just before war was declared two of these pocket battleships, the *Admiral Graf Spee* and the *Deutschland*, were secretly put to sea with the sole object of harassing and sinking British merchant ships, so forming an effective blockade of Britain. The Germans confused our captured merchant seamen by changing the names of these battleships and rapidly altering areas of operations so they did not know which was raiding where. Quite soon a number of our ships were sunk in areas as far apart as the North Atlantic, South Atlantic and the Indian Ocean. The most recent of these was the *Doric Star* whose last reported position was off South-West Africa. It was our objective to track down whichever pocket battleship was operating in this area and stop her.

Commodore Harwood anticipated that the raider would make for the River Plate estuary – a vital focal point for all shipping. If his assumption were correct, he estimated she could be intercepted in that area about the 12 or 13 December. He ordered *Ajax* and *Achilles* to rendezvous with *Exeter* off the River Plate on 12 December and transferred his ensign to our ship, *Ajax*. The three cruisers then exercised the action procedure to be taken should the enemy appear.

The following day, 13 December 1939, dawned bright, clear and calm. Shortly after 6am a ship was spotted on the horizon. The *Exeter* was sent to investigate and she reported back that it was a pocket battleship. 'Action Stations', and our three ships took up their positions with *Exeter* on our port beam and *Achilles* in line with us ahead. We set off at full speed with the battle ensigns flying at mast-head. My responsibilities at action stations were in the after end of the ship where, as the damage control officer, I was in charge of the after repair parties and their equipment below decks. My position was in the wardroom flat, which was just outside the wardroom and adjacent to the ammunition hoist carrying cordite and shells to 'X' turret above. My staff were scattered around the flat, sitting or lying on the deck in anticipation. We had no idea what was going on; all we could hear was the noise from our own guns blasting away. We were already in range of the German ship's deadly 11-inch guns and desperately speeding towards her to get in range for our 6-inch guns.

With the range rapidly closing, *Exeter* was put out of action by a direct hit. Down below in the wardroom the sick-bay staff had cleared away all the chairs and small furniture to make an auxiliary sick-bay. Someone had dumped a dining-chair near me so I thought 'I might as well sit down as stand up'. Then suddenly it happened. There was a horrible tearing noise followed by a mighty explosion. In the fraction of a second before all the lights went out, I saw that chair disintegrate and disappear. I found myself flying across the wardroom flat until I hit the far side bulkhead, closely followed by debris, shrapnel, bits of the ship's structure and I don't know what. All I can remember was calling out 'Jesus Christ'.

I could hear running water and the glug-glug of oil or hydraulic fluid from burst pipes. It was pitch dark except for an odd gleam overhead. Luckily my own hand torch was still on its lanyard around my neck. I shouted to the electrician, who was apparently still alive, for some emergency lighting which soon came on.

Then we saw the damage. An 11-inch delayed-action shell had ploughed through the upper deck, a distance of about ten feet over the wardroom flat, pierced the armoured ring of the ammunition hoist and exploded. All six handlers inside were killed; their bodies indistinguishable, disembodied and blown to hell. Why our own cordite and shells never exploded we shall never know. If they had it would have been the last of *Ajax*.

The dead could wait; we had lots of work to do. Sloshing around the flooded flat we managed to stem most of the flow from the ruptured pipes and clear away some of the torn structure and debris. Our wounded had to be transferred to our forward sick-bay for treatment. My own wounds were minor, in fact I thought the blood running down my leg was water or oil.

Whilst we were busy aft, the battle was still on and *Ajax* was steaming at full speed, zig-zagging to avoid being hit again. We were still firing from our two forward turrets; we didn't realise until later that the shell had dented the armoured ring of 'Y' turret, putting it out of action as well.

At the end of the day we heard the whole story. The captain broadcast over the ship's Tannoy that the pocket battleship had entered Uruguayan territorial waters at Montevideo. We later learned that the ship was the *Admiral Graf Spee*, retreating for a respite to repair her damaged hull. The *Ajax* and the *Achilles* remained as close as possible outside territorial waters at constant action stations, waiting for the *Graf Spee* to come out. During that time we managed to bury our dead comrades at sea.

After four days our spotter aircraft reported that the *Graf Spee* was leaving harbour. We stood by for further action for some considerable time only to learn that the *Graf Spee* steamed over a shallow sandbank, had her crew taken off, and blew up. Scuttled instead of coming out to fight. The following day her captain, Captain Hans Langsdorf, committed suicide.

Able Seaman Jack Napier

In 1938 during the Munich crisis HMS *Exeter* had been shadowing from Buenos Aires up to Rio de Janeiro some of the German merchant marine. We kept out of sight, of course, mostly what they saw was the top of our mast, but we maintained close contact. We – *Ajax* and *Exeter* – were the South American Squadron.

If ever the war came, we thought we were going to get a good hammering. We heard about the German ship-building and how their fleets were all modern. Our ships went back to the 1914–18 war. The *Exeter* was built in 1928 but she was in bad repair really, because she had been commissioned before on the South American station, and she was recalled for the Abyssinian crisis in 1935–36. Another time she went around Cape Horn. I wasn't on her then, but that would have been in 1934–35.

When the battle started my action stations were on the port 0.5 inch machine-guns, which were situated on 'B' gundeck right level with the port side of the bridge. It was a very bad position really. However, when the Germans opened up and the shells were coming quite close to us, the bridge shouted down to us to take shelter. So, I and my other two pals went into the lower part of the bridge and we stood behind a ladder where some lockers were. When the 11-inch shell penetrated the bridge and exploded on the 4-inch gun mounting, I was on the bridge, but, of course, we never realised what had happened until it was too late. The first thing I realised, that most of the bridge personnel were wiped out, was when a head came rolling down the ladder. And I recognised the head. Then I left there and I went on to the port waist and started helping with the casualties and at the same time the torpedo tubes on the starboard side had suffered a near-miss. Splinters were all over and killed quite a lot of the people on the tubes themselves. I was helping with the wounded, but splinters penetrated the hydrants and the hydrants which were leaking and the hoses useless. Our decks were flooded. The wounded were lying down on the deck and getting covered in water. Some of them must have died from pneumonia. There were so many casualties around, you see, we were trying to do our best for them, getting them down to the wardroom and the sick bay. Of course some casualties never made it at all. Two or three of us would get hold of the person and get them down. There was one person I remember vividly, now. Part of the shells went through the Chief Petty Officers' mess and exploded in the locker-room. The blast blew this person up through the ladder of the hatchway from just below and he caught his leg on the conning of the hatch after it had blown up. It was the Chief Torpedo Gunner's mate, and I remember him well. He had a compound fracture in the leg. Well, he never survived. This happened all in about half an hour. We didn't have time to think properly. But being so well trained I suppose, the discipline was there and we were looking for jobs to do. We couldn't hit back at all. So, the captain in the meantime had gone to the after-control tower and found that everything was all out of order there and he got a boat's compass and he started giving orders for steering. As the main steering position was manned we formed a chain of men from the control tower, along the quarterdeck to the after-steering position. The captain would give the orders, and we passed the orders on, one by one. The orders were short and sweet – just, port 15 or starboard 15. We had to bellow because 'Y' turret was still firing.

I remained like that until we pulled out of the action altogether. There was one period when we were on the reciprocal bearing to the *Graf Spee*, and when I looked over to her, I thought the battle ensigns they were flying were so close, you could pick up a snowball and throw it at them. Of course she was a couple of miles away. We were going to go in to ram. The Captain said, when our guns stop firing, we've still got the speed of the ship, so we can go in and ram. Of course, if we had done so, there wouldn't be very much of us left.

The *Ajax* and the *Achilles* at that time saw what was happening. They went in as close as possible to draw fire. We were actually on fire from the bowels of the ship up to about the bridge. They were fighting fires continually, all the time. One of our midshipmen went forward to try and douse the fire in the paint shop and the next thing we knew, he had disappeared, by the blast of another shell. There was nothing found of him whatsoever.

It happened so quickly and time was so precious. We were kept busy, every man jack of us. All the time. And of course, when we pulled out we were told we were going down to the Falklands to patch up. Then we started finding the dead, going round collecting them. All these damage control parties, quite a lot of them were killed. We were picking up their remains and putting them in sacks. We knew them all. We'd been together for nearly two years and eight months. I joined as a boy and finished as an Able Seaman on *Exeter*. So, we weren't strangers, we knew each other.

I can still smell the stench of the burned flesh now. I'd recognise the stench right away, anywhere. It's one of those things you know. They talk now about the Falklands war and people under stress and strain; but we didn't talk about such things in those days. It comes back to you. Just imagine the ship being struck and seeing people mowed down alongside you and yet you're still standing up in one piece.

We stopped the ship twice and buried the dead on the way back to the Falklands. But there's one officer, a Lieutenant in the Marines, who was wounded and nursed by one of the nurses in the Falkland Islands and he married her and he stayed down there. In fact he's still alive and very much in action.

We lost three or four more men, who had been wounded, while we were in the Falklands. We repaired ourselves from the ironplate of the SS *Great Britain*. We left home for Plymouth in February and it took three weeks to get there. We received a wonderful welcome. People lined the dockyard for what seemed miles and miles. We felt like heroes.

Surgeon Lieutenant Roger Lancashire

I joined the *Exeter* on 13 December 1936, exactly three years before the battle of the River Plate. We were under the command of Commodore Harwood who was absolutely certain that at some time we would finish up at war with Germany. He told us all about their three Pocket Battleships. It would be our job to tackle those. A hell of a lot happened during the next three years. After I got married in Bermuda on 17 April 1937 I got a fortnight's leave and we went to New York for our honeymoon. *Exeter* had a lovely cruise mapped out to go through Panama, but then strikes and riots blew up at an oilfield in Trinidad. So off we were sent. It would normally have taken us seven or eight days at normal cruising speed from Bermuda to Port of Spain, but we did it in forty-six hours. She was absolutely flat out, doing about twenty-six knots which was exhilarating, but with the heat generated down below, we had to keep on changing watches and it had a bad effect on me. I caught a bug and finished up in hospital.

In the West Indies the whole thing was rather like the Royal Tournament. We'd barely docked before the Royal Marines were ashore, then the field gun and finally the stokers. We had two Walrus aircraft which then dropped leaflets. We didn't have any casualties and we didn't have to fire our guns in anger. It was, however, a bloody good experience.

The next big thing was the earthquake on 24 January 1939 at Concepción in Chile near the naval base of Talcahuano. It was very nearly one hundred years after the earthquake graphically described by Charles Darwin in the 'Voyage of the Beagle'.

During the earthquake I stayed on board to receive the casualties and one of them was a young woman whose husband had been killed. Their little house fell about them. She managed to get clear and gave birth prematurely to a little boy in the main square. They arrived on board with a lot of other casualties. The chief sick-berth Petty Officer and I cleaned this little baby up. We also had some patients from a hospital which had been evacuated and one of them was a Roman Catholic priest. His mate came up with him to the sick-bay and decided that they had better christen this little fellow. One of his various names was Exeter. Soon all the ship's company knew what was going on and they all wanted to have a peep. Without any prompting from anyone many donated a day's pay to this lad because they knew that he wouldn't have a dad. We gave the money to the British Consul in Valparaiso and asked him to deal with it.

There were a lot of casualties coming on board and we were really busy. This was the first time I had had to deal with so many; certainly more than in Trinidad.

To make matters more exciting for me our pay lieutenant had appendicitis on the way back. We did two trips down so I landed him in Valparaiso because I knew there was a British hospital there. We got him in there and I gave him the anaesthetic. The surgeon operated on him and back we went for another lot. We took the Chilean soldiers down with us to stop looting but they were all very seasick on board. All this for me was good training. After this we circumnavigated South America twice, went round the Horn the last time back and down to the Falklands several times. We then sailed for New York in May 1939 for the British Empire Exhibition. The King and Queen were there before us so we missed their ticker-tape welcome. My wife had arrived and we and my fellow officers were rewarded with a thrilling police motorcade and given a hearty welcome at the 'Aquacade' where we saw Johnny Weissmuller, who had become famous as Tarzan, in a high diving act.

The *Exeter* arrived back in Plymouth in August 1939, flying our paying off pennant. We got four days at home and I had time to go to Liverpool because Gieves' had a branch there and I organised a new uniform for myself. My wife and I were staying with my parents because we lived within half a mile of each other in South Manchester. When we got back – we'd been to a cinema show in town – there was a policeman patrolling the drive at our house with a telegram telling me to report back at once. So we had to go into Moss Bros where my only uniform was being repaired. My wife had to come with me on the train down to Plymouth to stitch it together and put the sleeves back on. I never got my new uniform from Gieves' until on the way home again.

When we got to Plymouth after being summoned to rejoin the *Exeter*, one or two failed to turn up. Our sick berth attendant was one of them. We set sail and this time Harwood had been up to the Admiralty and got a flag captain for us: F. S. 'Hookie' Bell who had been commander of *Repulse* before he took us over. He was a magnificent man, a splendid fellow. We were told that we were going back to our war station. During the three years we'd been out there, we'd created a tremendous liaison with all the British merchantmen. Harwood was very keen on that. It was my job along with 'Torps', the torpedo officer, to go aboard every ship flying the Red Ensign and make ourselves known to the captain, to let him know that we were around.

We were halfway between Freetown and Rio de Janeiro when war was declared. Since we had been into Rio the regulations said we could not go into any Brazilian port for another three months. So we went down to Montevideo in Uruguay where we had carried out our squadron exercises in the River Plate area. We already knew that a Pocket Battleship had sailed from her home port bound for the South Atlantic to be ready to attack our merchant ships when war was declared on 3 September. She sank nine without a single loss of life, which says much for the humanity of Captain Langsdorff. The Germans tried to make us think there were two of them because they had different nameplates. She could either have been the *Graf Spee* or the *Admiral Scheer*. During the whole battle we thought we were fighting the *Scheer*. The previous time that she had been sighted was by a Dutch merchantman after the *Graf Spee* had sunk the *Africa Shell* off Mauritius in territorial waters. She'd been sighted at close range coming back round the Cape. Then she was wearing the nameplate of the *Scheer*. We were never deceived into thinking that there were two of them. We knew that she had a supply ship, the *Altmark*. We bottled up the other supply ships in Montevideo.

We were long overdue in the *Exeter* for a refit because our starboard outer propeller had a bit of a kink in it, which wouldn't have slowed us down by itself, but also the bottom needed scraping. So one of the other ships, it could have been the *Dorsetshire* or *Cumberland*, had come across to relieve us. We were halfway across to Simonstown from the Plate when the *Graf Spee* came back again to the South Atlantic. She'd been wasting her time over in the Indian Ocean but had sunk the *SS Doric Star* and *Doric Star*, God bless her, gave a magnificent display, keeping her radio going all the time to pinpoint herself exactly. Without waiting for further orders Hookie Bell turned us right about and back we went to the Plate. We were unaccompanied – we hadn't even seen the *Achilles* – but *Ajax* were old pals of ours by then. Harwood had worked out the various options that were open to us. The Germans are great ones for doing the magnificent thing on the right day and Harwood reckoned that on 8 December they would be thinking of how they could extract their revenge off the Falklands Islands for the sinking of the *Scharnhorst* and *Gneisenau*, twenty-five years earlier almost to the day. So on 8 December the *Exeter* went round and round the Falklands looking for smoke or anything suspicious, but nothing happened at all. We then rejoined Harwood who had shifted his flag from *Exeter* to *Ajax*. It was a good thing that he did. Together with *Achilles* we rendezvoused about 200 miles off the mouth of the Plate on 12 December. The obvious thing that we had to do was to get the *Graf Spee* to divide her fire. We were steaming in line ahead when the enemy was sighted.

Harwood had decided what we were going to do twenty-four hours in advance. We detached ourselves and steamed away as fast as we could in order to close the range; but their opening fire was so accurate that in the first ten minutes of the battle we lost five officers and fifty-six ratings killed outright. That was ten per cent of the ship's company. I was squatting on my haunches close to the wardroom door taking drugs and instruments out of a cupboard when the *Graff Spee*'s first salvo fell short and burst on impact with the water. There was a loud crash and a blast of air blew my cap off and threw me backwards. Later on, I found part of an 11-inch shell fuze-cap embedded in the fanlight casing. Had I been standing, it would certainly have beheaded me. Unfortunately, other fragments came hurtling inboard, killing all the fire party assembled in the stokers' bathroom on the same deck.

The next salvo struck 'A' turret and blew up and started a fire right forward. We never saw one of the team of shipwrights again, nor Sub-Lieutenant Morse whose father was C-in-C in Freetown. The second one hit 'B' turret manned by the Royal Marines which was immediately below the bridge. It was lucky that anybody came out of it alive. On the bridge, there were only three survivors and old Hookie Bell had splinters in both eyes and his leg. I suppose there were about ten men on the bridge including those from the plot just aft, one of whom was our sub-lieutenant. The three survivors went aft to control, which was just forward of 'Y' turret. I didn't go up to the bridge, I stayed down in the wardroom. Thank God we had rehearsed 'Action Stations' prior to this battle because we'd rigged up the sick-bay so many times in the last three years, that everything went like clockwork. Fortunately, to take the place of our missing sick-birth attendant, we had an extra war complement from *Ajax*. Some of the wounded were treated in the sick-bay up forward but most of them were brought down to the wardroom. Every now and then the Master-at-Arms, who was part of my team, thank God, would call me up to see if I could identify somebody, especially if he was on his last legs.

The casualties were fairly devastating. There were two or three who literally died in my arms. These were people who I'd been living with, as it were, for three years. There were cases where, if I'd had the facilities and an endless supply of blood transfusions, things might have been different, but it wasn't like that. I did a quick assessment of who was most likely to benefit and then went to work on them. We had no nursing orderlies with us. But the Royal Marine bandsmen came up after their transmitting station had been put out of action. I took over 'Hookie' Bell's day and sleeping cabin. A lot of the casualties were in there. There was quite a lot of stitching up and other tasks which merged into one another.

As the day crept on and night fell I had, with the help of the bandsmen, got a good team going. We had a problem with the morphine. Instead of being in bottles with a rubber-topped diaphragm so that you could plunge the needle through, they were in ampoules. That was one of the things that I spent a day complaining about, when I returned to Devonport, with an RNVR Surgeon Rear-Admiral who listed our requirements. The first thing I told him was, that morphine should not be dispensed in the ampoules because to break them open we had to use a file which was very time-consuming. In a hurry it was much easier to use bottles. Thank God we had a ruddy great packing case which we'd had on board since we commissioned in 1936, which was only to be opened in action. A character came along to deliver a message. He was rather badly shot up so I put a few stitches in him and tied him up and made him as comfortable as possible. Then when he had come to, he said, 'Well, let me do something, Doc, for heaven's sake'. So I said, 'All right. Open that crate for me.' Right at the very top was the very thing we wanted; a ruddy great big pair of tailor's scissors used for cutting open serge trousers. It was beautifully planned. I remember putting that down in my report. There was also enough morphine in there. I operated on a fellow called Causton. I was wondering whether I ought to amputate his foot but then I saw that there was a good blood supply. Several of his tendons had gone. I knew that I had three or four ampoules of anaesthetic – which was quite new in those days – to give an injection into a vein. I got them myself in Rio and there was one left up in the sick bay. So I sent a messenger up to get it. With the assistance of the sick-berth PO, we operated on Causton and laid him out on the deck of 'Hookie' Bell's sleeping cabin. I got the finest sutures and needles which we could get hold of and stitched the tendons together again. It was a nice clean wound and kept his foot on for him. In 1943 I was sent out to Durban. I spent a fortnight in the transit camp near Capetown, so I went down most days to the naval hospital and this fellow Causton was still there. He had found work in an office and was walking about with a stick. I felt about ten yards tall.

The only time I left the sick-bay was when I got the message that 'Hookie' Bell and Commander Graham had been blown off the bridge and were wounded in the legs. 'Hookie' went to the after-conning position and the Commander went to his cabin. As I poked my head through the hatch on my way from the wardroom to the quarterdeck, a hand shoved my head down again with a yell, 'Port Twenty'. I passed the message on to the chain of men for transmission to the two perspiring heroes who were manning the massive steering wheel way back aft.

On deck I had never seen anything like it before. The immaculate *Exeter* I'd known for three years was an absolute shambles. All the aircraft who had been told to stay on their catapults were now riddled and high octane fuel was pouring out of them. Richard Jennings, 'Guns', was standing on the lid of 'Y' turret giving his orders. Hookie Bell and I went up to see him and he gave me a running commentary of what was going on. It was fantastic. I was spellbound. There in the distance you could see the *Graf Spee*, firing every now and again. The exciting thing was that *Ajax* and *Achilles* had made a smokescreen and they were taking it in turns to dodge in and out of it and give a rapid and accurate six-inch broadside, which the *Graf Spee* didn't like very much. 'Hookie' Bell said to me, 'You see what position we're in: "A" and "B" turret are out of action (which I already knew), so we've only got one gun here in "Y" turret. All the power's gone, so even that's got to be trained and loaded by hand. But it's all we've got now.'

Then he said, 'If he gives me half a chance and heads this way I intend to ram the bugger.'

I fixed up his legs to stop them from bleeding and said, 'Now look, when you can, let me know when you're under control and I'll come and do what I can for your eyes'. At about midnight he came below. We were swinging about all over the place, but fortunately, as part of my job years ago, I'd done quite a lot of eye work, so with the chief steward holding a torch I was able to clear one eye and reminded 'Hookie' that Nelson had managed pretty well with only one. It was not until the following Sunday night, when he was staying as the guest of Hennicker-Heaton, the governor at Port Stanley, that I was able to do the other eye under much easier conditions.

There were a number of facial injuries from the battle. I had to stitch an ear back on and there were quite a few scalp injuries. A Royal Marine came in, brought by his mates, and they couldn't think what the matter was. He was the most mild-mannered chap but he suddenly started behaving very oddly and using the most terrible obscene language. So I thought there must be something the matter with him. They couldn't find any sign of a wound or scar so I had a jolly good look at his scalp and sure enough there was a tiny hole in the front. A fragment of shell had gone right through into the frontal lobe like a leucotomy. I left it there like that; that was the cause of his problem. I wanted to take him back home because we could have looked after him and my friend Sir Geoffrey Jefferson who was a neuro-surgeon could have helped. They sent him down to the Falklands Hospital where they couldn't do anything. We took him up to Buenos Aires where he was operated upon and died on the table. He should have been left as he was. I was furious because, once we got down to Port Stanley, I was not allowed to see any of my patients at the hospital. They wouldn't allow me near them. There was a Royal Marine from 'B' turret whose forearm had been blown off completely. He should have been left alone or given a transfusion. He'd lost an enormous amount of blood. A Canadian pathologist, who was chief of the hospital, thought he knew better and insisted on doing something or other on the table and, of course, he died. That was tragic.

I was constantly on the go from that Tuesday and the wee small hours of Wednesday until the following Sunday night. Harwood made a signal to Hookie Bell and said, 'Can you make it to the Falklands?' We had a very dangerous list to port and our main mast was whipping about in a terrible state. We were navigating by a boat's compass.

You see, we had been struck by seven 11-inch shells, three of which passed straight through the ship without exploding. One of them went clean through the sick-bay, through where the heads (toilets) were, removing all the bedpans and the bath. The blast of the things did a hell of a lot of damage. We weren't holed below the water-line but the place was absolutely incredible. The *Exeter* was a damned well-built ship.

When we were down at Port Stanley afterwards, Commodore Harwood sent for me and 'Hookie' Bell. Governor Henniker-Heaton was there and they asked me what we were going to do with all the patients. Some of them could be taken back but they were not allowed unless they were capable of looking after themselves, which was fair enough. So I suggested that since there were lots of fracture cases, they should send out an orthopaedic surgeon. 'Good God,' he said, 'They'll never do that.' I said, 'Of course they would. They'd be most interested to see their injuries.'

They sent a pal of mine who I'd met many times in my RNVR days in Liverpool. They put them all in one of the cruisers, the *Dorsetshire* I think, and took them over to the Cape.

The only reason that I am able to tell this story now is that we in *Exeter* had basically been the same ship's company for three years, so here was a lot of rapport and camaraderie which there wouldn't have been the case if we had been a new commission. Without that, we could not have survived the punishment we took.

Chronology of Naval Events 1914–1939

1914
July
29 Admiralty send 'Warning Telegram' to Fleets.

Aug.
1 Government order Naval Mobilization.
4 Great Britain declares war on Germany.
5 Minelaying in open sea begun by Germans. Minelayer KÖNIGIN LUISE sunk.
6 HMS AMPHION mined off Yarmouth. Action between HMS BRISTOL and SMS KARLSRUHE in West Indies.
7 Action between HMS GLOUCESTER and GOEBEN and BRESLAU off Greece.
9 HMS BIRMINGHAM sinks first enemy submarine (U-15) in North Sea.
16 Landing of original British Expeditionary Force in France completed.
26 HMS HIGHFLYER sinks German armed merchant cruiser KAISER WILHELM DER GROSSE.
28 Action off Heligoland. German KÖLN, MAINZ and ARIADNE sunk.

Sept.
3 HMS SPEEDY mined off Humber.
5 First British warship (HMS PATHFINDER) sunk by submarine in North Sea.
14 Action between armed merchant cruisers CARMANIA and CAP TRAFALGAR in South Atlantic: latter sunk.
20 HMS PEGASUS sunk by KÖNIGSBERG.
22 HM Ships ABOUKIR, HOGUE and CRESSY sunk by submarine U-9.

Oct.
3 Royal Naval Division reaches Antwerp.
15 HMS HAWKE sunk by submarine in North Sea.
17 HMS UNDAUNTED and destroyers sink four destroyers off Holland. First British submarines E.1 and E.9 enter Baltic. German submarines attempt raid on Scapa Flow.
20 First merchant vessel (British SS GLITRA) sunk by German submarine.
27 HMS AUDACIOUS mined off Donegal.
31 HMS HERMES sunk by submarine in Straits of Dover.

1914
Nov.
1 Action off Coronel. HMS GOOD HOPE and MONMOUTH sunk by von Spee's squadron. Admiral Craddock and over 1,600 lives lost.
3 First German naval raid on England.
6 Submarine B.11 is first British warship to enter Dardanelles.
9 SMS EMDEN destroyed by HMAS SYDNEY at Cocos Islands.
11 HM Torpedo Gunboat NIGER sunk by submarine off Deal.
21 Naval air raid on Friedrichshaven.
26 HMS BULWARK destroyed by internal explosion in Sheerness harbour.

Dec.

8 Battle of the Falklands. German Ships SCHARNHORST, GNEISENAU, LEIPZIG, NÜRNBERG sunk.

13 Turkish battleship MESSOUDIEH sunk by B.11 in Dardanelles.

25 British seaplane raid on Cuxhaven.

1915
Jan.

1 HMS FORMIDABLE sunk by submarine in the Channel.

24 Action off the Dogger Bank, German Cruiser BLÜCHER sunk.

Feb.

19 Naval attack on Dardanelles begins. First ship (Norwegian SS BELRIDGE) torpedoed without warning.

Mar.

14 DRESDEN, last cruiser of Admiral von Spee's squadron, sunk.

18 Naval attack on Dardanelles repulsed. French BOUVET and HMS IRRESISTIBLE and OCEAN sunk.

23 First kite-balloon ship, HMS MANICA, commissioned.

28 First passenger ship (British SS FALABA) sunk by submarine.

April

25 Allies land on Gallipoli.

May

1 First US ship (SS GULFLIGHT) torpedoed.

7 SS LUSITANIA sunk by U.20.

13 HMS GOLIATH sunk by Turkish destroyer in Dardanelles.

25 HMS TRIUMPH sunk by submarine off Dardanelles.

27 HMS MAJESTIC sunk by submarine in Dardanelles. Minelayer PRINCESS IRENE destroyed by internal explosion at Sheerness.

June

7 L. Z. 37 destroyed by Lieut. Warneford, RNAS, near Ghent (first occasion of airship successfully attacked by aeroplane).

July

11 German Lt. Cruiser KÖNIGSBERG destroyed by monitors.

Aug.

8 Turkish battleship BARBAROUSSE-HAIREDINE sunk by British submarine E.11 in Dardanelles.

13 HMS ROYAL EDWARD sunk in Aegean by submarine.

19 E.13 attacked by warships while aground in Danish waters. SS ARABIC sunk by submarine. HM Q-ship BARALONG sinks U.27.

21 First ship's crew in open boats (British SS RUEL) fired on by submarine.

Oct.

23 German Cruiser PRINZ ADALBERT sunk by E.8 in Baltic.

Nov.

7 SMS UNDINE sunk by E.19.

17 Hospital ship ANGLIA mined off Dover. German Cruiser BREMEN sunk by British submarine in Baltic.

30 HMS NATAL destroyed by internal explosion in Cromarty harbour.

1916
Jan.

6 HMS KING EDWARD VII sunk by mine off North of Scotland.

8 Evacuation of the Gallipoli Peninsula.

15 SS APPAM captured by raider MŒWE.

Feb.

11 HMS ARETHUSA mined in North Sea.

29 Action in North Sea between raider GREIF and British auxiliary cruiser ALCANTARA; both sunk.

1916
April

25 Lowestoft and Yarmouth raided by German battle cruiser squadron.

27 HM RUSSELL mined in Mediterranean.

May

31 Battle of Jutland. *(British casualties: 6,097 killed, 510 wounded.) Loss in Ships:–British: 3 battle-cruisers, 3 cruisers, 8 destroyers. German: 1 battleship, 1 battle-cruiser, 4 light cruisers, 2 destroyers.
*Cf. Trafalgar; 449 killed, 1,241 wounded.

June

5 HMS HAMPSHIRE mined off Orkneys. Earl Kitchener drowned.

July

27 Capt. Fryatt of SS BRUSSELS shot.

Aug.

19 HMS FALMOUTH and NOTTINGHAM sunk by submarine in North Sea.

Oct.

26 First destroyer raid in Dover Straits.

1917
Jan.

9 HMS CORNWALLIS sunk by submarine in the Mediterranean.
23 Harwich flotilla action in North Sea; British Destroyer SIMOOM sunk.

Feb.

25 British SS LACONIA sunk (immediate cause of America's entry into war).

Mar.

16 Raider LEOPARD sunk by HMS ACHILLES and Armed Boarding Steamer DUNDEE.
21 Hospital ship ASTURIAS torpedoed.
30 Hospital ship GLOUCESTER CASTLE torpedoed.

April

3 Torpedo Gunboat JASON mined off west coast of Scotland.
17 Ambulance transports LANFRANC and DONEGAL sunk in Channel.
20 Destroyer raid on Dover Straits; action by SWIFT and BROKE.

May

15 14 British drifters sunk by Austrian light forces in Straits of Otranto.
26 Hospital ship DOVER CASTLE sunk in Mediterranean.

July

9 HMS VANGUARD sunk by internal explosion in harbour.

Aug.

2 Sqn. Cdr. E. H. Dunning first pilot to land aircraft on ship underway.

Sept.

4 German submarine shells Scarborough.

Oct.

2 HMS DRAKE sunk by submarine.
17 HMS STRONGBOW and MARY ROSE sunk in North Sea convoy raid.

Nov.

2 Kattegat raid by naval light forces.
17 Light cruiser action off Heligoland.

Dec.

6 US Battleship Division joins Grand Fleet in Scapa Flow.
12 HMS PARTRIDGE sunk in North Sea convoy raid.

1918
Jan.

4 Hospital ship REWA sunk.
14 German destroyers bombard Yarmouth.
20 Naval action outside Dardanelles. SMS BRESLAU and HMS RAGLAN sunk. GOEBEN mined and beached.

Feb.

5 SS TUSCANIA sunk off Irish coast. (Only loss of US transport under British naval escort.)
16 Dover shelled by German submarine.
26 Hospital ship GLENART CASTLE sunk.

April

15 Kattegat raid by naval light forces.
23 Raid on Ostend and Zeebrugge

May
9 Raid on Ostend. HMS VINDICTIVE sunk to block harbour.

June
27 Hospital ship LLANDOVERY CASTLE sunk off Irish coast.

Aug.
3 Ambulance transport WARILDA sunk.

Sept.
16 HMS GLATTON sunk by explosion in Dover harbour.

Oct.
31 Armistice with Turkey.

Nov.
2 Last British merchant vessels (SS SURADA and MURCIA) sunk by submarine (in the Mediterranean).
4 Armistice with Austria.
9 HMS BRITANNIA sunk by submarine in the Atlantic (last warship so lost).
11 Armistice with Germany.
15 KÖNIGSBERG with German delegates enters Firth of Forth to arrange surrender of German Fleet.
20 First contingent of German submarines surrender at Harwich.
21 High Seas Fleet arrives at Rosyth for internment in Scapa Flow.

1919
June
4 HMS/M L.55 sunk in Baltic by Bolshevik destroyers.
17 Lieutenant Agar, Captain of CMB 4, torpedoed and sank the Russian cruiser OLEG in Kronstadt: Agar awarded VC.
21 German High Seas Fleet scuttled at Scapa Flow. 11 battleships, 5 battlecruisers, 5 cruisers and 22 destroyers sunk: 3 cruisers and 18 destroyers beached.
24 Coronation review at Spithead.

July
30 Aircraft from HMS VINDICTIVE attacked Kronstadt Naval Base.

Aug.
3 During a strike by Liverpool City Police, HMS VALIANT, VENOMOUS and WHITLEY, anchored in River Mersey to protect the docks and support the civil power.
18 HMS KENT's detachment reached Vladivostock, from service in the Urals 4,500 miles West.

Oct.
1 WRNS disbanded.

1920
Jan.
12 Combined operation of all three Services against the 'Mad Mullah' of Somaliland.

June
16 HMS REVENGE, RAMILLIES, ARK ROYAL and WESTCOTT in action against Turks at Istria.
24 Start of operation against Turks on South coast of Sea of Marmara.
25 HMS REVENGE, ROYAL SOVEREIGN, MARLBOROUGH assist landing of 8,000 Greek troops to occupy Panderma.

Oct.
1 HMS GREENFLY captured by insurgents in Mesopotamia.

November
10 Body of the Unknown Warrior carried by HMS VERDUN from Calais to Dover for burial at Westminster Abbey.

1921
Jan.
20 HMS/M K5 lost on exercise.

April
1 RNVR reconstituted.
29 Mutiny by RNR battalion at Newport during Miners' strike.

May
20 RN College Osborne, opened in 1903, closed.

June

25 HMS/M K.15 sank in Portsmouth
Harbour.

Sept.

11 Admiral of the Fleet Prince Louis of
Battenberg died.

1922
Jan.

12 HMS VICTORY moved into No.2
dock in Portsmouth Yard.

Mar.

23 HMS VERSATILE accidentally
rammed and sank HMS/M H.42 off
Europa Point.

Sept.

4 To protect British interests, Royal
Navy concentrates ships at Smyrna.
24 HMS SPEEDY lost in collision in Sea
of Marmora.

1923
April

1 Naval responsibility for HM
Coastguard transferred to Board
of Trade.

May

1 HMS HERMES commissioned. First
aircraft carrier purpose built and first
with island superstructure.

June

22 Amalgamation of RMA (Blue
Marines) and RMLI (Red Marines)
to reform the Royal Marines. The
ranks of Gunner and Private were
replaced by Marine.

Oct.

1 HMS VERNON established ashore,
on the Old Gunwharf at Portsmouth.

Dec.

25 HMS CAPETOWN ordered to
Mexico to protect British interests.

1924
Jan.

10 HMS RESOLUTION rammed and
sank HMS/S L.24 off Portland Bill.

April

1 HMS CAROLINE, last survivor of
Jutland, became drillship of Ulster
Division, RNVR.
1 Shipborne element of RAF
recognised as Fleet Air Arm.

1925
Oct.

4 Rates of pay reduced for new entries
on advice of Anderson Committee.

1926
July

1 First night deck landing: Flight
Lieutenant Boyce in Blackburn Dart
N9804 on HMS FURIOUS.

Aug.

9 HMS/M H.29 foundered in two
minutes alongside at Devonport: loss
of civilian and naval personnel.

Sept.

5 Wanhsein incident on Tangtze:
HMS WIDGEON and COCKCHAFER
with naval brigade from DESPATCH,
SCARAB and MANTIS involved.

Oct.

22 HMS VALERIAN foundered in
hurricane off Bermuda.

1927
Mar.

11 'Heart of Oak' and 'A Life on the
Ocean Wave' officially recognised as
the marches of the RN and RM.

Oct.

27 HMS WILD SWAN repulsed Chinese
attack on mission hospital at
Swatow, China.

1928
Mar.

1 HMS COURAGEOUS
recommissioned and became first
carrier with transverse arrester wires.

1929
July

9 HMS/M H.47 lost in collision with
HMS/M L.21 off Pembrokeshire.

26 Midshipman Cobham and Able
Seaman awarded GC for gallantry
in turret explosion in HMS
DEVONSHIRE in which 18 killed.

1930
Jan.
21 HMS ST. GENNY foundered in the
Western Approaches. 23 lost.

Aug.
27 HMS HAREBELL evacuated
population of St. Kilda.

1931
June
 9 HMS/M POSEIDON lost in collsion
with SS YUTUA off Wei Hai Wei:
first use of Davis' submarine escape
apparatus.

Sept.
15 Pay cuts led to mutiny in some ships
of the Atlantic Fleet at Invergordon.

Oct.
 1 Boy Servants became Boy
Stewards.
 1 On recommendation of
May Committee, all pay
to have been reduced to
1925 scales.
16 Rank of Mate abolished.

1932
June
 3 HMS IMPLACABLE (ex-DUGUAY-
TROUIN) arrived Portsmouth
and exchanged salutes with
HMS VICTORY, her adversary at
Trafalgar.

1933
Jan.
 2 HMS COURAGEOUS
recommissioned, with first
(hydraulically controlled)
arrester gear.

1934
April
17 First flight of Fairey Swordfish
nicknamed 'Stringbag' by Fleet
Air Arm.

1935
Jan.
23 HMS HOOD collided with
RENOWN.

Feb.
26 First British seaborne radar tested.

Sept.
 9 A Cierva C30A autogyro becomes
first service rotary wing aircraft to
land on carrier HMS FURIOUS.
19 For the first time since 1746 Royal
Marines exercise their right to
march through the City of London
with fixed bayonets. Kept Guard at
Buckingham Palace for first time.

Nov.
19 Admiral of the Fleet Earl Jellicoe of
Scapa died.

1936
Mar.
11 Admiral of the Fleet Earl Beatty,
died.

May
 7 Officer's cap and badge of present
design adopted.

1937
Feb.
 9 First flight of Blackburn Skua, FAA's
first monoplane.

April
27 National Maritime Musuem,
Greenwich opened by King
George VI.

June
22 HMS AJAX from Bermuda
to Trinidad in support of the
Civil Power.
24 Admiral Sir William Fisher died.

July
30 Fleet Air Arm come under Admiralty
control.

Aug.
23 HMS REPULSE and CODRINGTON
gain release of British ship

taken by Spanish republican
cruiser.

Oct.
28 HMS SEAGULL launched at
Devonport to become the first
all-welded ship in the RN.

1938
May
10 An RAF Anson detected aircraft
taking off from and landing on HMS
COURAGEOUS at eight miles with
first side-scan ASV radar.

July
19 First appointment of Fifth Sea
Lord responsible for naval aviation.
Vice-Admiral the Hon. Sir Alexander
Ramsey, Chief of Naval Air Services.

Aug.
15 HMS SHEFFIELD fitted with first
RN radar.

1939
June
 1 HMS/M THETIS foundered in
Liverpool Bay on acceptance trials.

Aug.
24 Home Fleet and all ships in Home
Ports proceeded to War Stations.
29 Admiralty ordered mobilisation
of Fleet.
31 Admiralty ordered general
mobilisation of naval Reserves.

Sept.
 3 War declared against Germany. Mr
W. S. Churchill again became First
Lord – "Winston is back".
 3 HMS PLOVER laid first British
minefield, off the Bass Rock in the
Firth of Forth, and remained in
commission for thirty-one years.
 3 ATHENIA sunk by U.30. First British
merchant ship to be sunk in WWII.
 3 HMS AJAX sank the German
OLINDA in the Plata area.
 3 HMS SOMALI captured the blockade
runner HANNAH BLOGE in North
Atlantic. First capture of enemy
vessel in World War II.

14 HMS FAULKNOR, FIREDRAKE
and FOXHOUND sank U.39 off the
Hebrides, the first U-boat sunk in
World War II.
20 HMS FORESTER and FORTUNE sank
U.27, 60 miles west of the Hebrides.
26 First German aircraft destroyed in
World War II shot down by Lt.
McEwen in a Skua of 803 Sq. FAA.

Oct.
13 HMS ILEX and IMOGEN sank U.42
in Western Approaches.
15 HMS ROYAL OAK sunk at Scapa
Flow by U.47, with loss of 833 men.
20 HMS TRANSYLVANIA (AMC)
captured the German BIANCA in
Denmark Strait and sank POSEIDON
next day.

Nov.
20 HMS/M STURGEON sank the
German trawler GAULEITER
TELSCHOW 30 miles N.W. of
Heligoland: first RN submarine
success of World War II.
23 RAWALPINDI (AMC) sunk by
the SCHARNHORST in Iceland-
Faroes gap.
23 HMS CALYPSO captured
the German KONSUL
HENDRIK FISSER north of
the Faroes.
23 First German magnetic
mine, Type A, located at
Shoeburyness: rendered
safe by Lt-Cdr Ouvry
and Chief Petty Officer
Baldwin.

Dec.
 4 HMS SALMON sank U.36 in
North Sea.
 4 HMS NELSON severely
damaged by mine entering
Loch Ewe.
 7 First German Type B magnetic
mine rendered safe in Thames
estuary by Lt. Glenny and
Lt. Armitage of HMS
VERNON.
12 HMS DUCHESS sunk in collision
with ROSEMARY off N.W.
Ireland.

13 HMS SALMON torpedoed the German cruisers LEIPZIG and NURNBERG 130 miles west of Jutland.

13 Commodore H. H. Harwood engaged the ADMIRAL GRAF SPEE off the River Plate and drove her into Montevideo, where she was scuttled on the 17th. Ships: HMS AJAX, ACHILLES (NZ), EXETER.

Index

INDEX